Chuck and Blanche Johnson's

Wilderness Adventures
Wild Game Cookbook

©Fred McCaleb

Wilderness Adventures Press, Inc.
Belgrade, Montana

Published by Wilderness Adventures Press, Inc.™
45 Buckskin Road
Belgrade, MT 59714
1-800-925-3339
Web site: www.wildadv.com
E-mail: books@wildadvpress.com
First Edition

Printed in South Korea

ISBN 1-932098-95-2

TABLE OF CONTENTS

-Big Game -

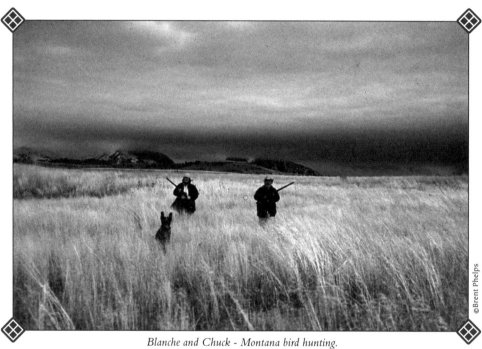

Blanche and Chuck - Montana bird hunting.

©Brent Phelps

INTRODUCTION

The first version of our wild game cookbook came out in 2004 and surprised us with its success. We heard from so many hunters who commented on how much they enjoyed the recipes in the book. So, after several reprints of *Savor Wild Game Cookbook*, we decided that it was time to update the book with a lot of new recipes, and some changes to existing ones.

There is nothing like the feeling of bringing your harvest of wild game to the family table, especially when you have enjoyed the pleasures of the hunt together. For close to fifty years now we have been hunting and cooking together. This mutual bond has strengthened our relationship immeasurably.

Although Chuck's family had a long hunting tradition, Blanche had never been exposed to the sport. In the first fall of her new married life, Chuck announced to her that he intended to spend every weekend hunting. He invited her to join him, but warned her that if she declined, she would have no right to grumble that he wasn't home on weekends. It didn't take long for her to discover the excitement of the hunt, and the fun of sharing it with her best friend.

Since that first season, we have enjoyed hunts all over this country and Canada; from elk in British Columbia to quail in North Carolina. The memories continue to pile on each other: the quiet of a squirrel hunt in the woods of Ohio and Pennsylvania; the rustic elegance of a quail hunt using mule-drawn quail wagons on a cotton plantation in Tennessee; the pent-up excitement of watching a huge flock of mallards work the blind on a sandbar in the Missouri River in South Dakota; the splendor of a horse-pack trip for trophy elk during bugling season in British Columbia; and especially the feeling of being on top of the world as you watch your German wirehaired pointers lock up on point in the wide open prairies of Montana.

Through all these hunts, our philosophy has stayed constant: Do not take game unless you intend to use it. This has led us on a continuing search for new recipes to use with each season's harvest. This book is the compilation of the successful end products of that search. We have also included favorite recipes that some of our hunting friends have shared with us. Another addition to this book comes by way of our daughter, Tracy. Through her connections with the wine industry, Tracy has provided access to a number of wonderful wineries who have suggested wine pairings for most of the recipes. These pairings will satisfy a variety of palates and purse strings.

We hope you enjoy reading the book and trying the recipes. We would also enjoy your comments on these recipes, and would love to have you share your culinary wild game experiences with us.

Chuck Johnson
Blanche Johnson
Belgrade, Montana

THE CARE OF GAME FROM FIELD TO TABLE

Field Dressing and Keeping Game Birds – *Chuck*

Over the years I have tried a number of methods to keep my birds from getting freezer burn. Now I use a method that I read about in the L.L. Bean Game and Fish Cookbook. I like to field dress my birds shortly after they are killed. This is especially important when the weather is warm. I use a pocketknife with a gut hook. After I field dress the birds I put them in a loose plastic bag and put them in my cooler. When I get home I cut off the head, wings and the legs, using a pair of tin snips instead of game bird sheers. Tin snips can handle large game birds far better than the smaller game sheers. After I have cut off the appendages, I place the bird with the feathers still on it in a gallon freezer bag. I seal the bag tight, getting as much air out as possible, then mark the bag and put it in my freezer. The feathers will protect the bird from freezer burn and keep it fresh. We cook most of our birds with the skin off. However, if I want a bird to roast with the skin on I can take one out of the freezer and pluck it. I find that plucking a bird while it is frozen is easier than when it is warm. Normally, a gallon freezer bag will easily hold one pheasant, two grouse, or four quail. Using this method, I am able to keep game birds fresh for as long as a year.

Preparing Your Furred Game – *Chuck*

For small game, rabbits and squirrels, I use the same method for storage as I do for my game birds. I field dress the animal and leave the skin on. I put the game into a gallon freezer zip lock bag, mark it with the date, and freeze it.

For deer, antelope, and elk, I field dress them immediately after they are shot. I now butcher all of my own animals. I will hang the animal in a cool place in my garage for two to four days. There are many good books and a few videos that will take you step by step through the process of butchering your game. Blanche and I love game short ribs, spare ribs, and braised shanks. I found that most butchers would not take the time to cut the ribs for you. The last two times that I asked for the ribs I did not get them. The butchers' excuses were that they did not have enough time or they didn't remember. Now, by doing it myself, I get the cuts of meat that I want. This includes the large joint bones that are great for soups or stocks. The cuts that we intend to use for stew and burgers we leave in large chunks. We wrap and freeze the chunks of meat in one-pound packages. If we want burger, we simply take out the amount of frozen chunks and put them in a food processor to grind them up for burger. By freezing them in chunks we find that the meat stays fresher, without getting freezer burn.

Deboning a Game Bird - *Blanche*

Many recipes call for the meat of the game bird to be cut away from the bone and then cut into strips, chunks, or flattened as for use in a scaloppini recipe. The following method works for any game bird – pheasant, chukar, grouse, ducks, geese, etc. If you make your own stock, be sure to save the bones in the freezer until you accumulate enough to use in stock or soup.

Cut the breast and the thighs from the carcass. In most cases, the drumstick on a wild bird is full of tendons with very little meat, so I usually just leave them on the carcass for stock or soup. You will end up with eight pieces of usable meat.

Use a small, sharp knife, preferably a boning knife. Its thin profile lets you get between the meat and the bone without tearing up the meat. On each thigh, make a slit down the inside of the thigh, right to the bone. Then carefully use the tip of your knife to separate the meat from the bone by cutting the thigh all around the knee joint and again at the joint of the thigh and pelvic bone. Then carefully cut around both sides of the thighbone until the meat falls off in one piece. Repeat with other thigh.

For the breast, insert the tip of your knife at the top of the breastbone. Working slowly, slide your knife between the breast meat and the breastbone and continue working it down and to the end of the breastbone. Then turn and work the knife from the top of the breastbone in the same manner back to where the breastbone connects to the wing and shoulder. Continue to separate as much meat as possible in one piece until it is free. Repeat with the other side of the breast.

Now you are going to make three pieces out of each half breast. First, separate the smaller tenderloin of the inner breast. Then cut the rest of the breast in half, widthwise. Repeat with other half of breast.

Grilling Wild Game – *Chuck*

Wild game has very little fat compared to domestic chicken or red meat. Most people make the mistake of overcooking wild game. We have found that game prepared and served on the rare side tastes best. When I grill game steaks I have a hot fire around 350 to 400 degrees. I cook my steaks about three minutes a side and burgers about four minutes a side. Game birds are best cooked at 300 degrees for four minutes a side. Ducks and geese get very tough and tasteless when over-cooked. A.J. McClane in his great cookbook, *A Taste of The Wild*, recommends cooking duck on the barbecue for no more than three minutes per side. When we cut the time on our ducks back to three minutes we found the meat to be juicy and delicious. We barbecue wild game once or twice a week. I always marinade any wild game for at least several hours before I put it on the grill. The marinade adds flavor and tenderizes the meat and adds juices to keep the meat from drying out while cooking. You can make a little extra marinade, set it aside in a separate dish, and baste it on the game while cooking or when you serve it.

Cooking Wild Game – *Blanche*

Preparing meals with wild game is not really that different from preparing any nice dinner. You just need to remember a few principles. First, the quality of the meat that you serve is entirely in your hands. Game meat that has not been properly field-dressed and kept at cool temperatures until cooked or frozen will not provide the quality of meat that you have come to expect from your domestic butcher. Second, you can expect to spend a little more time preparing game meat than you would a cut of domestic meat that comes wrapped in plastic. No matter how good the butcher, there are always a few things that need to be cleaned out. In preparing furred game meat, look for stray hairs that might have escaped the butcher's eye. Remove as much of the silverskin that you can without damaging the cut of meat. Cut away any area of the meat that looks as if it has been freezer burned or may be damaged from the bullet entry. In preparing game birds, use a pair of tweezers to extract any shot that has penetrated the meat. Along with the shot, also look for small pieces of feathers that have been imbedded into the meat by the shot. Hold the bird under cool running water, and carefully remove any of the internal organs or lining that may still be in the cavity, such as parts of the lungs. You want to be able to see the tiny rib bones that emanate from the backbone. If the bird has been plucked, check for any quill ends that are still imbedded in the skin. For turkey or goose, you may have to use matches to burn away any of the silky down feathers that remain. After cleaning the game meat, let it drain on some paper towels, and then pat dry before starting your preparations.

The third and most important principle is the fact that all wild game is much leaner than domestic meats. Unlike domestic animals, wild game has had to use its muscles to survive. Consequently, you will not find in any big game the rich marbling of fat that you find in beef. And you will not find the layer of fat under the skin of truly wild birds that you find in domestic poultry. This gives you a much more nutritious cut of meat, but one that has to be cooked a little differently.

For quick cooking, such as grilling, frying, or sautéing, be sure that you cook the meat for only a few minutes. Without the extra marbled fat, game meat will dry out more quickly and become tough and tasteless. Cooking so that the meat is still rare to medium rare will bring out the sweet and delicious taste in game meat. In reading the recipes that call for relatively quick cooking, you will see a pattern that you can adapt to any domestic meat recipe that will keep your game meat moist and flavorful. This method basically employs searing the meat in some type of fat, then putting it in a dish with a cover to hold the moisture, and keeping the dish warm while the other ingredients are cooked. Adding the meat back into the mixture toward the end of the cooking process lets the meat combine its flavors with the other ingredients, but keeps the meat from overcooking.

As far as slow-cooking methods, such as stews and braised dishes that employ liquids, reverse the process and plan to cook the meat a little longer than domestic meats. Slow-cooking methods are used to break down the connective tissues of tougher or older cuts of meat. Since wild game animals use their muscles, the connective tissues tend to be larger and stronger than the connective tissues of domestic animals. This extra cooking time will help break those down. Just be sure to keep the level of liquid up during the process so that the meat does not dry out.

Use of Liquids in Cooking Wild Game – *Blanche*

We always keep a selection of stocks, broths, and cooking wines on hand. The stocks are homemade, using the carcasses of both big game and game birds. We have also made great stock out of veal bones when available. This is discussed in the chapter on stocks and sauces. We also keep some commercial beef and chicken broth on hand; buying the broth that has a minimum amount of salt in it.

As you read the recipes, you will see that we like to use a lot of different wines and spirits. When used in cooking, the alcohol evaporates but adds a special flavor to the sauce. If you prefer not to use alcoholic beverages in cooking, you can substitute stock or broth for the wine. If the recipe calls for a flavored spirit, you can always substitute some stock or broth mixed with a fruit jam or marmalade similar in flavor to the spirit.

In using wine, do not buy the "cooking wines" that you see on the grocery shelves. These are poor imitations of wine and also have extra salt and preservatives in them. You do not need to buy expensive wines for cooking, either. We usually keep the following bottles of medium-priced wines on hand for cooking:

> Tawny Port
> Cream Sherry
> Dry Sherry
> Madeira

Apple cider is another liquid that complements wild game. In the fall, we keep a bottle in our refrigerator. You can substitute it for stock, or use it in place of half of the stock in a recipe. It also works well in marinades. And, it's great warmed in a mug with a stick of cinnamon and enjoyed while you are cooking.

Fat Substitutions in Recipes – *Blanche*

As you read the recipes, you will see that we have usually specified certain ingredients such as butter, olive oil, sour cream, and heavy cream or half and half. Feel free to substitute the ingredient that best suits your own diet. We used the term "butter" but often use one of the healthier non-hydrogenated margarines in its place. One word of caution: If you are using the margarine to brown the meat or vegetables, use a regular "full-fat" margarine. The "light" margarines do not have enough fat in them to achieve the desired result. You will just see the light margarine disappear before your eyes in the hot skillet. You can use the light margarines to swirl into a sauce, however. That will add the richer taste without the extra fat and calories.

We like to use a lot of olive oil. If you find the taste of olive oil too intense, feel free to substitute another type of vegetable oil, such as canola or safflower.

We usually use a light sour cream instead of the full-fat variety. It doesn't seem to make that much difference in the taste (unless you really want an exceedingly rich dish). I have also replaced heavy cream with a mix of about two parts light sour cream to one part 2% milk. I know that it is not as rich and creamy as the real thing, but my conscience feels better about it!

Substitutions of Big Game Meats – *Chuck and Blanche*

Unlike the very different textures of the various types of game birds and waterfowl, big game meat tends to be more similar. Buffalo, moose, and elk bear the closest resemblance to beef. The fat in these meats tends to taste good even when used as a leftover in a cold sandwich. On the other hand, the fat in deer and antelope seems to have a slightly grainier texture. Other than that, you can easily substitute one type of game meat for another in any of the recipes. So, don't ignore the section on elk just because you don't have any in your freezer. Have fun experimenting with all the different recipes. We had fun putting this cookbook together, and we hope you have as much fun using it.

~Upland Game Birds~

Pheasant

CLAY POT PHEASANT WITH APPLES

Clay pot cooking is a fun way to cook a meal in one pot. The unglazed clay pot is immersed in water for 20 minutes before you add your ingredients. Then you put it in a cold oven and turn the heat up to 450 degrees, usually cooking the ingredients for about 1 hour. This results in a delicate blending of the various flavors. With wild game, however, you don't have the luxury of the extra fat to keep the birds moist during this process. So, we have found that, like so many of our recipes, it is best to remove the birds from the cooking utensil for part of the cooking time. Try this recipe, and then have fun experimenting with other ingredients to vary the taste.

Ingredients

1 pheasant, cut into 8 pieces	½ cup sherry
2 apples, peeled, quartered, and cored	2 tablespoons tarragon
1 orange, quartered	2 tablespoons brown sugar
½ cup orange juice	1 teaspoon nutmeg
½ cup dry white wine	1 cup pearl onions, frozen or canned

Preparation

PRE-SOAK clay pot and lid in water for 20 minutes. Drain pot and put some of the apple and orange quarters in the bottom. Put the pheasant in next, followed by the rest of the apple and orange quarters. Sprinkle the tarragon, brown sugar, and nutmeg over the top. Pour the orange juice, wine, and sherry over all. Put the lid on and put in a cold oven. Turn the heat to 450 degrees. The total cooking time is 1 hour, but it will be divided into thirds.

AFTER the first 20 minutes, remove the pheasant to a covered dish. Add the pearl onions, put the lid back on and return to 450-degree oven.

AFTER next 20 minutes, return the pheasant to the pot, stirring to combine the ingredients. Cover and return to oven for the last 20 minutes.

WHEN done, remove to a trivet or hot pad. Be careful. The clay pot is very hot. It may crack if placed on a very cold surface, or it may burn some counters. Let the pot sit, covered, for a few minutes, so that you can move it to the table.

SERVE with a green vegetable and noodles or pasta, which can be covered with the juices from the pot.

Serves 2 to 3

Wine Suggestions: Sauvion Rose d'Anjou or Irony Pinot Noir

MONTANA HUCKLEBERRY PHEASANT

In good years, huckleberries are plentiful in the Northwest and a great compliment to wild game dishes. However, if you cannot obtain them, blueberries make an excellent substitute.

Ingredients

- 1 pheasant – cut in 8 pieces (2 thighs, 2 legs, 2 breasts cut in half)
- ½ cup flour, seasoned with salt, pepper and garlic powder
- 2 tablespoons butter
- 1 tablespoon olive oil
- 3 large shallots – thinly sliced
- 1 cup mushrooms, sliced

- ½ cup port wine
- 1 cup game bird stock or chicken broth
- 1 teaspoon dried tarragon
- ¾ cup huckleberries (or blueberries)
- ⅔ cup heavy cream
- brown sugar to taste
- balamic vinegar to taste

Preparation

DREDGE the pheasant pieces in the seasoned flour. Brown the pieces in the butter and olive oil in skillet on medium high. Remove to covered dish and keep in a 300-degree oven.

ADD the shallots and mushrooms to the skillet and sauté for 3 to 4 minutes. Pour port wine in and deglaze the pan, scraping any browned bits from bottom.

STIR in the stock and tarragon. Add the cream and stir to combine. Add the huckleberries and simmer to reduce liquid by half.

IT IS important to taste the sauce at this time. Huckleberries can vary in tartness and sweetness. Season to taste with a little brown sugar and/or balsamic vinegar to balance.

RETURN the pheasant pieces and any accumulated juices to skillet. Spoon the sauce over the pheasant pieces, and simmer on low for a couple of minutes.

THIS is great served over wild rice.

Serves 2 to 3

Wine Suggestions: Loredona Viognier or Ruta 22 Malbec

Orange-Simmered Pheasant

Ingredients

- 1 pheasant, cut in 6 pieces (2 breasts, 2 legs, 2 thighs)
- ½ cup flour, seasoned with ½ teaspoon nutmeg, and salt & pepper
- 4 slices bacon, chopped
- 8 green onions, sliced lengthwise, including green tops
- 1 cup game bird stock or chicken broth
- ½ cup orange juice
- ¼ cup Drambuie
- 1 tablespoon honey
- ½ teaspoon dried tarragon, or 1 sprig of fresh
- 1½ teaspoons arrowroot, mixed with a little water
- balsamic vinegar – to taste
- ⅓ cup parsley
- ½ cup toasted almond slivers

Preparation

BROWN bacon pieces in skillet until crisp. Remove to a paper towel to drain. Roll pheasant pieces in seasoned flour. Brown in bacon fat for 3 minutes; turn and brown for 2 minutes. Remove legs and thighs, and brown breasts 1 more minute. Put pheasant in covered dish in warm oven.

SAUTÉ the green onions in the skillet for 2 minutes on low. Add stock, orange juice, and Drambuie. Stir, scraping up brown bits from bottom of skillet. Add honey, bacon crisps, and tarragon. Cover and simmer 10 minutes. Spoon a small amount of sauce into arrowroot-water mixture and stir. Pour mixture back into sauce, using spatula to be sure you get all of the arrowroot. Stir to thicken.

RETURN pheasant and juices to skillet, putting breasts with bone-side up. Spoon the sauce over pheasant. Simmer, covered for 5 minutes.

ADJUST sauce by adding a touch of balsamic vinegar if the sauce is too sweet. Add the parsley and almonds for the last couple of minutes.

GREAT with wild rice or noodles.

Serves 2 to 3

Wine Suggestions: Sauvion Vouvray
or
Gnarly Head Pinot Noir

BRAISED PHEASANT LEGS – ITALIAN STYLE

Too often the legs of game birds are neglected, as hunters concentrate on the tender breast meat. This is a shame, since the legs hold a lot of great flavor. They just need to be cooked slowly.

An option introduced with this recipe is the use of a piece of Parmigiano Reggiano rind in the cooking liquid. This imparts a rich, nutty flavor to the broth as well as slightly thickening it.

Ingredients

3 slices bacon, chopped	1 bay leaf
8 pheasant legs	5-6 fresh sage leaves
olive oil	1 15-ounce can diced tomatoes with
1 large carrot, chopped	liquid
2 celery stalks, chopped	1 cup port
1 small parsnip, chopped	2½ cups chicken broth
1 red onion, chopped	1 piece of Parmigiano Reggiano rind
1 bell pepper, chopped	(optional)
2 large garlic cloves, chopped	2 tablespoons flour (optional)
¼ cup brandy	1½ cups fresh or frozen peas

Preparation

IN A skillet, brown the bacon over medium heat until crisp. Remove bacon and drain on paper towel. Pour off all but a tablespoon of the bacon fat. Raise the heat to medium-high.

GENEROUSLY salt and pepper the pheasant legs and brown them for 1 minute per side. Remove to a plate. Add a small amount of olive oil, if necessary, and sauté carrot, celery, parsnip, onion, and pepper over medium heat, adding garlic during the last couple of minutes. Spoon vegetable mixture into crockpot.

ADD brandy to the skillet and deglaze the pan, then pour liquid and any brown bits into crockpot. Add bay leaf, sage leaves, and diced tomatoes with liquid to crockpot, stirring to combine. Add port, chicken stock, and optional Parmigiano rind, and then add browned pheasant legs, tucking them into the liquid and vegetables. Sprinkle bacon on top, and stir in. Cover and cook on low for 5 hours, or until meat is almost ready to fall off the bone. Remove Parmigiano rind and discard.

IF thicker sauce is desired, mix flour with a little water and stir to get rid of lumps. Add some cooking liquid to the mix, and then add to crockpot, stirring to combine. Raise heat to high and cook for about 10 minutes. Turn back to low and add peas, cooking for 10 minutes.

Serves 4 to 6

Wine Suggestions: Foghead Pinot Noir or Poggio alle Sughere Splendido

Pheasant Francaise with Fettuccini

Can substitute 2 chukar partridge or 3 ruffed grouse.

This recipe is fun to do for company, since it is so quick. That is, as long as you prepare the pheasant pieces before your guests show up. Save the pheasant pieces in a zip-lock bag in the refrigerator until you are ready to do the final prep.

Ingredients

1 pheasant, deboned into 8 pieces	½ cup dry white wine
cooking spray	2 tablespoons lemon juice
1 tablespoon butter	2 teaspoons capers
2 tablespoons flour	¼ cup parsley, chopped
2 cups game bird or chicken stock	8 ounces fettuccini
4 large shiitake mushrooms	2 cloves garlic, sliced

Early Preparation

FOLLOW the instructions for deboning a game bird. You will find these in the front of this book under the section: The Care of Game from Field to Table.

PAT the 8 pieces of pheasant dry and place them on a cutting board that has been covered with wax paper. Place another piece of wax paper over the pheasant pieces. With a meat mallet, pound the pheasant pieces to about ¼ inch thickness, just as you would do for veal scaloppini.

Final Preparation

SPRAY a skillet that can be used for serving with cooking spray and heat to medium-high heat. Brown the pheasant pieces for no more than 2 minutes per side. Remove to covered dish and put in a warm oven.

LOWER the heat to medium and melt the butter in the skillet and stir in the flour. Stir constantly for 1 to 2 minutes. Slowly stir in ¼ cup of the stock and then add the mushrooms. Cook over medium heat for 2 more minutes. Now add the rest of the stock, the wine, and the lemon juice, scraping the bottom of the skillet to loosen any bits. Cook for a couple of minutes to thicken, then turn down the heat to a simmer and cook uncovered for 10 minutes. Stir in parsley and capers.

WHILE this is simmering, place the garlic slices in a large pot of boiling water. Add the fettuccini and cook until al dente (usually 10 to 12 minutes). Drain pasta and garlic slices, and add to the sauce in the skillet, stirring to mix. Remove the pheasant from the warming oven and drain the accumulated juices into the skillet and combine with the sauce. Place the pheasant pieces on top of the pasta and sauce and serve with crusty bread and a green salad.

Serves 4

Wine Suggestions: Barone Fini Pinot Grigio
or
Massimo Rioja

©Fred McCaleb

Pheasant Hollandaise

Can substitute 2 chukar partridge.

Ingredients

- 1 pheasant, boned and meat cut in 1-inch chunks
- ¾ cup flour, seasoned with salt and pepper
- 2 tablespoons olive oil
- 2 ounces pancetta, if unavailable, you can substitute deli ham
- 1⅓ cups white wine
- 1 teaspoon tarragon
- ¼ teaspoons thyme
- 1¼ cups game bird or chicken stock
- 3 egg yolks, room temperature
- juice of 1 lemon
- ½ cup parsley, chopped

Preparation

HEAT olive oil in skillet over medium heat. Cut the pancetta into strips and fry until it begins to crisp. Remove and set aside. Pat pheasant pieces dry and dredge them in the seasoned flour. Turn the heat to medium-high and brown the pieces in the skillet for about 3 minutes. Remove the pheasant and set aside.

TURN the heat down to medium-low and add the wine, tarragon, and thyme, stirring to combine and to scrape up any brown bits on the bottom of the skillet. Return the pancetta to the pan and add the stock. Continue simmering until the liquid has reduced by half. Return the pheasant chunks to the skillet, cover, and simmer on medium-low heat for about 10 minutes more.

REMOVE the skillet from direct heat for the next step. Put the egg yolks, lemon juice, and one half of the parsley in a bowl and whisk together. Now add the mixture to the pheasant, stirring with a whisk to combine smoothly. Return the skillet to low heat and continue to stir gently for 2 minutes to thicken the sauce.

SERVE with a risotto cooked with shiitake mushrooms and green onions.

Serves 4

Wine Suggestions: Loredona Viognier
or
George Duboeuf Beaujolais-Village

Pheasant in Port Wine

Ingredients

1 pheasant, quartered	1 medium onion, chopped
4 strips bacon, chopped	1 pound fresh mushrooms, thickly sliced
2 tablespoons olive oil	1 14-ounce can beef broth
½ cup flour – seasoned with:	¾ cup port wine
¼ teaspoon allspice	1 teaspoon tarragon
½ teaspoon garlic powder	2 tablespoons cherry or currant jelly
⅛ teaspoon black pepper	1 14-ounce jar boiled pearl onions

Preparation

SAUTÉ chopped bacon in skillet over medium-high heat until crisp. Set aside on paper towel to drain. Drain off all but 2 tablespoons of bacon fat. Add olive oil to skillet.

DUST pheasant pieces in seasoned flour and brown in the bacon fat and olive oil. Remove pheasant and set aside.

ADD onions and mushrooms to skillet and sauté until onions are translucent, adding extra olive oil if necessary.

ADD one half of beef broth, ½ cup of the port, and the tarragon to skillet, stirring to loosen any crusted bits. Add jelly, stir to combine and simmer about 10 minutes to reduce. Add rest of beef broth, remaining ¼ cup port, and boiled onions. Stir. Return pheasant pieces to skillet, using spoon to cover pieces with the sauce. Cover and simmer for 20 minutes.

GREAT served over wild rice mixed with toasted pecans.

Serves 2 to 3

Wine Suggestions: Hob Nob Pinot Noir,
Noble Vines 181 Merlot,
or
Black Stallion Chardonnay

PHEASANT MARSALA WITH DRIED CHERRIES

Three Hungarian partridge can be substituted.

Ingredients

1 pheasant – cut in 6 pieces (2 breasts, 2 thighs, 2 drumsticks)
½ cup dried cherries
½ cup Marsala wine + a splash
¾ cup flour (combination of white and whole wheat, if available)
¼ teaspoon cinnamon
¼ teaspoon nutmeg
¼ teaspoon allspice
2 tablespoons olive oil
1 cup mushrooms, sliced (about 5 large)
1 cup onions, chopped
1½ cups game bird stock or chicken broth
⅓ cup toasted almond slivers

Preparation

SOAK dried cherries in ½ cup Marsala wine for 1 hour.

COMBINE flour with cinnamon, nutmeg and allspice. Dust the pheasant pieces with the seasoned flour.

HEAT olive oil in large skillet over medium high heat. Brown the pheasant 3 minutes per side. Remove to a covered dish, and keep in warm oven.

SAUTÉ the onions and mushrooms in the skillet, using a splash of Marsala if skillet gets too dry. When the onions are translucent, add the cherries and Marsala wine, along with the stock. Cover and simmer for 15 minutes.

RETURN the pheasant to the skillet along with any juices. Add another small splash of Marsala. Spoon the sauce over pheasant pieces. Cover and simmer on low for 3 to 5 minutes.

SPRINKLE the toasted almonds over the pheasant, and serve.

THIS is great served over orzo, tossed with grated Parmesan and a small amount of olive oil that has been heated with a few garlic slices.

Serves 2 to 3

Wine Suggestions: Black Stallion Chardonnay
or
Poggio alle Sughure Morellino di Scansano

PHEASANT TARRAGON

Ingredients

1 pheasant – cut in 6 pieces
4 tablespoons flour seasoned with
  garlic powder, Lawry's Seasoned Salt,
  paprika and pepper
2 tablespoons butter
1 tablespoon olive oil
2 shallots, cut in half and sliced
1 cup mushrooms, sliced
1 carrot, grated

1 cup pearl onions – either from jar or
  can, or frozen
2 tablespoons brandy
1 cup game bird stock or chicken broth
½ cup sherry
1 tablespoon dried tarragon
2 tablespoons sour cream, mixed with 2
  tablespoons flour
¼ cup chopped parsley
¼ cup toasted sunflower seeds (optional)

Preparation

PAT pheasant pieces dry, and lightly coat with seasoned flour. Heat butter and olive oil in skillet. Brown the pheasant 2 to 3 minutes per side. Remove pheasant, cover, and place in warm oven.

ADD shallots, mushrooms, and grated carrot to skillet. Sauté, stirring, for 2 minutes. Add pearl onions. Add brandy to pan, and deglaze. Then add stock, sherry, and tarragon. Cover and simmer for 15 minutes.

SPOON about ¼ cup of the sauce into the sour cream and flour mixture, mixing with a small whisk or fork to combine. This helps to warm the sour cream so that it doesn't curdle. Add the sour cream mixture to the sauce and stir to combine.

RETURN pheasant and juices to skillet. Cover and keep on low until serving. When ready to serve, add parsley and stir in. Sprinkle toasted sunflower seed on top, if desired.

Serves 2 to 3

Wine Suggestions: Llai Llai Pinot Noir
or
Loredona Pinot Grigio

Cajun Pheasant

Ingredients

1 pheasant – cut in 8 pieces (2 legs, 2 thighs, 2 breasts cut in half)	1 tablespoon olive oil
½ cup flour	1 tablespoon butter
1 teaspoon Lawry's Seasoned Salt	6-8 green onions, sliced
1 teaspoon paprika	6 large mushroom caps, sliced
1 tablespoon Cajun seasoning, such as Emeril's	½ cup game bird stock or chicken broth
	½ cup sherry
	¼ cup chopped parsley

Preparation

HEAT butter and oil in skillet on medium-high. Combine flour with the seasonings. Dust pheasant pieces with the seasoned flour. Brown pheasant in the skillet for 2 to 3 minutes per side. Remove pheasant, placing in covered dish in warm oven.

ADD the green onions and mushrooms to the skillet and sauté until onions have softened. Add the stock and the sherry, scraping up any brown bits on bottom of the skillet. Simmer for 10 minutes, stirring occasionally. Return the pheasant and any juices to the skillet. Simmer for another 5 minutes. Sprinkle chopped parsley over top just before serving.

SERVE with Zahtarain's Black Beans & Rice with a side of salsa.

Serves 2 to 3
Wine Suggestions: Loredona Riesling or Ramón Bilbao Valiñas Albariño

©Brett Smith

Opening Day Pheasants

PHEASANT WITH OYSTER MUSHROOMS

Ingredients

2 pheasants, cut in 8 pieces each
1 cup flour, seasoned with salt and
pepper
2 tablespoons olive oil
6 cloves garlic, thickly sliced

4 shallots, sliced
⅓ cup brandy
2 cups game bird or chicken stock
½ teaspoon tarragon
2 cups oyster mushrooms, cut in half

Preparation

HEAT the olive oil in a large skillet and add the garlic slices. With heat on low, let the garlic infuse the olive oil without browning. If the garlic is sizzling at all, the temperature is too high. As the garlic is warming, press each slice with a fork to extract some of the garlic oil. Remove the garlic and set it aside.

WHILE the oil is heating, dust the pheasant with the seasoned flour. Turn the heat to medium-high and brown the pheasant pieces in the oil for about 3 minutes per side. Remove to covered dish and keep in oven at 300 degrees.

SAUTÉ the shallots in the skillet, adding a little more oil if needed. Add the brandy and deglaze the pan. Stir in the stock and add the tarragon and mushrooms. Cover the skillet and simmer on medium-low heat for 10 minutes. Return the pheasant and any accumulated juices to the skillet and simmer for another 5 minutes.

Serves 4 to 6

Wine Suggestions: Vidal-Fleury Côtes du Rhône Rouge,
Handcraft Chardonnay,
or
Symphony Obsession

PHEASANT WITH SAFFRON RISOTTO

Ingredients

1 pheasant
½ cup flour, mixed with salt and pepper
4 tablespoons butter
1½ cups mushrooms, sliced
¾ cup Arborio rice
¼ cup cream sherry
½ cup white wine

1 cup pearl onions, frozen or canned
2 cups game bird stock or chicken stock
1 tablespoon tarragon
1 pinch saffron
½ cup sour cream, thinned slightly with
  a little milk

Preparation

FILET each breast from the pheasant, and then cut each half in half (4 breast pieces). Starting in the middle of the inner thigh, cut through to the bone. Then run your knife in a circle around the knee joint and then at the top of the thigh where it attaches to the pelvic bone. By loosening the meat in both places, you can then remove it in one piece by cutting the meat away from the thigh bone. Repeat with the other thigh. You now have 6 pieces of meat. Save drumsticks for soups.

MELT 2 tablespoons butter in Dutch oven or large casserole with lid. Dredge the pheasant pieces in the seasoned flour and sauté over medium-high heat for about 2 minutes per side. Remove pheasant to a covered dish in a warm oven.

MELT 1 tablespoon butter and sauté mushrooms in pan for 1 to 2 minutes, adding a little stock if they get too dry. Now add 1 last tablespoon of butter to the pan and add the rice. Stir over medium heat until rice is clear on the outside, about 2 to 3 minutes. Add the white wine and the sherry, stirring to scrape up any bits. Add pearl onions, tarragon and saffron, and ¾ cup of the stock. Cover and simmer for 10 minutes. Add ¾ cup of the stock. Cover and simmer for another 5 to 10 minutes more.

WHEN rice is done, adding more stock if necessary, add a splash of sherry, and keep at a lower simmer. Warm the last ½ cup of stock and add to the sour cream, whisking to blend. Add the heated mixture to the rice.

RETURN the pheasant, and any accumulated juices, to the pan. Cover and simmer for about 5 minutes.

Serves 2 to 3

Wine Suggestions: Twisted Moscato or Volteo Tempranillo

Pheasant with Shiitake Mushrooms and Garlic

Ingredients

1 pheasant – cut in 8 pieces (2 drumsticks, 2 thighs, 2 breasts cut in half again)
1 tablespoon olive oil
1 tablespoon butter
6 large shiitake mushrooms – sliced thickly (about 1½ to 2 cups)

5 cloves garlic – peeled and split in half
1½ cups chicken broth
½ cup sherry wine
2 tablespoons brandy
   seasoned flour – seasoned with salt, pepper, garlic powder, and a pinch of Cajun seasoning if preferred

Optional

1½ teaspoon arrowroot mixed with a small amount of water for thickening

Preparation

PLACE olive oil in large skillet on low heat. Add garlic pieces. Let the garlic infuse the warm olive oil for about 15 minutes. Make sure that it does not brown. Remove the garlic and set aside. Add the butter to the skillet.

DUST the pheasant pieces with the seasoned flour and brown in the oil & butter mixture at medium-high heat. Brown approximately 2 minutes per side. Remove pheasant and place in covered dish in a warm oven. Put brandy into skillet, stirring to scrape up any brown bits. Add the garlic, the chicken broth, and the sherry. Reduce the mixture by a third on medium-high (about 5 minutes).

RETURN pheasant to pan, along with the shiitake mushrooms. Cover and simmer about 10 minutes.

IF YOU want the sauce to be a little thicker, mix the arrowroot with a small amount of water and add to the sauce, stirring constantly to dissolve. Let sauce simmer for another minute or two to thicken.

THIS recipe is great served with steamed asparagus and roasted new potatoes.

Serves 2 to 3

Wine Suggestions: Nobles Vines 446 Chardonnay or
Vidal-Fleury Côtes du Rhône Blanc or Rouge

ROAST PHEASANT WITH DRAMBUIE ORANGE SAUCE

Ingredients

2 pheasants
8 sprigs parsley
4 garlic cloves, peeled
2 bay leaves
2 sprigs fresh tarragon
2 oranges, halved – zest saved for sauce
¼ cup orange juice

salt and pepper to taste
olive oil
6 bacon slices
⅔ cup game bird stock or chicken broth
½ cup orange juice
4 tablespoons Drambuie

For Sauce

½ cup game bird stock or chicken broth
2 tablespoons orange juice
½ cup clover honey (or less, depending on sweetness)

3 tablespoons Drambuie
1 tablespoon orange zest
2 tablespoons butter, chilled & cut in small cubes

Preparation

PREHEAT oven to 350 degrees. Squeeze 2 orange halves over each bird and into the cavity. Season birds inside and out with salt and pepper. In each cavity, place 4 parsley sprigs, 2 garlic cloves, 1 bay leaf and tarragon sprig. Brush birds with olive oil. Place 3 bacon slices over each bird, securing with toothpicks. Place breast-side up in roasting pan.

MIX the game bird stock, orange juice and 4 tablespoons of Drambuie, and pour over birds. Bake in 350-degree oven for 1 to 1¼ hours, basting every 20 minutes, until breast meat is no longer bright pink. Remove the bacon for the last 15 minutes to let the breasts brown.

MEANWHILE, combine the game bird stock, orange juice, honey, orange zest, and 2 tablespoons of Drambuie in a small saucepan on low heat. Cook for about 2 minutes, stirring constantly, until the honey thins out. Swirl in the butter, and cook 2 more minutes until the sauce thickens. Hold lowest setting to keep warm. If you like the taste of Drambuie, add 1 tablespoon to sauce as you add the pan juices, just before serving.

WHEN birds are done, remove to a serving platter. Remove the herbs from cavities. Pour juices from roasting pan into honey/Drambuie mixture. Turn up heat to low simmer, and blend the juices with the sauce.

TO SERVE, place roasted potatoes or wild rice around pheasants on platter. Drizzle a small amount of the sauce over the pheasants. Serve the rest of the sauce on the side. It has a strong (but great) flavor, so each diner can regulate the amount per serving.

Serves at least 4

Wine Suggestions: Massimo Sauvignon Blanc or
Chateau Bonnet Blanc

FARMHOUSE ROAST PHEASANT

Ingredients

1 pheasant, either plucked or skinned
3 bacon slices, cut in half
3 tablespoons butter
1 carrot, finely chopped
1 celery rib, finely chopped
1 garlic clove, minced

2 mushrooms, stems removed and finely chopped
2 green onions, finely chopped
1 small tomato, finely chopped
¼ cup Kentucky bourbon
1 tablespoon brown sugar

Preparation

HEAT the oven to 350 dgrees. Rinse and pat pheasant dry. Season the bird with salt and pepper and place in roasting pan. Fix bacon slices to breast and legs with toothpicks. Place in preheated oven and turn temperature down to 325 degrees. Roast for about 45 minutes.

WHILE pheasant is roasting, melt butter in a saucepan and add carrot, celery, and garlic. Cover and sweat vegetables over medium heat for 3 minutes. Add mushrooms, green onions, and tomato. Cover and continue to cook on medium for 3 more minutes. Add bourbon and sugar, stirring to combine. Simmer, covered, for 3 more minutes.

REMOVE pheasant from oven and take off bacon. Pour the vegetable mixture over the pheasant and return to oven and continue to roast for another 10 to 15 minutes.

FOR A rustic serving, serve as it comes out of the oven. If a more refined method is desired, scoop the vegetables into a blender or food processor and purée. Place in saucepan and rewarm. To serve, you can drizzle some of the sauce over the pheasant and serve the rest on the side.

Serves 4 to 6
Wine Suggestions: Hob Nob Merlot
or Noble Vines 337 Cabernet Sauvignon

ROAST PHEASANT

Ingredients

1 pheasant, preferably plucked not skinned
stuffing – see Grandma's Turkey Dressing

3-4 bacon strips
½ cup sherry
½ cup game bird stock or chicken stock
1-2 teaspoons arrowroot

Preparation

PREHEAT oven to 350 degrees.

SALT the inside of the pheasant and stuff with your favorite stuffing. Tie the legs together with kitchen twine. Place in a roasting pan and lay the strips of bacon over the breast and legs, securing with toothpicks.

AFTER 25 minutes, pour ¼ cup of sherry over the pheasant. After 15 more minutes, pour the rest of the sherry over bird, basting with the pan juices.

IN A saucepan, mix the arrowroot with the stock, and keep on low heat.

WHEN pheasant is done, remove the bacon strips and toothpicks. Pheasant is done when breast meat is just barely pink. Overcooking will only dry out the meat. Put the bird on a serving platter and keep warm while you finish the sauce.

POUR the roasting pan juices into the heated stock, scraping the bottom of the pan to include all crusted bits. Bring the stock to a boil and lower to a simmer, until reduced by about a third.

SERVE the sauce on the side.

Serves 2 – 3

Wine Suggestions: George Duboeuf Château des Capitans Juliénas
or
Irony Chardonnay

CLAY POT PHEASANT
WITH PEARS AND CRANBERRIES

As mentioned with other clay pot recipes in this cookbook, the low fat content of wild game requires a little different cooking method than domestic meats in a clay pot. You don't want wild game cooked as long, or it will toughen up. In this version, we add the pheasant toward the end of the cooking process, keeping the meat moist and juicy and letting the other ingredients steep together in the slow-cooking process of the clay pot.

Ingredients

1 teaspoon ground cinnamon
1 teaspoon powdered ginger
½ teaspoon grated nutmeg
2 tablespoons brown sugar
2 pears, barely ripe with core removed, peeled and quartered
1½ cups cranberries

1 cup pearl onions, frozen or canned
½ cup chicken broth
½ cup dry white wine
½ cup cream sherry or Madeira
1 pheasant, cut in 6 pieces
1 tablespoon olive oil

Preparation

SUBMERGE clay pot in water and soak for 20 minutes. Mix spices and brown sugar in small bowl. Remove the clay pot from the water and place half of the cranberries, pears, and drained pearl onions in the bottom. Sprinkle half the brown sugar mixture over the fruit. Repeat with a second layer of fruit, onions, and spice. Pour broth and wine over all and cover with top of clay pot. Place pot on middle rack of cold oven and turn heat to 400 degrees. Cook for 40 minutes.

PAT pheasant pieces dry and season with salt and pepper. Heat olive oil in a skillet over medium-high heat and brown pheasant about 2 minutes per side. Remove skillet from heat.

OPEN oven and carefully remove top of clay pot, placing it on a trivet to keep it from cracking on a cold surface. Place pheasant pieces in pot, spooning fruit and liquid over the meat. Replace clay top and continue cooking for 15 minutes to finish the pheasant and to blend the flavors.

REMOVE from oven, remove top, and let rest a few minutes before serving.

Serves 2 – 3

***Wine Suggestions: Irony Chardonnay
or Kunde Estate Zinfandel***

Pheasant Medallions with Cranberry Cream Sauce

Cranberries are not just for Thanksgiving and Christmas. They can be frozen for use throughout the year, and work well with most wild game. This recipe is for two people, but can easily be doubled to serve four or more.

Ingredients

1 full pheasant breast, deboned & cut in half

½ cup flour, seasoned with 1/4 teaspoon each of nutmeg, ginger, dry mustard, and thyme

1 tablespoon butter

1 tablespoon olive oil

1 cup cranberries

3 green onions, sliced into 1/4-inch pieces, green pieces separated from white

2 tablespoons brandy

1 cup gamebird stock or chicken stock

⅓ cup Madeira wine or sherry

1 tablespoon brown sugar, with extra for seasoning

¼ teaspoon ground nutmeg

¼ teaspoon ground ginger

¼ teaspoon dry mustard

¼ teaspoon ground allspice

1 teaspoon arrowroot or cornstarch

½ cup whole milk or half and half

balsamic vinegar, optional

Preparation

FOR breast meat that is more tender, pound meat as for scaloppini. Dust in the seasoned flour. Heat butter and oil in a skillet over medium-high heat and fry the dusted pheasant meat for 1 to 1-1/2 minutes per side. Remove to a warm pan and cover.

PLACE cranberries and the white parts of the onions in skillet and sauté for 1 minute. Add the brandy and deglaze the pan, scraping up any brown bits. Add the broth, wine, brown sugar, and spices, stirring to combine. Bring to a low simmer and cook until reduced to about half, and cranberries have popped open.

MIX arrowroot into the milk until dissolved. Mix a little of the hot stock into the milk and then add the mixture to the skillet, stirring to combine. Simmer gently until it thickens. Taste sauce and adjust sweetness by adding more brown sugar or a touch of balsamic vinegar, if necessary.

JUST before serving, add the pheasant back into the sauce, heat through, and then sprinkle green onion tops over all. Serve with fettuccine tossed with a little olive oil and sprinkled with freshly grated Parmigiano Reggiano.

Pheasant

20

Serves 2

Wine Suggestions: Hob Nob Pinot Noir or Massimo Sauvignon Blanc

Clay Pot Pheasant with Root Vegetables

Depending on how much heat you want in this dish, you can include some or all of the chipotle peppers that are used in the marinade to the vegetables in the clay pot.

Ingredients

1 pheasant, quartered
½ cup olive oil
2 cups red wine, divided
2 dried chipotle peppers
4 new potatoes, cut in half
1 turnip, cut in quarters
  fresh sage leaves

1 carrot, cut in large chunks
1 celery stalk, cut in large chunks
1 yellow onion, peeled and quartered
1 14-ounce can fire-roasted tomatoes
1 cup gamebird stock
5 mushrooms

Preparation

PUT chipotle peppers in a small bowl and pour 1/2 cup of the red wine over them. Let soak for half an hour. Combine olive oil and 1 cup of the red wine in a sealable plastic bag. Add the peppers and wine and then add pheasant and marinate for several hours.

SOAK clay pot in water for 20 minutes. Boil potatoes and turnip in water for 10 minutes. Remove and drain. Take clay pot out of water and line the bottom with sage leaves. Place the potatoes and vegetables (except for the mushrooms) on top of the sage. Pour the tomatoes and their juices over all. Add the remaining wine and the stock and cover with the clay pot top. If desired, remove chipotle peppers from marinade, chop, and add to the vegetables.

PLACE in cold oven and turn temperature to 425 degrees. Cook for 40 minutes. Remove pheasant from marinade and season with salt and peper. Brown pheasant quarters in a skillet with a small amount of olive oil. Carefully remove clay pot from oven and place on a surface that is not cold. Remove the top and add the mushrooms, stirring them into the vegetables. Nestle the browned pheasant into the vegetable mix and cover with some of the liquid. Cover clay pot and return to oven and cook another 20 minutes.

REMOVE from oven and let cool for few minutes before serving.

Serves 4
Wine Suggestions: Brazin Monte Rosso Zinfandel
or
Volteo Tempranillo-Cabernet Sauvignon

Pheasant with Artichokes and Olive Tapenade

This delicious one-dish dinner can be baked in the oven or on the grill with very little more than a food processor or blender and some heavy duty aluminum foil. It could also be prepared ahead, packed in its foil packets and cooked over a campfire. While pheasant is used in this recipe, any upland game bird would combine well with the other ingredients. The sealed, moisture-filled packets keep the meat very tender and moist.

Ingredients

- 4 18-inch pieces of heavy-duty aluminum foil coated with vegetable oil spray
- 1 12-ounce jar marinated artichokes
- ½ cup black olives, pitted
- ½ cup green olives, pitted
- 2 pheasant breasts, halved and fileted from the bone
- 12 ounces yams, peeled and cut into 1-inch cubes

- ¾ cup fresh green beans, cut in 1-inch pieces
- 2 teaspoons, fresh rosemary, chopped fine
- 1 teaspoon salt
- 4 Roma tomatoes, chopped
- ½ medium sweet onion, chopped
- ½ cup chicken broth
- ½ cup white wine

Preparation

DRAIN the marinated artichokes and reserve the liquid. Place the olives and 1 tablespoon of the artichoke liquid in a food processor or blender and process until it reaches the consistency of a paste.

FOLD the coated foil pieces in half, with the coating on the inside. Now open them back up and put a boned pheasant breast half in the middle of the left half of the foil. (Two combinations of vegetables will go on either side of the breast, but all is on the left half of the foil.) Spread an equal amount of the olive tapenade on the top of each breast. Combine the yam and green beans with ¼ cup of the artichoke liquid, the rosemary, and 1/2 teaspoon of the salt. Divide this mixture evenly among the four packets, placing it to one side of the pheasant breast. Combine the artichokes, tomatoes, and onion with a tablespoon of the artichoke liquid. Place the mixture to the other side of the pheasant breast.

START to close the packets by folding the other half of the foil over the food and crimping the two long sides, leaving one side open. Combine the chicken broth and wine in a measuring cup and pour an equal amount in each packet. Crimp the remaining side to seal in the liquids.

PLACE on a preheated 400-degree grill and close the lid. Cook the packets for about 12 to 15 minutes, depending on the temperature of the grill. When done, carefully unfold each hot packet and place on plate.

Serves 4
Wine Suggestions: Yellow Tail Bubbles Rose or Domino Merlot

Roast Pheasant with Peppers, Tomatoes, and Onions

This recipe works equally well for both pheasant and chukar partridge. Just reduce the cooking time a little for the smaller birds.

Ingredients

1 pheasant, quartered
2 tablespoons olive oil
1 onion, chopped
1 green bell pepper, chopped
5 garlic cloves, chopped
9 ounces cherry tomatoes
½ cup sherry
1 cup gamebird stock

¼ teaspoon savory
¼ teaspoon marjoram
¼ teaspoon basil
⅛ teaspoon ground red chipotle (or more as desired)
1 teaspoon cornstarch, mixed with a little water
3 tablespoons parsley, chopped

Preparation

HEAT oven to 325 degrees. Season pheasant with salt and pepper. Heat olive oil in braising pan over medium-high heat. Brown pheasant 2 minutes per side and remove from pan. Lower heat to medium and sauté onion and pepper for 3 to 4 minutes. Add garlic, stir, and sauté another 2 minutes. Add tomatoes and sauté another minute. Add sherry, stock, and spices, stirring to combine. Simmer for a couple of minutes and then return pheasant to pan. Cover and place in oven for about 25 minutes.

REMOVE pheasant and cover to keep moist. Simmer the liquid and vegetables for a few minutes. Add the cornstarch slurry and stir to combine. Continue cooking a few minutes more to thicken. Return pheasant to pan, spooning mixture over the pieces. Remove from heat and sprinkle with parsley.

SERVE with cooked orzo mixed with olive oil and a little garlic, with freshly grated Parmesan on top.

Serves 4

*Wine Suggestions: Domino Shiraz
or Llai Llai Chardonnay*

CROCKPOT PHEASANT WITH TARRAGON SAUCE

Ingredients

2 cups mushrooms (about 3 large or 6 medium), thickly sliced

1½ cups frozen or canned pearl onions

2 tablespoons butter, divided

1 tablespoon olive oil

1 pheasant

2 shallots, sliced thin

2 carrots, fine chop

2 celery stalks, fine chop

½ onion, fine chop

¼ cup brandy

3 tablespoons flour

1 cup dry vermouth or other dry white wine

2½ cups chicken stock

1 tablespoon white Worcestershire sauce

1 bay leaf

1 tablespoon dried tarragon

3 tablespoons sour cream combined with 1 tablespoon flour

Preparation

PLACE mushrooms and pearl onions in large crockpot, leaving room in center for the pheasant. In a large skillet, heat 1 tablespoon of the butter with the olive oil over medium-high heat. Season pheasant with salt and pepper and place in skillet on its side. Brown meat for 2 minutes, and turn to the other side, browning it for 2 more minutes. Place pheasant in crockpot, breast side down.

LOWER heat in skillet to medium and add remaining butter. Sauté shallot, carrot, celery, and onion for about 4 minutes. Add brandy and use to deglaze pan. Simmer 1 minute. Sprinkle flour over the mixture, stirring to combine. Cook for about 1 more minute. Add vermouth and stir to combine. The flour will start to thicken the liquid, so add a cup of the broth and keep stirring. Add white Worcestershire sauce, bay leaf, and tarragon and bring mixture to a slow boil. Pour this mixture over pheasant in the crockpot. Pour remaining broth over pheasant, cover and cook on low for 3 hours or until juices run clear when breast is pricked with a fork.

TRANSFER pheasant to a platter and tent with aluminum foil to keep warm. Remove and discard bay leaf. Turn heat to high. Combine a small amount of the liquid from the crockpot with the sour cream and flour mixture, stirring so that no lumps form. Add a little more liquid, stir to combine, and then add this mixture to the crockpot. Stir to combine and continue to cook mixture to reduce and thicken the liquid.

THIS dish can be served two ways. You can remove the meat from the pheasant carcass, cut it into bite-size pieces and return it to the vegetable-broth mixture. Place wild rice in individual bowls and ladle the pheasant, vegetable, and liquid over the rice.

OR, YOU can place the pheasant on a serving platter and carve at the table, with the vegetable mixture in its own serving bowl.

Serves 4
Wine Suggestions: The Crossings Unoaked Chardonnay or
Bota Box Redvolution

PHEASANT BREAST WITH PINEAPPLES & PEPPERS

After prepping your ingredients, this makes a delicious and quick stir fry. Fresh pineapple is much better in this recipe than canned, and is now available almost year round. The ginger-flavored schnapps is a handy staple to have in your culinary liquor cabinet. It adds a spicy-sweet flavor when cooking many dishes using game birds.

Ingredients

- 1 tablespoon peanut oil
- 6 thin slices peeled, fresh ginger
- 2 large garlic cloves, sliced
- 1 pheasant breast, deboned and cut into thin strips
- ½ large bell pepper, cut in strips ¼-inch wide
- ½ cup sweet onion, cut into thin strips
- 2 thin slices of fresh pineapple, cut into chunks
- ⅓ cup ginger-flavored schnapps
- ½ teaspoon Chinese five-spice powder
- 1 cup chicken stock
- ½ cup cashews

Preparation

IN SKILLET or wok, heat peanut oil on low to medium-low heat. Add ginger and garlic slices and continue heating slowly to infuse the oil with the flavors, about 20 minutes. Be sure that the garlic is not burning – turn your heat down if you see the slices start to sizzle.

PAT pheasant strips dry. Remove garlic slices from wok and discard. Turn heat up to medium-high and add pheasant slices, spreading out to an even layer. Let cook for 2 minutes, and then stir to cook other side for another minute. Place in a serving dish and set aside. Add pepper and onion strips and stir fry for 2 minutes. Lower heat to medium, add pineapple and continue stir frying for another minute.

ADD ginger-flavored brandy and deglaze wok for about 2 minutes, or until most of the liquid has evaporated. Sprinkle the Chinese five-spice over the ingredients, stir to combine and then add stock. Simmer for about 5 minutes and return pheasant and juices to wok, stirring until pheasant is just heated through. Add cashews to heat through just before serving.

Serves 2 – 3
Wine Suggestions: Loredona Pinot Grigio or Josh Cellars Chardonnay

ROAST PHEASANT WITH CITRUS CREAM

This can be served both as a hot and a cold dish. We have presented it here as a hot entrée, but it works just as well served as a dinner salad on a warm summer evening. Just toss some mixed greens with a little olive oil and a small amount of balsamic vinegar. Cut the pheasant meat into bite-size chunks and add to the greens, topping this with a sprinkling of toasted pecans.

Ingredients

1 pheasant	1 cup frozen pearl onions, thawed
5 cups apple cider, divided	¼ cup brandy
¾ cup fresh lemon juice	2 cups orange juice
6 garlic cloves, finely minced	1 lemon
¾ cup sugar	1 lime
3 tablespoons kosher salt	1 cup sour cream
olive oil	powdered sugar (optional)

Preparation

MAKE a marinade by combining 3 cups of the apple cider, lemon juice, garlic, sugar and kosher salt. Place pheasant in a non-reactive bowl or large sealable plastic bag. Pour marinade over pheasant and marinate for 4 hours – 2 in refrigerator and last 2 at room temperature.

HEAT oven to 400 degrees. Remove pheasant from marinade and wipe dry. Rub olive oil over pheasant and season with salt and pepper. Place pheasant, breast side up, in lightly greased roasting pan. Place pearl onions around pheasant and roast in 400-degree oven for 10 minutes.

LOWER heat to 350 degrees and pour brandy over pheasant. Stir onions to coat them with the brandy and pan juices. Continue roasting until juices run clear – about an hour.

MEANWHILE, make citrus cream by combining the remaining apple cider with orange juice in a medium saucepan. Squeeze the juice from the lemon and lime into the pan. Turn heat to high and reduce the liquid to a little less than 1 cup. Remove from heat and let cool for about 10 minutes. Whip sour cream into the reduced liquid. If too thick, you can add a little apple cider. Taste the sauce and, if it is too tart, whip in a little powdered sugar.

TO SERVE, place the pheasant on a platter and drizzle a small amount of the sauce over the breast. Pass the remaining sauce in a gravy boat. Wild rice makes an excellent accompaniment.

Serves 2 – 3
Wine Suggestions: Kunde Magnolia Lane Sauvignon Blanc or
Gnarly Head Merlot

SOUTHWEST PHEASANT STEW

This hearty strew utilizes the whole bird, including the additional flavor that comes from slow-cooking the pheasant bones. I like to use black beans that are made with a Caribbean or Cuban sauce instead of just plain black beans. If you use this kind, don't drain them. The extra sauce adds to the flavoring in the stew. You can serve it with a variety of garnishes to please just about every palate: sour cream, hot sauce, shredded cheese, avocado, green onions, toasted tortilla strips or chips.

Ingredients

1 pheasant, skinned and quartered
1 medium red onion, chopped
1 green bell pepper, chopped
3 cloves garlic, minced
1 15-ounce can, roasted tomatoes
2 15-ounce cans, black beans – drained
1 16-ounce bag frozen corn (about 3 cups)
1 4-ounce can green chilies

1 28-ounce can enchilada sauce
2 cups chicken or gamebird stock
2 teaspoons ground cumin
1–2 teaspoons chili powder, to your taste
1½ teaspoons oregano
3 large corn tortillas, cut in half & then cut in ½-inch strips
1 lime, juiced
garnishes as noted above

Preparation

PAT pheasant dry and sprinkle lightly with salt and pepper. Place the rest of the ingredients – except the lime juice and garnishes – in a large crockpot. Stir the ingredients well to combine, and then place the pheasant quarters in the mixture. Cook on low for about 6 hours.

REMOVE the pheasant quarters from the crockpot and let them cool enough to handle. Pull the meat from the bones and shred or chop. When working with the drumsticks, be sure to remove the tiny little tendons from the drumstick meat. Discard bones and return meat to stew.

SERVE in bowls with garnishes as described above.

Serves 6 – 8

Wine Suggestions: Domino Moscato
or
Villa Pozzi Pinot Grigio

ROAST PHEASANT WITH GRILLED PEACHES AND PEPPERS

Be sure to keep a pheasant or two in your freezer to cook with the summer's ripe peaches. A vertical roaster works ideally for this recipe. It has a center cup for the flavoring liquid, with a cone that sits upright to hold the bird in a vertical position. This keeps the drier breast meat away from the direct flame of the grill. Or, you can use the prototype of this kitchen tool – the handy beer can. Just put the chosen liquid in the can and place the bird over the can.

Ingredients

- 1 pheasant
- 1 dried ancho chile, seeds removed
- ½ cup olive oil
- 2 garlic cloves, minced
- 1 teaspoon oregano
- 1 teaspoon thyme
- 1 teaspoon ground ginger
- 1½ teaspoons ground cumin, divided
- ¼ cup lime juice
- 1⅓ cups orange juice, divided
- ½ teaspoon ground cinnamon
- 1 tablespoon brown sugar
- ⅓ cup orange liqueur
- 1 teaspoon balsamic vinegar
- 2 peaches, skin removed and quartered
- 1 red bell pepper, cut in 3-inch chunks
- ½ cup beverage of your choice – wine, beer, juice
- 3 strips bacon

Preparation

PLACE the seeded chile in a small bowl and cover with warm water. Soak until soft. Remove chili and cut into small pieces or blend in a blender. Place in a marinade bowl and add the olive oil, garlic, oregano, thyme, ginger, and 1 teaspoon of the cumin. Whisk together and add the lime juice and 1/3 cup of the orange juice. Place the pheasant in the marinade, turning to coat. Cover and marinate in the refrigerator for 4 to 6 hours, turning occasionally.

COMBINE remaining orange juice with the remaining cumin, and the cinnamon, brown sugar, orange liqueur, and balsamic vinegar. Whisk to combine. Add peaches and bell pepper, stirring to coat. Cover and marinate for 2 hours.

HEAT grill to 400 degrees. Remove pheasant from marinade and season with salt and pepper. Pour the 1/2 cup of wine, beer, or juice into the center cup of a vertical roaster (or use a beer can). Wrap the bacon pieces over the breast of the pheasant, securing them with toothpicks, and place the bird vertically on the cone (or beer can).

REMOVE the peach and pepper from the marinade. The pheasant will take about 20 to 25 minutes of roasting and the peach/pepper mixture about 8 minutes. While you can coordinate cooking both at the same time, you might find it easier to grill the peach/pepper mixture in a grilling basket first, and remove it to a bowl to keep warm in the oven while you roast the bird. Pheasant meat can dry out if cooked too long. This way – grilling the peach/peppers first – you can finish the pheasant to perfection.

PLACE the bird in its upright position on the grill. Roast, with lid covered, turning one-half circle every 3 to 4 minutes until the juice from the leg runs only slightly pink when pricked.

WHEN done, place on platter and surround with the grilled peaches and pepper chunks.

Serves 2 – 3
Wine Suggestions: The Calling Chardonnay or Foghead Pinot Noir

ROAST PHEASANT ON GRILL

Roasting a pheasant on a barbeque grill is a great way to get the wonderful roasted pheasant taste without heating up your kitchen on a hot day. The best way to do this is to use one of the vertical roasting cones available online and in most culinary stores. This was originally called "beer can chicken" because an opened can of beer was used as the vertical base, allowing the beer to add moisture and flavor to the chicken. The advantage of the store-bought roaster – besides the stability – is the tray around the base that can also hold vegetables to roast along with the meat.

Ingredients

1 pheasant, plucked or skinned
3 bacon strips
½ cup wine or beer for center of roaster

fresh thyme sprigs
chipotle fruit sauce or fig balsamic sauce (see note below)

Preparation

ON A gas grill, light the back burner and one burner on each side and heat to 300 degrees.

PAT pheasant dry and season with salt and pepper. Place thyme sprigs in center cup of vertical roaster and fill with your favorite wine or beer. Place roasting cone on top and put pheasant on the cone. Wrap strips of bacon around pheasant, securing them with toothpicks.

PUT roaster in center of grill, close cover, and roast for 20 – 30 minutes, until inner temperature of pheasant reaches 150 degrees. Remove from grill and place pheasant on a serving platter. Remove and discard bacon strips. Baste pheasant with the chipotle fruit sauce of fig balsamic sauce. Finish in low-temperature oven for about 5 minutes before serving.

NOTE on the sauces: Most well-stocked grocery stores carry a variety of sauces that can be used for basting or finishing roasted meat. You can also view some great online sources in the Culinary Sources section in the back of this book.

Serves 2 – 3
Wine Suggestions: Massimo Sauvignon Blanc or Yellow Tail Sauvignon Blanc

Hawaiian Pheasant

Cutting the pheasant into eight pieces allows the meat to cook more evenly. You have four pieces with the drumsticks and thighs. Then you cut each half-breast in half, making your eight pieces. You will note that this recipe includes a small amount of ground chipotle pepper, which adds a slightly smoky kick to it. Feel free to add more if you want more heat.

Ingredients

1 pheasant, plucked or skinned and cut in 8 pieces
¼ cup coconut rum
⅓ cup dried cherries
2 ½-inch thick slices pineapple, quartered
2 tablespoons brown sugar
¼ cup shredded coconut
2 tablespoons butter

1 2-inch piece fresh ginger, peeled & sliced
1 garlic clove, thinly sliced
2 shallots, thinly sliced (about 1/3 cup)
¼ cup dry white wine
¼ teaspoon ground nutmeg
½ teaspoon ground cumin
⅛ teaspoon ground red chipotle
1½ cups game bird stock

Preparation

IN A small bowl, soak cherries in coconut rum. Place the pineapple on a plate and baste both sides with a little of the coconut rum. Sprinkle half the brown sugar on one side of the pineapple, turn and sprinkle the rest on the other side.

HEAT oven to 200 degrees. In a dry skillet, toast the shredded coconut until it turns a golden brown. Remove and set aside. On low, heat the butter in the skillet until melted. Add garlic and ginger slices, and cook on low to infuse the butter with their flavors, about 10 minutes. Do not let the garlic burn.

PAT the pheasant pieces dry and season with salt and pepper. Remove garlic and ginger from skillet, discarding the garlic. Turn heat to medium-high and brown the pheasant pieces for 2 minutes on each side. Remove to a covered dish and place in the warm oven.

LOWER heat to medium, and add shallots to skillet. Sauté shallots until translucent. Deglaze the pan with the white wine, cooking until most of the liquid has evaporated. Remove shallots to plate with the reserved ginger. Place pineapple in skillet and cook until the pieces have caramelized – about 3 minutes on the first side and 2 minutes on the other side. Add soaked cherries and rum to skillet and deglaze pan again. Return shallots and ginger to pan and sprinkle spices over all. Add stock, stirring to combine. Bring mixture back to a simmer and reduce stock by about half. Add pheasant and any accumulated juices to the mixture and simmer for a couple of minutes.

TO SERVE arrange pheasant on a platter with the pineapple pieces. Pour sauce over all and sprinkle with toasted coconut.

Serves 2 – 3

Wine Suggestions: Yellow Tail Moscato or Loredona Viognier

BRAISED PHEASANT LEGS WITH ROASTED PEPPERS

Ingredients

6 pheasant legs	1 tablespoon olive oil
½ cup flour	3 garlic cloves, sliced
½ teaspoon garlic powder	2 roasted red peppers, thickly sliced
½ teaspoon ground cumin	¼ cup dry white wine or vermouth
½ teaspoon sweet paprika	½ cup cream sherry
½ teaspoon dried tarragon	1 cup game bird stock
¼ teaspoon salt	1 teaspoon dried tarragon
¼ teaspoon ground pepper	1 teaspoon arrowroot
1 tablespoon butter	⅓ cup sour cream

Preparation

PAT pheasant legs dry. Combine flour with the spices and dust pheasant legs with mixture. Heat butter and oil in braising pan over low heat. Add garlic slices and continue cooking on low to infuse fats with garlic flavor.

REMOVE garlic slices and set aside. Raise heat in pan to medium-high and brown the pheasant legs about 3 minutes per side. Add roasted pepper slices and sauté for 2 minutes. Add white wine, stirring to loosen any brown bits, and continue simmering until liquid is reduced by half. Add sherry, stock, and tarragon and return garlic to pan, stirring to combine. Cover and simmer on low until legs are tender – about an hour and a half. If necessary, add extra stock.

COMBINE arrowroot with sour cream. Stir a little of the hot liquid into the sour cream mixture. Add mixture to pan and stir to combine. Bring mixture back to a simmer and allow liquid to thicken.

Serves 4
Wine Suggestions: Foghead Chardonnay or Josh Cellars Chardonnay

Springer spaniel rests after a morning Montana hunt.

32

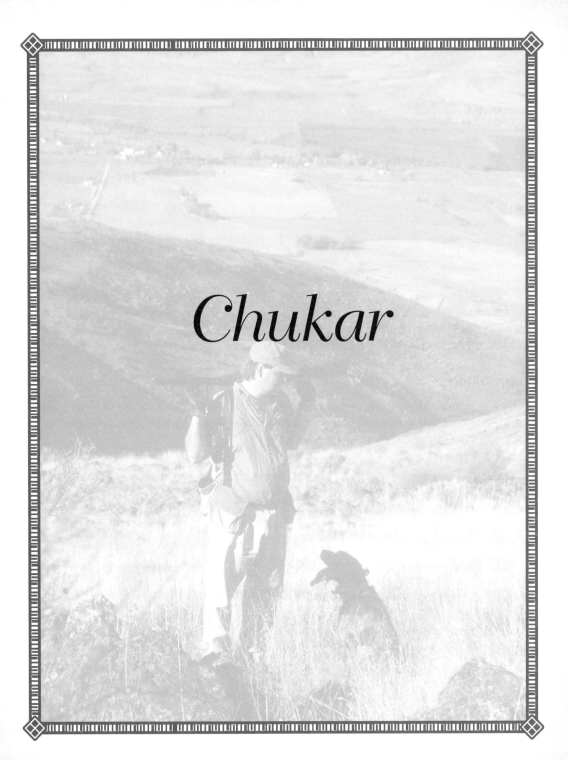

Chukar

CHUKAR BREASTS WITH SAUTÉED MUSHROOMS

Ingredients

2 chukar partridge, breasts filleted and
    rest of carcasses quartered
1 tablespoon olive oil

2 tablespoons butter
8 ounces mushrooms, any combination,
    chopped thickly

For the Marinade

¼ cup olive oil
2 cloves garlic, minced
1 tablespoon Worcestershire sauce

1 tablespoon brandy
    salt and pepper

For Stock

1 tablespoon olive oil
1 carrot, chopped
1 small onion, chopped
    couple of sprigs of parsley
3 tablespoons brandy

2 cups game bird or chicken stock
1 tablespoon tomato paste
1 bay leaf
½ teaspoon thyme

Preparation

THE night before, or at least 4 hours before, combine the ingredients for the marinade. Fillet the breasts from the partridge and place in the marinade. Save the rest of the carcasses to be used when preparing the dinner.

QUARTER the carcasses. You will have the 2 breastbones, split and the four legs with the meat still on. To make the stock, brown the carcasses in a large saucepan in the olive oil, over medium-high heat. Add the carrot and onion, and continue browning. Add the parsley and the brandy, stirring to deglaze. Then add the rest of the ingredients, and simmer until the liquid is reduced by half. Remove the bones from the saucepan, saving the legs for a pre-dinner snack. Strain the stock and set aside.

PUT the tablespoon of olive oil in a skillet and heat to medium-high. Remove the chukar breasts from the marinade, pat dry, and sear in the skillet on both sides for a total of only 2 to 3 minutes. Remove to covered serving dish and keep warm in oven.

PUT 2 tablespoons of butter in the same skillet and add the mushrooms, sautéing over medium high heat until they start to soften. Add half of the stock and continue cooking until soft. Pour the mushrooms and the rest of stock over the birds in the serving dish.

SERVE with noodles tossed with a little butter and chopped parsley, and a green veggie.

Serves 2

Wine Suggestions: Noble Vines 667 Pinot Noir or Chateau Bonnet Rose

CHUKAR TARRAGON
with Saffron Risotto and Pine Nuts

Can substitute 3 pheasant breasts.

When cooking the risotto, you can substitute ¾ cup of a sweet white wine, like a riesling, for the combination of the dry white wine and the cream sherry.

Ingredients

> 4 chukar partridge breasts, filleted and halved
> ½ cup flour, seasoned with salt, pepper, and garlic powder
> 2 tablespoons butter

For the Risotto

> 1 cup Arborio rice
> 2 tablespoons butter
> ½ cup dry white wine
> ¼ cup cream sherry
> 1 tablespoon tarragon
> 1 pinch saffron

> 2-3 cups game bird or chicken stock
> 1 cup shiitake mushrooms, sliced thinly (optional)
> 1 cup sour cream, combined with ⅓ cup milk
> ¼ cup pine nuts, toasted

Preparation

PAT breast pieces dry, and dust with the seasoned flour. Heat 2 tablespoons butter in a large skillet until sizzling. Add the breasts and brown 1½ minutes per side for chukar (2 minutes per side for pheasant). Remove to a covered dish and put in warm oven.

TURN heat down and add 2 tablespoons butter to the skillet. Add the rice and sauté until lightly browned, about 4 minutes. Add the white wine and the sherry along with the tarragon and saffron, stirring to combine. Cover and simmer over low heat until the liquid is almost entirely absorbed. Meanwhile, heat at least 2 cups of stock in a small saucepan. Add stock in ½-cup batches, as the liquid is absorbed. Keep covered and simmering until rice is softened but still has a slightly firm interior. Toward the end of this process, you can add the mushrooms, if you like.

BLEND the milk and sour cream. Add some of the heated stock to this mixture to even its temperature. Add this to the rice, stirring to blend. Add more stock if you want more sauce with the finished dinner.

JUST before serving, add the chukar breasts to the rice and sauce to reheat, covered. Then sprinkle the toasted pine nuts on top and serve in the skillet.

THIS is excellent served with a plain green veggie and a fresh fruit salad.

Serves 4

Wine Suggestions: Kunde Estate Chardonnay or Loredona Riesling

Chukar with Orange and Paprika Sauce

Ingredients

3 chukar – quartered
4 tablespoons flour
2 tablespoons paprika
2 tablespoons butter or margarine
1 large clove of garlic – minced
1 medium onion or 3 shallots – chopped
1 cup game bird stock – or chicken broth

½ cup orange juice
½ cup dry vermouth or other dry white wine
1 can mandarin oranges - drained
2 tablespoons parsley - chopped
3 tablespoons sour cream

Preparation

SEASON the flour with salt, pepper and 1 tablespoon of the paprika. Lightly flour the chukar pieces and brown in the skillet over medium-high heat, about 3 minutes per side. Remove birds, cover, and keep in a warm oven.

LOWER heat to medium and sauté the garlic and the onion until limp. Add the game stock or broth and ¼ cup of the vermouth, stirring to scrape any browned bits in the pan. Add the other tablespoon of the paprika and stir to combine. Cover and simmer on medium low for 20 minutes.

ADD the orange juice, cover, and simmer for another 10 minutes.

ADD the last ¼ cup of the vermouth, the mandarin oranges, and the parsley. Cover and simmer another 10 minutes for a total of 40 minutes.

PUT the chukar and the collected juices back into the skillet. Cover and heat for a couple of minutes. Take a couple of spoonfuls of the heated broth and mix with the sour cream to even the temperature. Then stir into the rest of the sauce.

SERVE with orzo tossed with a little garlic, olive oil, parsley and grated Parmesan cheese.

Serves 3 to 4

*Wine Suggestions: Foghead Sauvignon Blanc or
Sonoma Coast Vineyards Sauvignon Blanc*

Orange and Ginger Chukar

You can substitute 6 quail.

Ingredients

2 chukar partridge
1 1-inch piece of fresh ginger root, peeled and sliced into 5 pieces
2 tablespoons peanut oil
½ cup flour
⅛ teaspoon cayenne or red pepper
½ teaspoon paprika
salt and pepper

1 large shallot, sliced
6 large mushrooms, sliced
½ cup sherry
¾ cup game bird or chicken stock
¼ cup Grand Marnier + 1-2 tablespoons
1 orange, sectioned, or 1 11-ounce can mandarin oranges

Preparation

QUARTER chukars and pat dry. Combine the seasonings with the flour.

WARM the ginger slices in the peanut oil in a large skillet on low for about 15 minutes, without browning. Smash the slices as they warm to infuse the oil. Remove the ginger slices from the skillet and discard.

RAISE the heat in the skillet to high. Dust the chukar with the seasoned flour. When the oil in the skillet is hot enough that it sizzles when a few drops of water are sprinkled on it, lower the heat to medium-high and immediately add the chukar pieces to the skillet and brown, about 4 minutes per side. Remove chukar to a covered dish in a warm oven.

SAUTE the shallot in the skillet over medium heat, stirring for about 1 minute. Add the mushrooms and stir for about 1 more minute. Pour ¼ cup of sherry over the shallots and mushrooms, and deglaze the pan. Add the rest of the sherry, the stock and the ¼ cup Grand Marnier. Stir until blended and simmer for 10 minutes, uncovered. Add the orange sections and simmer for another 10 minutes.

RETURN the chukar and any accumulated pan juices to the skillet, spooning the sauce over the chukar. Cover and simmer on low for 5 minutes.

SERVE with asparagus tossed with butter and lime juice, and a saffron risotto.

Serves 2 to 3

Wine Suggestions: Gnarly Pinot Grigio
or Flirt Red Blend

CLAY POT CHUKAR

Any game bird can be cooked in this manner, but chukar seems to work particularly well with this recipe. Clay pot cooking requires an unglazed clay pot with lid. You must immerse the pot in water for about 20 minutes before filling it with your ingredients. You will then place it in a cold oven and turn the heat up to 450 degrees, usually cooking the ingredients for about 1 hour. That may seem awfully hot, but the wet clay and the liquids inside will keep your ingredients moist and tasty. But, you are still working with wild birds with very little fat. That extra fat in chicken allows you to keep cooking it for a much longer time without drying it out. For recipes using wild birds, we recommend removing the birds for the middle 20 minutes, so that they don't overcook.

Ingredients

3 chukar, quartered with the back discarded
fresh sage leaves
6 medium-sized red potatoes cut in half
1½ cups pearl onions, frozen or canned
2 carrots, peeled and quartered
fresh tarragon

¾ cup port wine
2 tablespoons soy sauce
½ cup chicken broth
salt and pepper
1½ cups mushrooms, halved
½ cup olive oil

Preparation

COMPLETELY immerse the clay pot and lid in water for 20 minutes. Parboil the red potatoes in salted water for 5 minutes.

REMOVE the clay pot from the water and line the bottom with fresh sage leaves. Place the chukar, potatoes, carrots, and pearl onions in the pot. Sprinkle liberally with fresh tarragon leaves. Whisk to combine the olive oil, port, soy sauce, and chicken broth. Pour over the ingredients in the pot. Cover with clay lid and put in cold oven. Turn the heat to 450 degrees. And cook for 20 minutes.

AFTER 20 minutes, remove the chukar pieces from the pot, cover and set aside. Add the mushrooms to the pot and stir. Cover and replace in oven, baking for another 20 minutes. Then return the meat to the pot for the last 20 minutes, stirring to let the sauce and vegetables coat the chukar.

AFTER 1 hour, check to see if meat is done. When removing clay pot from oven to counter, be sure that the surface it is put on is not too cold. It could crack the pot. Also, be careful of the heat from the pot on your counter. It is best to put it on a raised rack or trivet, which will let the air circulate until the pot is cool enough to take to the table.

SERVE this with biscuits and honey, and a chilled green salad.

Serves 4

Wine Suggestions: Chateau la Louveire Blanc or Brazin Old Vine Zinfandel

FRIED CHUKAR

You can substitute any game bird; just adjust the cooking time to the size of the pieces.

Ingredients

3 chukar partridge, quartered
½ cup flour
⅓ cup cornmeal
1 teaspoon salt
1 teaspoon garlic powder
½ teaspoon ground chipotle pepper, or cayenne

1 teaspoon paprika
¼ teaspoon each – thyme, marjoram, savory
1 egg
2 tablespoons milk
4 tablespoons butter-flavored Crisco

Preparation

COMBINE the flour, cornmeal, and the seasonings. Place on a dinner plate. Break the egg on a dinner-size plate. Add the milk, and whisk to combine. Put both plates on the counter next to the stove.

PUT Crisco or other lard into an iron skillet, and turn the heat to high. Pat the chukar pieces dry, and place on another dinner plate, and put on the counter next to the other plates.

WHEN the oil has heated so that it sizzles intensely when a few drops of water are sprinkled, you are ready to cook the chukar. Working quickly, dip the chukar pieces into the egg/milk mixture and then dredge in the flour mixture until coated. Put the floured pieces in the skillet and fry about 2 to 3 minutes per side. Then turn the heat down to low and cover for 3 minutes, or until done.

DRAIN on paper towels.

Serves 4

***Wine Suggestions: Gnarly Head Zinfandel or
Yellow Tail Rose Bubbles***

Grilled Chukar with Pear Sauce

Ingredients

4 chukar partridge, halved

For the Marinade

¼ cup olive oil
1 cup sweet vermouth
½ cup sherry

1 shallot, minced
1 teaspoon lemon zest
1 teaspoon cracked peppercorns

For the Sauce

1 tablespoon olive oil
3 shallots, thinly sliced
1½ cups mushrooms, thinly sliced
4 ripe pears, peeled, cored, and sliced
½ teaspoon tarragon
½ teaspoon ground chipotle pepper

¾ cup sweet vermouth
1½ cups game bird or chicken stock
2 tablespoons butter, cut in pieces & chilled
brown sugar and balsamic vinegar (optional)

Preparation

COMBINE the ingredients for the marinade. Rinse chukar pieces, pat dry, and place in the marinade for 8 hours or overnight.

SINCE the sauce keeps well, you can make it ahead of time and either keep warm or reheat. Just wait until you are ready to serve before you swirl in the butter.

TO MAKE the sauce, heat the olive oil in a large saucepan and add the shallots. Cook over medium-high heat for about 1 minute. Add the mushrooms and cook an additional 2 minutes, stirring frequently.

ADD a small amount of the vermouth to the pan to keep the mixture from sticking, and add the pears, tarragon, and chipotle pepper. Then add the rest of the vermouth and the stock. Simmer on low for about 10 to 15 minutes to reduce the sauce and blend the flavors.

DEPENDING on your taste and the sweetness of the pears, you can add a little brown sugar to increase the sweetness or a little balsamic vinegar to cut the sweetness.

REMOVE the chukar from the marinade and pat dry. Pre-heat your grill and grill the chukar pieces for a total of about 8 to 10 minutes, turning once.

JUST before the birds are done, swirl the butter pieces into the sauce. Continue on low heat to thicken.

SERVE the sauce in a separate bowl. This is great accompanied by asparagus with lemon butter and a simple pasta coated with garlic-infused olive oil, toasted pine nuts, and grated Parmesan cheese.

Serves 4 to 6

Wine Suggestions: Flirt White Blend or Noble Vines 667 Pinot Noir

End of the day.

JIM'S INDIAN CURRIED CHUKAR
with Basmati Saffron Rice

Jim Tenuto has been a customer and friend of ours for many years. As he has become enamored with wingshooting, he has turned his gourmet talents to creating delicious wild game recipes. We have traded recipes over the years, and this is one I particularly liked. I think you will, too.

Ingredients

6 chukar partridge breasts, sliced into strips
1 tablespoon Emeril's Essence
1 tablespoon canola oil
1 tablespoon butter
1 small onion, chopped
1 tablespoon fresh ginger, peeled and minced

2 tablespoons curry powder
1 tablespoon Thai curry paste (Jim uses the green, but feels the red would also work)
1 13.5 ounce can unsweetened coconut milk
2 tablespoons cilantro, chopped

Preparation

MIX the chukar strips with the Emeril seasoning and sauté quickly in the canola oil. Remove from skillet and set aside.

HEAT the butter in the skillet over medium-high heat. Add onion and sauté until soft, about 4 to 5 minutes. Add ginger, curry powder, and curry paste. Sauté for 1 minute. Stir in the coconut milk and simmer for 3 to 4 minutes. Jim comments that, if you want to thicken the sauce, you might mix in a pinch of cornstarch at this stage.

RETURN the chukar strips to the skillet and heat through. Add cilantro and season to taste with salt and pepper.

SERVE over Basmati Saffron Rice.

Ingredients

1 cup Basmati rice
1½ cups water

salt
pinch of saffron

Preparation

BOIL water with salt and saffron. Add rice, bring back to boil, and reduce heat to low. Cook for 15 to 20 minutes.

Serves 4

Wine Suggestions: Enza Prosecco or Loredona Viognier

Raspberry Chukar

Can substitute 3 Hungarian partridge or 6 quail.

Ingredients

2 chukar partridge, quartered
2 tablespoons butter
6 tablespoons honey
14 ounces game bird or chicken stock
1 cup cream sherry

1 tablespoon tomato paste
¼ cup Drambuie or Grand Marnier
¾ cup raspberries, fresh or frozen
  balsamic vinegar to taste

Preparation

PREHEAT oven to 350 degrees. Melt butter in skillet over medium-high heat and brown birds on all sides, a total of about 4 minutes. Put the birds in a Dutch oven. Pour the butter remaining in the skillet over the birds, and then drizzle the honey over them. Cover and roast in 350-degree oven for 30 minutes at the most. Birds are done when meat is barely pink.

MEANWHILE, place the stock, sherry, and tomato paste in a saucepan. Stir to combine and then simmer on medium until reduced by half.

POUR the Drambuie or Grand Marnier into the skillet that you used to brown the birds. Do not have it on the heat. Carefully light a match and ignite the liquor, letting the flames go out on their own. Add the reduced stock and deglaze the pan. Simmer for 2 to 3 minutes. Add the raspberries and heat through.

REMOVE the Dutch oven and pour the raspberry mixture over the birds. Stir gently to mix the sauce with the honey and pan drippings. Taste to determine the sweetness. If too sweet, add a touch of balsamic vinegar.

THIS is delightful served over shredded cabbage that has been boiled in salted water and drained.

Serves 2 to 3

Wine Suggestions: Massimo Malbec
or
Villa Pozzi Nero d'Avola

ROAST CHUKAR PARTRIDGE

Can substitute 2 pheasant breasts, bone in.

Ingredients

3 chukar partridge, preferably plucked
   garlic powder
   tarragon
   ground sage (or fresh sage leaves)
   salt and pepper
4 tablespoons butter, melted
2 tablespoons brown sugar

1 tablespoon soy sauce
1 tablespoon Angostura bitters
½ cup sherry
1 tablespoon lemon juice
½ teaspoon tarragon
1 tablespoon balsamic vinegar
   pinch of thyme

Preparation

IF partridge have been skinned, wrap bacon around them to keep them from drying out. You do not need bacon if they have been plucked.

PREHEAT oven to 375 degrees. Sprinkle garlic powder, tarragon, and sage in the cavities. Sprinkle salt and pepper on the outside of the birds.

IN A small saucepan, combine the rest of the ingredients and bring to a simmer. Stir to combine and keep warm.

PLACE the birds in a shallow roasting pan in the oven at 375 degrees. After 15 minutes, turn heat down to 350 degrees and baste with the heated mixture.

ROAST in 350 degree oven until done, basting every 10 minutes with sauce. Birds are done when juices run clear and breast meat is just barely pink next to the bone.

Serves 2 to 3

Wine Suggestions: Yellow Tail Reserve Shiraz
or
Twisted Zinfandel

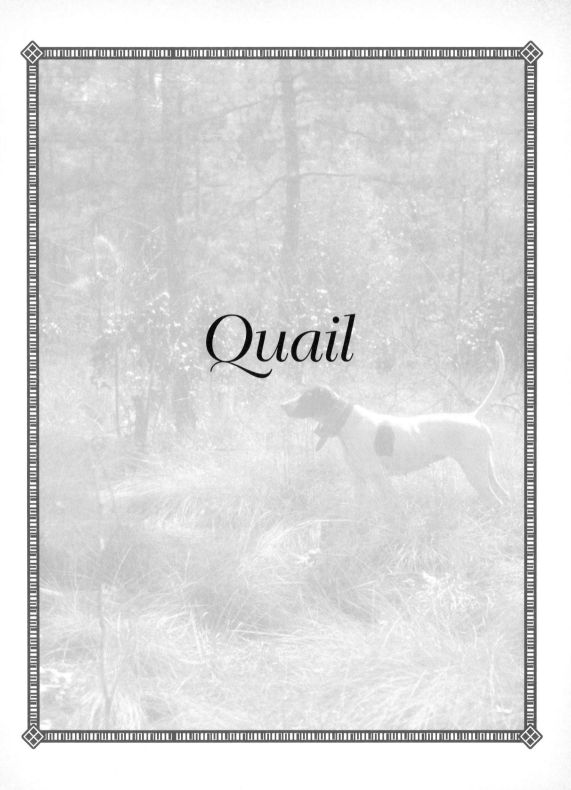

Quail

Blanche's Grilled Quail

This marinade also works well with pheasant.

Ingredients

8 quail, split in half

For the Marinade

¼ cup peanut oil
2 tablespoons soy sauce
2 tablespoons sherry
½ cup orange juice
small amount of brown sugar, no more
than 1 tablespoon, depending on how
sweet you desire

1 clove garlic, minced
1 tablespoon grated fresh ginger root
1 tablespoon Dijon mustard
1 teaspoon thyme, or several fresh
thyme sprigs

Preparation

MIX the marinade ingredients together, and marinate the quail for at least 2 hours. Grill over very hot fire, 3 minutes on one side and 2 minutes on the other side. Check to see if they are done by cutting into the thickest part of the breast. They are done when the meat is still slightly pink. Don't overcook.

Serves 4
Wine Suggestions: Noble Vines 667 Pinot Noir
or Ramón Bilbao Crianza

"FETCH HERE"

Fetch Here

©Fred McCaleb

CHUCK'S GRILLED QUAIL

Can substitute one chukar, quartered, usually 1 per person.

This is a quick and easy recipe that can be adjusted for the "heat level" that you and your guests like. You can adjust the chipotle pepper in both the marinade and the honey sauce. If available, the chipotle pepper adds a nice smoky taste that you don't get with just cayenne pepper.

Ingredients

    8 *quail, split in half*

For the Marinade

    ½ *cup canola oil*
    1 *tablespoon garlic powder (or 2 garlic cloves, crushed)*
    1 *tablespoon Italian seasoning (mixture of marjoram, thyme, rosemary, sage, oregano, and basil)*

    1 *teaspoon 4-peppercorn blend*
    1 *teaspoon ground chipotle pepper, or cayenne pepper*

For the Basting Sauce

    1 *cup honey*
    1 *tablespoon ground chipotle pepper, or cayenne pepper*

Preparation

MARINATE the quail halves for 2 to 4 hours. Just before grilling, put the honey and chipotle pepper in a small saucepan. Blend and simmer on low for about 10 minutes. Keep warm.

REMOVE the quail from the marinade and grill over very hot fire for 3 minutes per side. Baste the quail with the sauce and grill 1 more minute per side. Bring the remaining basting sauce to a simmer, cooking for about 5 minutes on a low simmer. Serve this sauce with the quail.

Serves 4

Wine Suggestions: The Crossings Pinot Noir
or
Loredona Viognier

GRAND MARNIER QUAIL

Ingredients

6-8 quail, split in half
1 inch ginger root, peeled and cut into 5 slices
2 tablespoons peanut oil
½ cup flour
1 teaspoon paprika
½ teaspoon ground chipotle pepper, or cayenne pepper
salt and pepper

1 shallot, thinly sliced
6-8 large mushrooms, sliced
½ cup sherry
¾ cup game bird or chicken stock
¼ cup Grand Marnier, plus 1 tablespoon to add at end of cooking
1 orange, sectioned, or 1 can mandarin oranges

Preparation

WARM the ginger slices in the peanut oil in a large skillet, smashing the ginger several times to infuse the peanut oil. Do this on low heat so the ginger does not burn. Let it heat for about 15 minutes. Meanwhile, split the quail in half and pat dry. Combine the flour with the paprika, chipotle pepper, and salt and pepper. Dust the quail halves in the seasoned flour.

REMOVE the ginger from the skillet and set aside. Raise the heat to high. As soon as the oil "spits" when a drop of cold water is added, lower the heat to medium high and brown the quail in the oil for about 2 minutes per side. Remove quail to a covered dish and place in a warm oven.

SAUTÉ the shallot in the remaining oil, stirring frequently, for about 1 minute. Add the mushrooms and stir frequently for about 1 more minute. If the skillet gets too dry, you can add a little stock. Lower heat to medium low and pour ¼ cup of the sherry into the pan and deglaze, scraping all brown bits from bottom of pan. Add the rest of the sherry, the stock, and the ¼ cup of Grand Marnier. Stir until blended. Return the ginger slices to the skillet along with the orange sections. Cover and simmer for about 15 minutes. Remove the ginger slices and discard. Add the quail and any accumulated juices back into the pan. Spoon the sauce over the quail, cover, and simmer on low for about 5 minutes.

THIS is great served with steamed asparagus tossed with a little butter and lime juice and a saffron risotto.

Serves 4

Wine Suggestions: Loredona Pinot Grigio
or Sauvion Chinon

Orange and Sage Stuffed Grilled Quail

Ingredients

8 quail
gin

For the Marinade

4 tablespoons olive oil
1 tablespoon soy sauce

1 tablespoon lemon juice
black pepper

For the Stuffing

1 large orange, cut in 8 pieces
2 medium slices of yellow onion,
chopped

16 fresh sage leaves
black pepper

Preparation

MARINATE the quail in the marinade for 2 to 4 hours. Remove from marinade, pat dry, and wash each bird out with gin. Stuff each bird with an orange piece, 2 sage leaves and some chopped onion and pepper. Tie the legs together.

GRILL the quail over a very hot fire for 3½ minutes per side, depending on fire. Don't overcook, breasts should just barely be pink.

THIS is great served with wild rice mixed with sautéed mushrooms and cooked asparagus tips.

Serves 4

Wine Suggestions: George Duboeuf Fleury
or
Irony Chardonnay

QUAIL WITH SUN-DRIED TOMATOES

Ingredients

6 quail
flour – seasoned with garlic powder,
   pepper and paprika
1 tablespoon olive oil
1 tablespoon butter
3 shallots, sliced thin
¼ cup sun-dried tomatoes, sliced

½ pound mushrooms, sliced
¾ cup port wine
1 tablespoon tomato paste
1 teaspoon ground chipotle pepper
¾ cup veal stock or beef stock
   ground savory to taste

Preparation

RINSE quail and pat dry. Dredge quail in seasoned flour. Heat butter and oil in large skillet over medium-high heat. Quickly brown quail on all sides. Remove and set aside. Lower heat to medium and sauté the shallots, sun-dried tomatoes and mushrooms for 1 to 2 minutes, stirring to combine. Add small amount of the port to the skillet and stir to deglaze. Add the tomato paste and chipotle pepper, and stir to combine. Return the quail to the pan. Pour the rest of the port and the veal stock over the quail. Lightly sprinkle the savory over all.

COVER and simmer on low for about 25 minutes, turning a couple of times so that the breasts are immersed in the sauce.

Serves 3 to 4
Wine Suggestions: Hob Nob Pinot Noir or Massimo Rioja

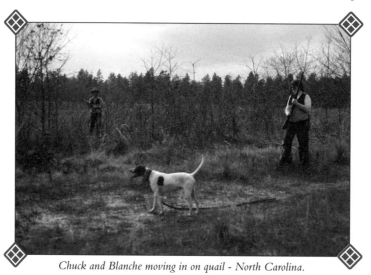

Chuck and Blanche moving in on quail - North Carolina.

Quail Stuffed with Wild Rice, Dried Cherries, and Pecans

Can substitute 1 chukar for 2 quail, and increase roasting time.

This is an elegant presentation that shows quail off at their best. If you use a roasting pan that can also be used as the serving dish, you can bring the presentation to the table and wow your guests by flaming the quail at the table. Just be sure you haven't had too much brandy yourself!

Ingredients

6 quail
1 stick butter

½ cup cognac or brandy

For Stuffing

1 cup Madeira wine
½ cup dried cherries
2 cloves
1 cup cooked wild rice

1 tablespoon melted butter
½ cup chopped pecans
1 teaspoon orange zest
juice of one orange

Preparation

PRE-HEAT oven to 450 degrees.

PUT the Madeira, cherries, and cloves in a small saucepan and bring to a boil. Turn heat down to medium low and simmer for 5 minutes. Set aside. In a small bowl, mix the wild rice, the melted butter, the pecans, and 1 teaspoon zest from the orange. Strain the wine mixture, discarding the 2 cloves and putting the cherries in the wild rice mixture. Squeeze the juice of the orange into the Madeira and set aside. Mix the wild rice mixture and stuff the cavities of the quail.

MELT the stick of butter in a small saucepan. In a roasting pan or Dutch oven with a cover, put stuffed quail in a circle with legs facing the outside. Pour the butter over the quail and put in 450-degree oven, uncovered, for 5 minutes. Pour the Madeira-orange mixture over the quail and roast, uncovered another 5 minutes at 450 degrees. Reduce heat to 300 degrees, cover the pan, and roast until quail is done, approximately 30 minutes.

REMOVE quail from oven and pour brandy over the birds. Carefully light with a match and serve.

Serves 3 to 4
Wine Suggestions: Handcraft Petite Sirah
or Windsor Sonoma Russian River Pinot Noir

QUAIL WITH ORANGE MARMALADE, GINGER AND BRANDY

Ingredients

5 quail
  flour seasoned with salt and pepper
2 tablespoons peanut oil
6 green onions, chopped including green
  tops
1 inch fresh ginger, peeled and minced
3 tablespoons brandy

¾ cup game bird or chicken stock
¼ cup orange marmalade
¼ teaspoon nutmeg
1 teaspoon ground chipotle or cayenne
  pepper
3 tablespoons Grand Marnier

Preparation

DUST outside of quail with seasoned flour. In skillet over medium-high heat, brown quail in peanut oil, turning to brown all sides; approximately 6 minutes total. Remove to covered dish and place in 300-degree oven.

ADD green onions to skillet and sauté for about 1½ minutes. Deglaze the pan with the brandy. Add the rest of the ingredients except the Grand Marnier. Cover and simmer over low heat for about 15 minutes. Uncover, stir, and add the Grand Marnier. Leaving uncovered, simmer the mixture for about 5 minutes more. Strain sauce and pour over quail.

Serves 2 to 3
Wine Suggestions: Windsor Sonoma Russian River Chardonnay
or Gnarly Head Pinot Noir

"WATCH THE SINGLES"

©Fred McCaleb

Watch the singles

QUAIL WITH ORANGE-GINGER SAUCE

Ingredients

5 quail, split in half
2 tablespoons butter
¼ cup brandy
2 cups game bird or chicken stock
¾ cup orange juice

2 teaspoons grated fresh ginger
dash of nutmeg
3 tablespoons balsamic vinegar
salt and pepper to taste
2 tablespoons butter to finish (optional)

Preparation

PUT 2 tablespoons butter in a skillet over medium-high heat. Brown the quail pieces for 1 to 1½ minutes per side. Remove to covered dish and keep in warm oven.

DEGLAZE the skillet with the brandy. When brown pieces are loose, add the stock and the orange juice. Swirl to combine, adding the ginger, nutmeg and balsamic vinegar. Simmer uncovered until mixture is reduced by half – approximately 15 to 20 minutes. If desired, swirl in the extra 2 tablespoons of butter to thicken the sauce.

RETURN the quail and any accumulated juices to the skillet. Spoon the sauce over the quail and simmer on low for about 2 minutes.

Serves 2 to 3
Wine Suggestions: Flirt Red Blend or Gnarly Head Pinot Grigio

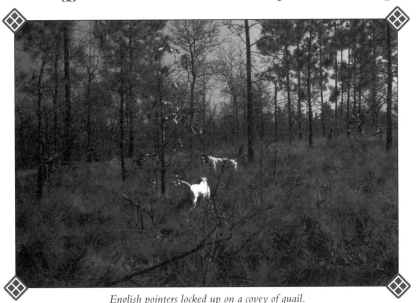

English pointers locked up on a covey of quail.

QUAIL WITH PEARS, ALMONDS, GINGER AND DRAMBUIE

Can substitute 1 pheasant, cut in 8 pieces.

Ingredients

8 quail
2 tablespoons peanut oil
5 ¼-inch slices fresh ginger
6 green onions, with top ⅓ cut off and
    sliced in half
½ dried ancho chili, sliced and
    reconstituted in a little stock

¼ cup Drambuie
½ cup sherry
1 cup game bird or chicken stock
2 pears, peeled, sliced, and cored
½ cup slivered almonds, toasted

Preparation

HEAT peanut oil in skillet on medium low. Add the slices of ginger and infuse the oil, smashing the ginger pieces as they warm up. Do not let the ginger brown. After about 10 minutes, remove the ginger and set aside.

TURN the heat up to medium-high. Pat the quail dry, and brown in the skillet on all sides. This should take about 5 to 6 minutes. Remove to a covered dish and put in a warm oven.

TURN the heat down to medium, and sauté the green onions and ancho chili in the oil for 2 minutes, stirring constantly. Add the Drambuie to the skillet and deglaze. Add the sherry, the stock, and the ginger pieces. Simmer, uncovered, for 5 minutes.

ADD the sliced pears. Cover and simmer on low for 10 to 15 minutes. Remove the ginger pieces and discard. Return quail and any accumulated juices to skillet and simmer for a couple of minutes, spooning the sauce over the quail. Sprinkle toasted almonds over top.

GREAT served with red potatoes roasted with butter and parsley, along with sugar snap peas simmered in a little chicken broth or stock.

Serve 4 to 6

Wine Suggestions: Bota Box Zinfandel or Cruz de Alba Crianza

QUAIL WITH QUINCE

Can substitute 1 pheasant cut in eight pieces.

Quince is not the easiest fruit to find, but when it is available, its delicate flavor pairs very well with light-meat game birds such as quail and pheasant. Quince is naturally a tart fruit, so the addition of a little honey toward the end of the cooking time will mellow out the flavor.

Ingredients

4 *quail, split in half*
½ *cup flour*
⅛ *teaspoon cinnamon*
⅛ *teaspoon allspice*
   salt and pepper
1 *tablespoon butter*
2 *tablespoons olive oil*

4 *green onions, chopped, with green tops chopped but separated*
6 *large mushrooms, sliced*
2 *tablespoons cognac or brandy*
½ *cup sherry*
¾ *cup game bird or chicken stock*
1 *quince, sliced*
   honey, to taste

Preparation

COMBINE the flour with the cinnamon, allspice, salt and pepper. Dust the quail pieces in the flour. Put the butter and olive oil in a hot skillet, and brown the quail approximately 2 minutes each side. Remove to covered dish and place in 300-degree oven.

SAUTÉ the white part of the green onions and the mushrooms in the skillet for 2 to 3 minutes, stirring frequently to keep from scorching. Turn down heat and add brandy and sherry to deglaze the pan. Add the stock and the quince. Simmer, uncovered, for about 8 minutes. Add the green tops of the green onions and simmer for 2 more minutes. Taste the sauce to check for seasoning. If it tastes too tart, add a tablespoon of honey, and recheck.

RETURN quail and accumulated juices to the skillet and simmer for about 2 minutes more. Return quail to the serving dish and pour the sauce over the quail.

Serves 2

Wine Suggestions: Girard Sauvignon Blanc or Gnarly Head Authentic Red

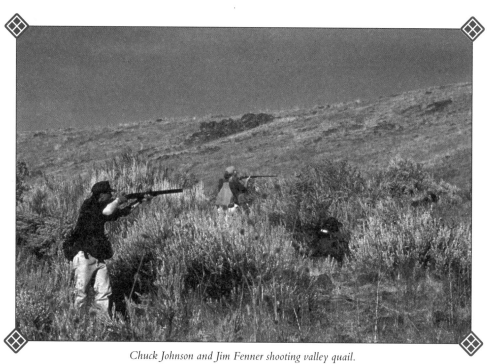

Chuck Johnson and Jim Fenner shooting valley quail.

56

Prairie Grouse

BAKED SHARPTAIL
WITH BLACKBERRY BRANDY SAUCE

Ingredients

2 sharptailed grouse, quartered
4 strips bacon, cut in small pieces
3 tablespoons melted butter
3 cloves garlic, sliced
3 green onions with green tops, sliced in
    half and then cut in half again
1¾ cups blackberry brandy, total
¾ cup game bird or chicken stock
1 tablespoon olive oil
¼ cup flour, seasoned with:
¼ teaspoon salt

¼ teaspoon garlic powder
½ teaspoon bouquet garni
½ teaspoon paprika
¼ teaspoon allspice
    ground pepper
2 shallots, thinly sliced
1 cup blackberries, fresh or frozen
½ cup sour cream
1 teaspoon arrowroot, mixed with a little
    water (optional)

Preparation

PRE-HEAT the oven to 350 degrees.

COMBINE the melted butter with the garlic, green onions, and ½ cup of blackberry brandy in a small saucepan. Warm on low just to blend the flavors. Do not boil.

PUT the bacon pieces in a large skillet and brown until crisp. Remove and drain on a paper towel. Drain off all but 1 tablespoon of the bacon fat and add the olive oil. Heat to high. Dredge the grouse pieces in the seasoned flour and brown 1½ minutes per side. Remove grouse to a shallow baking pan. Pour the warmed butter, garlic, green onion and blackberry brandy mixture over the pieces. Sprinkle the bacon pieces over the grouse and pour ¼ cup of blackberry brandy over all. Bake in 350-degree oven for 15 minutes. Don't overcook! Grouse is best when still rare.

WHILE grouse is baking, pour 1 cup blackberry brandy and ¾ cup stock into skillet, stirring to loosen any brown bits. Add shallots and reduce the liquid by half; about 10 minutes. When grouse is done, remove the pieces from the baking pan to a serving platter. Scrape all juices and the garlic and green onions into the skillet. Slowly stir in the sour cream until it combines with the sauce. Add the arrowroot if you want a thicker sauce. Simmer for 5 minutes, adding the blackberries for the last 2 minutes. Pour the sauce over the grouse on the platter.

SERVE with wild rice or orzo pasta seasoned with a little olive oil, parsley, and Parmesan cheese.

Serves 4 to 5

Wine Suggestions: Noble Vines 667 Pinot Noir or
Sonoma Coast Vineyard Freestone Hills Pinot Noir

Grilled Sharptail with Mango Sauce

Ingredients

> 2 sharptailed grouse, each cut into 8 pieces

For the Marinade

> 1 cup olive oil
> juice of 1 lemon
> 2 tablespoons soy sauce
> 2 tablespoons sherry

> ¼ teaspoon thyme
> ¼ teaspoon paprika
> ½ teaspoon ground chipotle pepper or
> cayenne pepper

For the Sauce

> 1 mango, chopped
> ½ cup orange or apricot marmalade
> 1 tablespoon Dijon mustard

> 2 tablespoons fresh chives, chopped
> 1 tablespoon soy sauce
> ½ cup game bird or chicken stock

Preparation

CUT each sharptail into 8 pieces by cutting each half-breast in half again. This will even out the grilling time, so that some pieces don't cook too quickly. Combine the marinade ingredients, and marinate the sharptail in the refrigerator for 6 to 8 hours, or overnight. Remove from the refrigerator at least one hour before grilling, so that the meat can come to room temperature.

COMBINE all the ingredients for the sauce in a medium saucepan and simmer over low heat for 15 minutes. Keep warm. When ready to grill, separate a small amount of the sauce to use as a basting sauce. Since you will be dipping your basting brush into this sauce, you want to keep it separate from the rest of the sauce.

REMOVE the sharptail from the marinade and grill over a very hot fire for 3 minutes. Turn and baste with the sauce. Grill the second side 3 minutes, turn and baste this side. Grill for 1 minute. Remove from grill and place in a shallow casserole. Pour the reserved sauce over the birds. Cover and keep in a warm oven for 5 to 10 minutes while finishing the rest of the dinner.

THIS is great served with red beans and rice and sugar snap peas. You can also vary the fruit, using pears or peaches instead of the mango.

Serves 4 to 5

Wine Suggestions: Mar de Frades Albariño or Massimo Rioja

Sage Grouse Marsala

We love hunting sage grouse, but limit our hunts and the grouse we take to a very few. Not because they aren't good to eat as so many people say; but, because their numbers seem to be growing smaller. Next to the wild turkey, sage grouse are the biggest upland game bird in North America. The meat is dark like the sharptail, and also needs to be kept on the rare side.

Ingredients

- 1 sage grouse breast, quartered (about 1¼ pounds)
- ½ cup dry Marsala wine
- ⅓ cup dried cherries
- 2 strips bacon, cut in small pieces
- ½ cup flour, seasoned with salt and pepper and a dash of allspice
- 2 shallots, halved and thinly sliced olive oil
- 1½ cups shiitake mushrooms, sliced
- ¼ cup brandy
- ½ cup game bird or chicken stock
- ½ teaspoon thyme
- ¼ teaspoon tarragon

Preparation

SOAK the dried cherries in the Marsala wine for at least 30 minutes. Brown the bacon pieces in a large skillet until crisp. Remove and drain on paper towel. Pour off all but 2 tablespoons bacon fat. Dust the sage grouse quarters in the seasoned flour and brown in skillet about 2½ minutes per side, being sure to brown thicker parts longer and the points of the breast less so that they don't overcook. Remove to a covered dish and place in a warm oven.

SAUTÉ the shallots for 2 minutes in the remaining drippings, using a little olive oil if needed. Then add the mushrooms and sauté another 2 minutes. Add the brandy and simmer until almost dry. Add the cherries and Marsala, along with the stock and the herbs. Cover and simmer 15 to 20 minutes.

CHECK the thicker part of the grouse breasts for doneness. The inside should still be rare. Add the grouse breasts and any accumulated juices to the skillet. Spoon the mixture over the grouse, cover and simmer gently for a few minutes until the inside of the grouse breast is pink. Do not over cook! The grouse will have much more flavor if too rare than too well done.

Serves 2

Wine Suggestions: Noble Vines 181 Merlot
or
Sauvion Vouvray

Sharptailed Grouse
with Portobello Mushrooms

The full-bodied flavor of this dish really works well with dark meat of the prairie grouse, but it can also be used for pheasant. These dark-meat birds need to be served almost rare, in order to taste their wonderful flavor.

Ingredients

1 sharptailed grouse, cut in 6 pieces
½ cup flour
¼ teaspoon allspice
¼ teaspoon garlic powder
⅛ teaspoon black pepper
¼ salt
¼ teaspoon paprika
4 strips bacon, cut into small pieces
1 tablespoon olive oil
1½ cups chopped white onion
1 shallot, chopped

1 garlic clove, minced
1 teaspoon dried tarragon, or 3 sprigs of fresh tarragon
1 large or 2 medium portobello mushrooms, sliced
1½ tablespoons red currant or cherry jelly
1½ cups game bird or beef stock
¾ cup port wine
2 tablespoons flour, mixed with a little water to form a paste (optional)

Preparation

BROWN the bacon pieces in a large skillet. Remove and drain on paper towel. Drain all but 2 tablespoons of the bacon fat from the skillet. Turn heat to medium high. Combine the flour with the allspice, garlic powder, pepper, salt, and paprika. Roll the grouse pieces in the seasoned flour and brown in the skillet, approximately 3 minutes per side. Remove to a covered dish and keep in a warm oven.

ADD the olive oil to the pan and sauté the onion, garlic, and shallot on medium heat until onion is translucent. Do not let the garlic brown, or it will turn bitter. Add the mushrooms and sauté for 2 minutes. If the skillet gets too dry, you can add a little stock. Add the jelly, stock and port to the skillet, stirring to combine and loosen any brown bits in the pan. Cover and simmer for 15 minutes.

IF YOU want a thicker sauce, add several tablespoons of the heated sauce to the flour paste, stirring to combine so that there are no lumps. Add the flour mixture to the sauce and blend. If the sauce is too thick, you can add a little more stock or port to the desired consistency. Return the grouse pieces and any accumulated juices to the skillet. Turn to coat with the sauce and leave skin-side down in the skillet. Cover and simmer very gently for about 7 to 8 minutes. Remember; be sure that the inside of the breast is still rare. Uncover, and turn pieces right side up to serve.

WILD rice is a perfect accompaniment for this dish, though the sauce also tastes great over a baked potato.

Serves 2 to 3
Wine Suggestions: Kunde Estate Merlot
or Noble Vines 446 Chardonnay

SHARPTAILED GROUSE WITH PEACH SAUCE

Fruit goes so well with all types of game birds. You can change the fruit in this recipe to use what is fresh and ripe in your area according to the season. Peaches are great in late summer; pears work equally well in late fall and winter. The recipe is fairly quick and easy, once you have prepared the grouse pieces. It is best to do this earlier in the day and then keep the pieces refrigerated, pounding them into thin pieces when you are ready to start cooking.

Ingredients

2 sharptailed grouse, bones removed
   olive oil
1 tablespoon butter
2 tablespoons flour
2 cups game bird or chicken stock
1 shallot, thinly sliced
½ cup dry white wine or dry vermouth
¼ teaspoon cinnamon

3 cups ripe peaches, peeled, stone
   removed and sliced
2 teaspoons fresh ginger, grated
2 tablespoons brandy
   brown sugar and balsamic vinegar, to
   taste

For the Marinade

2 tablespoons peanut oil
1 tablespoon soy sauce
3 tablespoons sherry
¼ teaspoon thyme

2 teaspoons fresh ginger, peeled and
   chopped
1 shallot, chopped
1 clove garlic, minced

Early Preparation

CUT the breasts and thighs from each sharptail carcass using the method described in The Care of Game from Field to Table in the front of this book. Freeze carcasses with drumsticks still on for stock. You will end up with 8 pieces per sharptail.

PLACE the 16 grouse pieces in the marinade for at least 2 hours or overnight.

Final Preparation

REMOVE the grouse pieces from the marinade and pat dry. Discard the marinade. In two batches, place the 8 pieces on a cutting board that has been covered with wax paper. Place another piece of wax paper over the sharptail pieces. With a meat mallet, pound the sharptail pieces to about ¼ inch thickness, just as you would do for veal scaloppini.

SPRAY a little olive oil in a large skillet. Brown the sharptail pieces over medium-high heat for about 1½ minutes per side. Remove to a covered dish and keep in a warm oven.

MELT the butter in the skillet over low heat. Add the flour, stirring to thicken for about 3 minutes. Add ¼ cup of stock, stirring to combine. Add the shallots and sauté over medium heat for 2 minutes. Add the rest of the stock and wine along with the peaches, ginger, and cinnamon. Stir to combine, and simmer over low heat, uncovered, for 12 minutes. Add the brandy, stir and simmer for 2 more minutes. Taste to correct the sweetness level, adding a touch of brown sugar if too tart, and balsamic vinegar if too sweet. The sweetness level has to be individually adjusted based on the sweetness of the peaches.

WHEN adjusted, add the sharptail pieces and any accumulated juices to the skillet. Spoon sauce over grouse and heat through.

THIS is delicious served over yellow rice seasoned with dash of cinnamon.

Serves 4 to 6

Wine Suggestions: Loredona Viognier
or

Vidal-Fleury Côtes du Rhône Pigeonnier

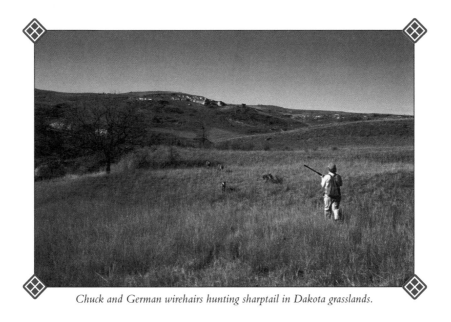

Chuck and German wirehairs hunting sharptail in Dakota grasslands.

SHARPTAIL WITH SPICY ORANGE SAUCE

Along with fruit, the big flavor of sharptail stands up well with spices. Combine the spices first, and then divide in half; using half for the flour and half in the sauce. Increase the chipotle or cayenne pepper to your individual comfort level. Also, the sauce for this dish can be made a day ahead. That will allow the orange rind to further infuse the sauce.

Ingredients

1 sharptail, cut in 8 pieces (4 pieces of breast, 2 thighs, 2 drumsticks)
½ cup flour
½ of the combined spice mixture (see below)
1 tablespoon olive oil

2 tablespoons butter
1 cup mushrooms, sliced
2 tablespoons sherry
cracked peppercorn to taste
thin slices of orange for garnish

Spices for Flour and Stock

7 juniper berries, finely ground
½ teaspoon thyme
½ teaspoon paprika

1 teaspoon chipotle or cayenne pepper
1 teaspoon nutmeg
1 teaspoon ground cloves

For the Spicy Orange Sauce

3 cups game bird or chicken stock
rind of 1 orange, peeled and julienned
3 tablespoons sugar
4 tablespoons balsamic vinegar
½ cup orange juice
¼ cup lemon juice

1½ teaspoons arrowroot
½ of the combined spice mixture (see above)
chipotle or cayenne pepper, extra if desired

Early Preparation

GRIND the juniper berries with a mortar and pestle or spice grinder. Combine with the other spices. Divide the mixture in half. You will save half for the flour in the final preparation, and use half in making the stock.

TO MAKE the sauce, put the 3 cups of stock in a medium saucepan. Over high heat, reduce the stock for about 5 minutes. Add the julienned orange rind, and keep reducing to about 1 cup of liquid. Reduce heat to a low simmer.

IN A small saucepan, combine the sugar and vinegar over medium-high heat. Stirring constantly, let the mixture caramelize to a very thick syrup. Slowly add a few tablespoons of the stock to the syrup and combine. Then add this mixture to the 1 cup of stock. Combine the orange juice, lemon juice, spice mixture, and arrowroot in a bowl or measuring cup.

Slowly pour this combination into the stock while stirring. Bring mixture back to a slow boil to allow the sauce to thicken slightly and reduce to a total of about 1½ cups. Keep warm. You can do this the day before and keep in the refrigerator. Then reheat before starting the final preparation.

Final Preparation

HEAT the olive oil and butter in a large skillet over medium-high heat. Combine the spice mixture with the flour. Pat the grouse pieces dry. Dredge the pieces in the flour mixture and brown them in the skillet for about 4 minutes per side. Remove and place in a 300-degree oven while completing the dish.

ADD the mushrooms to the skillet and sauté for 2 to 3 minutes. Add the sherry to deglaze the pan. Then add the sauce mixture to the skillet. Taste to correct seasonings, adding any extra chipotle pepper and cracked peppercorns if you wish more heat. Simmer for a couple of minutes, then add the grouse pieces and any accumulated juices back into the skillet. Simmer gently for a short time if grouse still needs more cooking time. Don't overcook. Grouse breasts should be pink inside.

Serves 2 to 3

Wine Suggestions: Volteo Viura or Gnarly Head Merlot

Rudy pins down a covey of sharptail.

SOUTHWESTERN-STYLE SHARPTAIL
WITH BLACK BEANS AND RICE

The southwestern flavors in this dish pair well with the dark meat of sharptailed grouse. In fact, any bird with dark meat will work – think waterfowl or any prairie grouse. The key is to cook the meat toward the end of the process, so it stays pink and tender. We like to use S & W's Caribbean Black Beans in this recipe because of its delightful seasonings and touch of lime. If you use this brand, don't drain, the thick liquid works well with the other ingredients.

Ingredients

1-2 sharptailed grouse, depending on size
3 tablespoons vegetable oil, divided
1 cup red onion, chopped
1 bell pepper, chopped
3 garlic cloves, minced
1 teaspoon chili powder, or more to taste

1 teaspoon ground coriander 3/4 teaspoon cumin seeds, toasted
1½ cups gamebird or chicken stock
1 15-ounce can black beans, drained
1-2 teaspoons lime juice
4 cups cooked brown rice
lime wedges
avocado slices

Preparation

SEPARATE the sharptail meat from the bones and slice into bite-sized strips. In a large skillet, heat 1 tablespoon of the oil and sear the meat for about 3 minutes the first side and 2 minutes the second side. Remove from skillet, cover, and place in a warm (250-degree) oven until needed.

HEAT the remaining 2 tablespoons of oil over medium heat and add the onion and pepper, cooking until they are soft – about 5 to 6 minutes. Add garlic, chili powder, coriander, and toasted cumin seeds. Stir and cook for 2 minutes. Add broth and beans, stirring to combine, and cook about 10 minutes, until sauce is thickened. Add sharptail meat and cook another minute or two. Add lime juice to taste.

TO SERVE, place brown rice in bowls and top with sharptail mixture. Serve with lime wedges and garnish with avocado slices.

Serves 4 – 6

Wine Suggestions: Loredona Viognier
or
Kunde Magnolia Lane Sauvignon Blanc

Bacon-Wrapped Sharptail with Grilled Pineapple

Depending on your desire or tolerance of heat, you can increase or decrease the amount of chipotle pepper in the marinade. If you like heat, you might enjoy sprinkling a little on the pineapple slices along with the brown sugar.

Ingredients

1 sharptailed grouse
1½ cups orange juice, divided
2 tablespoons peanut oil
1-2 teaspoons chipotle pepper

2-3 slices bacon
2 thick slices fresh pineapple
brown sugar

Preparation

COMBINE 1 cup of the orange juice, peanut oil, and chipotle pepper. Place sharptail in a self-sealing bag and pour in marinade. Close bag, squeezing out as much air as possible so liquid covers entire bird. Place in refrigerator for 2 to 4 hours. Remove bag from refrigerator about an hour before cooking.

HEAT grill to 300 degrees, leaving center burner off. Place remaining orange juice in container in center of a vertical roaster. Remove sharptail from marinade and place over vertical roaster with legs down. Place marinade in a saucepan and simmer for about 10 minutes. Wrap breast and legs with bacon, securing with toothpicks. Place in center of grill and close lid. Roast on grill for about 40 minutes, basting every 10 minutes with marinade.

CORE the center of each pineapple slice and remove the outer layer. Place on a plate and sprinkle with brown sugar. If more spice is desired, sprinkle a little chipotle pepper on pineapple slices also. When sharptail is about 10 minutes from being finished, place pineapple slices on tray of vertical roaster and close lid. After 5 minutes, turn slices and continue grilling for another 5 minutes.

Serves 2

Wine Suggestions: Yellow Tail Riesling
or
Twisted Moscato

OVEN-BAKED SHARPTAILED GROUSE

The key to cooking birds with dark meat is to not over-cook them. Often if you try to roast birds with dark meat, the outside of the meat is done too much before the meat closer to the bone is cooked enough. That's why this recipe calls for cutting the birds into pieces so they cook more evenly in a short time. Sharptailed grouse should be cooked no more than medium-rare – preferably rare.

Ingredients

2 sharptailed grouse, quartered
2 tablespoons smoked paprika
   chipotle pepper to taste
   salt and freshly ground pepper to taste
3 sage leaves, cut in strips

½ bottle red wine
2 tablespoons olive oil
1 onion, chopped
6 - 8 mushrooms, chopped
¼ cup brandy
2 cups cooked wild rice

Preparation

PAT sharptail meat dry and rub smoked paprika over all pieces. Sprinkle with salt, pepper, and chipotle pepper to taste. Place in bowl, sprinkle sage on top and pour red wine over all. Cover and keep in refrigerator for 6 to 8 hours, turning in the marinade several times.

HEAT oven to 350 degrees. Remove sharptail meat from marinade, reserving marinade. In a braising pan or skillet, place 1 tablespoon of the olive oil over medium-high heat and brown the sharptail quickly. Remove from skillet and add the remaining olive oil. Lower the heat to medium and add the onions. Sauté onions until they are soft and then add the mushrooms, stirring to combine. Cook for 3 to 4 minutes and add brandy, stirring to scrape any browned bit from skillet.

ADD wild rice, stir to combine, and then return sharptail to skillet. Pour marinade over all, cover, and place in oven for 12 minutes. Let rest for 4 minutes before serving.

Serves 4 – 8, depending on size of grouse

Wine Suggestions: Noble Vines 446 Chardonnay
or
George Duboeuf Beaujalois-Village

Roasted Black Raspberry Sharptail

Vertical roasters can be used both in the oven and on a closed grill, and help to cook the meat more evenly. They can be found in most good cookware stores as well as online. You can also use the vertical roaster's precursor – an empty soda or beer can. You can use an inexpensive raspberry liqueur in this recipe – it doesn't have to be Chambord.

Ingredients

1 sharptailed grouse
1 cup orange juice
1 cup black raspberry liqueur, divided
3 tablespoons olive oil

¼ teaspoon ground cinnamon
¼ teaspoon ground cloves
2-3 strips bacon
½ teaspoon dried tarragon

Preparation

IN A bowl mix together orange juice, ½ cup of the raspberry liqueur, olive oil, cinnamon, and cloves. Place grouse in a self-sealing bag and pour marinade in. Close bag, squeezing as much air out as possible, so marinade covers entire surface of the bird. Place in a bowl and marinate in refrigerator for 5 hours. Before cooking, remove bird and marinade from refrigerator for about an hour.

HEAT grill to 300 degrees, leaving center burner off. Pour remaining raspberry liqueur into container in center of vertical roaster and add tarragon. Remove sharptail from marinade and place on vertical roaster, with legs facing down. Wrap bacon slices around breast and legs of bird, securing with toothpicks.

PUT marinade in a saucepan and bring to a simmer. Continue simmering it for about 10 minutes. Place roaster in center of grill and close lid. Roast for about 40 minutes, basting with simmered marinade.

Serves 2 – 3

Wine Suggestions: Ruta 22 Malbec
or
Handcraft Petite Sirah

Spanish-Style Sharptail with Pomegranate Glaze

The flavors in this recipe are well suited to another dark meat – waterfowl. You just have to adjust the cooking time for smaller or larger birds. We have also used this on goose breast steaks (just slice each half of a goose breast in half the long way to make two "steaks").

Ingredients

1 large sharptailed grouse, cut in 6 pieces
¼ cup sweet paprika
1 tablespoon ground cumin
1 tablespoon dry mustard
3 teaspoons freshly ground pepper, divided

2½ teaspoons salt, divided
1 tablespoon ground chipotle pepper
1 cup pomegranate juice
⅓ cup horseradish
1 tablespoon Dijon mustard
olive oil

Preparation

IN A small bowl, combine paprika, cumin, dry mustard, 2 teaspoons of the salt, and 2 teaspoons of the pepper. Rub this mixture on the sharptail, place in a self-sealing bag, and place in refrigerator of 8 hours to overnight. Remove from refrigerator an hour before cooking.

HEAT grill to 375 degrees. In a small saucepan, whisk together the pomegranate juice, horseradish, Dijon mustard, and remaining salt and pepper. Bring mixture to a simmer and keep warm. When ready to use, divide into two bowls – one (a third) for the grill and one (two-thirds) for the finish.

REMOVE meat from bag and rub olive oil over all the pieces. Place meat on grill and baste with the pomegranate glaze. Grill for 2 to 3 minutes and turn, basting the second side. Grill for another 2 to 3 minutes.

REMOVE meat to a serving platter, pour the remaining glaze over the meat and let finish in a 300-degree oven for about 5 minutes, or until the meat is rare to medium rare.

Serves 2 – 3

***Wine Suggestions: Loredona Riesling or Flirt Red Blend
or a Pama Martini***

Five-month-old Camas retrieving her first sharptailed grouse.

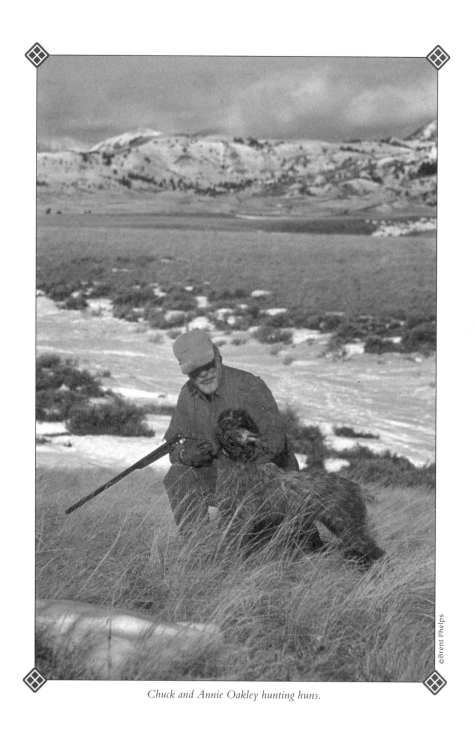

©Brent Phelps

Chuck and Annie Oakley hunting huns.

Hungarian
Partridge

BAKED HUNGARIAN PARTRIDGE
with Apple-Pear Delight

Ingredients

4 partridge
¼ cup olive oil
¼ cup gin
6 crushed juniper berries
4 tablespoons butter
9–12 mushroom caps

1 jar pearl onions, drained
½ teaspoon garlic powder
½ teaspoon tarragon
1 14-ounce can beef broth
⅓ bottle of Cabernet or Zinfandel wine
Apple-Pear Delight (Recipe follows)

Preparation

MARINATE the partridge in the olive oil, gin, and juniper berries for at least 2 hours. Remove from marinade and pat dry with a paper towel.

PRE-HEAT the oven to 350 degrees. Melt the butter in a skillet over medium-high heat. Brown the birds on all sides. Place the birds in an enamel pot or Dutch oven, along with the rest of the ingredients, except the Apple-Pear Delight.

COVER and bake in the oven for about 30 minutes, or until the interior breasts are slightly pink.

SERVE with wild rice and the Apple-Pear Delight.

Serves 3 to 4

Wine Suggestions: Brazin Old Vine Zinfandel or Girard Cabernet Sauvignon

Recipe for Apple-Pear Delight

Ingredients

2 Granny Smith apples, sliced
   horizontally to 1½-inch thickness,
   core removed
1 ripe pear, sliced the same

½ cup brown sugar
3 tablespoons butter
½ teaspoon cinnamon
¼ teaspoon nutmeg
   red currant jelly for garnish

Preparation

MELT butter in large saucepan. Add the brown sugar, cinnamon, and nutmeg. Stir to combine, and simmer for about 3 minutes. Add the fruit slices, spooning the sauce over them. Simmer for about 5 minutes until slices start to soften. Serve slices stacked with a dollop of red currant jelly in the center.

BAKED HUNGARIAN PARTRIDGE
with Lingonberry-Mushroom Sauce

Lingonberries are a perfect complement to dark-meat prairie birds. The sweet-tart fruit is always a winner since lingonberries taste like a subtle cranberry. This game sauce blends especially well when served with spinach fettuccini lightly coated with an Alfredo sauce. This creates a delightful mixture on the tongue of rich creaminess cut with the opposite texture of spicy sweetness. If you can't find lingonberries or lingonberry jam, you can substitute 1 cup of blackberries macerated with 2 teaspoons of sugar.

Ingredients

3 Hungarian partridge	1½ bay leaves
¼ cup flour, seasoned with salt, pepper, and ¼ teaspoon thyme	¼ teaspoon thyme
	½ teaspoon tarragon
2 tablespoons butter	½ cup game bird or chicken stock
1 tablespoon olive oil	1 cup Marsala wine
3 shallots or 6 green onions, sliced	½ cup lingonberries, preserved with a little sugar
½ pound mushrooms, sliced	
¼ cup brandy	

Preparation

PRE-HEAT the oven to 350 degrees. Dredge the birds lightly in the seasoned flour, and brown in the butter and olive oil in a heavy skillet over medium high heat. Remove to casserole, breast-side down.

IN THE skillet, sauté the shallots or green onions and the mushrooms for 2 minutes on medium heat. Add the brandy to deglaze the skillet. Add the Marsala wine and the stock, along with the herbs. Simmer for about 5 minutes to slightly reduce the mixture. Pour over the birds in the casserole, cover, and put in the 350-degree oven for 20 minutes. After the first 10 minutes in the oven, turn the birds breast side up and stir in the lingonberries. Spoon the mixture over the birds, cover, and continue cooking for the last 10 minutes.

SERVE with a side of steamed asparagus and spinach fettuccini Alfredo.

Serves 2

Wine Suggestions: George Duboeuf Moulin-a-Vent

or Massimo Rioja

GAME BIRD WITH CURRY CREAM SAUCE

Use any of the following types of birds

5 Hungarian partridge

1 pheasant - quartered

3-4 chukar partridge

6-8 quail

All birds should be cooked whole, varying the time according to the size of the bird. The pheasant could also be quartered to speed the process.

Ingredients

seasoned flour – about ½ cup seasoned with a sprinkle of salt, paprika, garlic powder and curry

3 tablespoons butter or margarine

3-4 green onions – sliced with green tops

1½ cups mushrooms – shiitakes are great, but regular button mushrooms can be used too

2 tablespoons dry vermouth – or any dry white wine

2 cans beef consommé

¾ cup water

2 teaspoons curry

1 cup sour cream (light or regular)

2 teaspoons arrowroot

Preparation

CLEAN birds and pat dry. Melt 2 tablespoons of the butter in a large skillet. Lightly coat the birds by rolling them in the seasoned flour.

BRING the melted butter to medium-high and brown the birds in the butter, varying the time based on the size of the birds. (Quail will only take about 1½ minutes per side, Huns about 3 minutes per side, chukar and the quartered pheasant about 4 minutes per side.) Remove the birds to a warm oven, keeping them moist by covering with aluminum foil or place in a covered bowl.

TURN down the heat in the skillet to medium and add the remaining tablespoon of butter. When it has melted, add the green onions. Sauté the onions for about 1 minute. Add the mushrooms and continue stirring for about another 2 minutes. Lower heat and add the vermouth to deglaze the crusted pieces in the pan. Add the consommé, the water, and the curry. (The curry will mix into the mixture better if you first mix in a little consommé to form a light paste.) Stir to combine all the ingredients in the skillet. Simmer on low for about 10 minutes.

PUT the birds, breast side up, back into the skillet along with any juices that have collected. Spoon the sauce over the breasts. Cover and simmer gently on low for about 8 minutes. Birds are done when the juices run clear if you prick the thickest part of the breast. Do not overcook. Uncover and remove birds to the warming oven while you finish the sauce.

MIX the arrowroot with the sour cream (If you don't have arrowroot, you can use flour, but you will need a couple of tablespoons to equal the arrowroot.) Add several spoonsful of the hot liquid to the sour cream to equalize the temperatures. This will keep the sauce from curdling.

SPOON the sour cream into the sauce and blend thoroughly. Bring to a low simmer to let it thicken. Put the birds on a serving platter and spoon the sauce over and around the birds.

Serves 2 to 4, depending on type of bird used

*Wine Suggestions: Handcraft Chardonnay or
Josh Cellars Cabernet Sauvignon*

FRIED HUNS

This recipe should serve four people, but you just might like to add a couple of extra partridge to the mix. It's hard to stop eating once you bite into this delicious bird.

Ingredients

6 Hungarian partridge, quartered	½ teaspoon ground cloves
¾ cup flour	1 teaspoon garlic powder
½ teaspoon thyme	½ teaspoon salt
½ teaspoon paprika	2 eggs, beaten with 2 tablespoons milk
1 teaspoon chipotle or cayenne pepper	4 tablespoons butter-flavored Crisco or
½ teaspoon nutmeg	other shortening

Preparation

COMBINE the flour with the seasonings on a dinner plate. On another dinner plate, put the eggs and milk mixture.

PAT partridge dry. Melt the butter-flavored Crisco in a cast-iron skillet on high heat. Dip the partridge quarters in the egg mixture and roll in the seasoned flour. When the melted shortening is very hot but not smoking, add the partridge to the skillet. Fry the breasts 3 minutes per side, and fry the legs 2 minutes on the first side and 1 minute on the second. Drain on paper towels and keep in warm oven until ready to serve.

Serves 4
Wine Suggestions: Enza Prosecco or Bota Box Riesling

GRILLED HUNGARIAN PARTRIDGE

Ingredients

6 Hungarian partridge, split in half
½ cup olive oil
1 tablespoon fresh rosemary, chopped –
   or 1 teaspoon dried

1 tablespoon fresh tarragon, chopped –
   or 1 teaspoon dried
5 juniper berries, crushed
¼ cup gin
¼ cup port wine

Preparation

COMBINE the ingredients and marinate the partridge for 2 hours. Fire the grill to high heat and grill the birds for about 4 minutes per side. Check for doneness. Birds are done when breast meat is still slightly pink. Don't overcook.

Serves 4

Wine Suggestions: Irony Merlot or Sauvion Muscadet

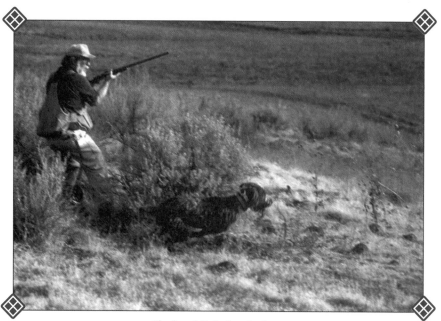

Chuck and Duke hunting huns.

Hungarian Partridge with Artichokes

Two pheasants, quartered, or 4 chukars, split in half, can be substituted.

Ingredients

6 Hungarian partridge
flour – seasoned with garlic powder,
paprika and black pepper
2 tablespoons butter
2 tablespoons olive oil
3 large shallots, sliced thin
¼ cup sun-dried tomatoes, sliced thin
2 cups mushrooms, sliced thin
1½ cups game bird or chicken stock

1 tablespoon Angostura bitters
2 teaspoons oregano
½ cup dry Marsala wine
½ cup cream sherry
1 14-ounce can of artichoke hearts,
drained and halved
½ cup toasted slivered almonds
salt and pepper to taste

Preparation

COAT the birds with the seasoned flour. Heat the olive oil and butter in a large skillet, and brown the birds on all sides. Remove birds from the skillet, and keep covered in a warm 300-degree oven.

ADD the shallots and the sun-dried tomatoes to the skillet and sauté for 3 minutes, stirring frequently. Add the mushrooms and ½ cup of stock stirring to loosen the crusted bits in the bottom of the skillet. Add the Angostura bitters and oregano, stirring to blend.

ADD the artichoke hearts, and pour the rest of the stock, the Marsala wine, and the sherry over the vegetables. Cover and simmer for 20 minutes to blend the flavors.

REMOVE the Huns from the warm oven, and return to the skillet, along with any accumulated juices. Spoon some of the sauce over the birds. Add the toasted almonds, and simmer gently for 5 minutes.

GREAT served over wild rice, with a green salad and rolls.

Serves 4

Wine Suggestions: Ramón Bilbao Valiñas Albariño
or
Loredona Viognier

Rotisserie Hungarian Partridge
with Raspberry Cider Sauce

Ingredients

6 Hungarian partridges
   salt and pepper to taste
¼ cup olive oil
2 cups orange juice

2 strips bacon, cut in thirds
   Raspberry Cider Sauce – recipe follows

Preparation

SEASON birds with salt and pepper. Combine oil and orange juice in a bowl and place birds in, breast side down. Marinate for 4 to 8 hours, turning occasionally.

HEAT grill to 400 degrees. Remove birds from marinade and pat dry. Place birds on rotisserie, tying legs together. Secure a piece of bacon on to each breast with toothpicks. Place rotisserie on grill and cook for about 15 to 20 minutes. Check with a meat thermometer and remove from grill when the birds reach 160-degree temperature.

TO SERVE, place on platter and drizzle some of the Raspberry Cider Sauce over the birds, passing the rest of the sauce in a bowl.

Serves 4

Wine Suggestions: Yellow Tail Riesling
or
Irony Chardonnay

RASPBERRY CIDER SAUCE

Ingredients

1 tablespoon butter
½ cup onion, chopped fine
3 cups raspberry cider

1 cinnamon stick, broken in half
1 cup frozen red or black raspberries

Preparation

Melt butter in saucepan. Add onion and sauté until soft, but not browned. Add cider and cinnamon stick. Bring to a simmer and reduce by half. Just before serving, remove cinnamon stick from sauce, stir in raspberries and heat through.

Serves 4

Chukar on point.

Fall Harvest

Forest Grouse and Woodcock

Blue Grouse Almandine

Can substitute ruffed grouse.

Ingredients

1 blue grouse, quartered
½ cup flour, seasoned with salt, pepper, and a dash of paprika and cinnamon
2 strips of bacon, cut in small pieces
¼ cup brandy

1 orange, ½ sliced thinly and ½ juiced
½ cup game bird or chicken stock
½ teaspoon thyme
⅔ cup slivered almonds, toasted

Preparation

BROWN the bacon pieces in a large skillet until crisp. Remove and drain on a paper towel. Discard all but 2 tablespoons of the bacon fat.

RINSE grouse quarters and pat dry. Dust in the seasoned flour. Over high heat, brown the grouse in the skillet. Remove to a covered dish and place in a 300-degree oven.

DEGLAZE the pan with the brandy, scraping up the loose bits. Add juice from the half of the orange, the stock, thyme, and bacon pieces. Simmer 10 to 15 minutes. Return the grouse and any accumulated juices to the pan. Spoon the sauce over the grouse. Cover and simmer for 2 minutes.

PLACE grouse on serving platter. Pour the sauce over the grouse and place the thin slices of orange over the grouse. Sprinkle the toasted almonds on top. Serve with wild rice.

Serves 2 to 3

Wine Suggestions: Noble Vines 337 Cabernet Sauvignon
or
Sonoma Coast Vineyards Gold Ridge Hills Chardonnay

GRILLED RUFFED GROUSE WITH PORTOBELLO MUSHROOMS

This is a simple recipe that lets the fantastic flavor of ruffed grouse stand out. It works just as well for other forest grouse.

Ingredients

> 2 grouse, quartered
> 2 large portobello mushrooms, cut in half

For the Marinade

> ½ cup olive oil
> ¼ cup soy sauce
> ¼ cup sweet Marsala wine
> 3-4 sprigs fresh tarragon, or ½ teaspoon dried

> 3-4 sprigs fresh thyme, or ½ teaspoon dried
> salt and pepper to taste

Preparation

ADD the grouse quarters to the marinade and marinate for at least 1 hour. Remove and pat dry. While your grill is heating up, add the portobello mushrooms to the marinade, spooning some of the marinade into the mushroom gills. Marinate only for 3 to 4 minutes. If you leave the mushrooms in the mixture too long, they will soak up so much marinade they won't grill properly.

OVER a very hot fire, grill the grouse for 3 minutes. Turn birds and add mushrooms and grill both for 2 minutes. Turn birds and mushrooms and grill for 2 more minutes. Check for doneness. The inside of the breast next to the bone should still be slightly pink. If you are grilling a larger blue grouse, add a couple of minutes to your timing.

SERVE with asparagus spears tossed with toasted pine nuts and a simple pasta with a light cream sauce.

Serves 4

Wine Suggestions: Ramón Bilbao Edición Limited Tempranillo
or
Noble Vines 446 Chardonnay

RASPBERRY-ZINFANDEL ROASTED GROUSE

Ingredients

    1 *grouse, preferably plucked, not skinned*
        balsamic vinegar

For the Marinade

2	*cups fresh raspberries*	1	*teaspoon Dijon mustard*
¼	*cup Zinfandel wine*	1	*teaspoon thyme*
2	*tablespoons oil*	½	*teaspoon salt*
1	*teaspoon sugar*	½	*teaspoon pepper*

Early Preparation

PURÉE the raspberries in a blender. Push through a sieve to remove the seeds. Return to the blender and add the rest of the ingredients. Purée until blended.

PLACE the grouse in a large plastic bag and pour in the marinade. Seal, removing all air, so that marinade will completely surround the bird. Keep in the refrigerator for 24 hours.

Final Preparation

PRE-HEAT oven to 350 degrees.

REMOVE the grouse from the marinade and pat dry. Place in a shallow roasting pan. And roast in oven for 30 to 40 minutes until done, brushing with the marinade twice. Mix a little balsamic vinegar with the marinade before using for the final basting. Breast meat should still be slightly pink on inside.

Serves 2

Wine Suggestions: Massimo Sauvignon Blanc or

Kunde Estate Century Vine Zinfandel

SAUTÉED GROUSE WITH PEACH BEURRE BLANC SAUCE

I originally created this dish for fish. We love the sweet flavor of escolar. After enjoying it as a fish dish, I realized that the mildly sweet sauce would be just as good with the delicate flavor of forest grouse. It also works well with pheasant and quail.

Ingredients

2 grouse, quartered
2 tablespoons butter
2 cloves garlic, sliced
¼ cup game bird or chicken stock
¼ cup dry sherry or white wine

2 teaspoons for fresh tarragon snips, or
1 teaspoon dried tarragon
¼ cup peach jam
1-2 teaspoons balsamic vinegar, to taste

Preparation

HEAT butter in large skillet on low until melted. Add garlic slices and continue heating on low for about 10 minutes, pressing to infuse the garlic into the butter. Remove the garlic and set aside.

PAT the grouse quarters dry. Heat the butter to medium-high and add the grouse. Brown on each side for about 3 minutes each. Remove to covered dish and place in warm oven.

TURN heat down and add the stock and sherry to the pan, stirring to scrape up any brown bits. Add the tarragon, the peach jam, and the garlic slices. Cover and simmer on medium low for 10 minutes. Adjust for sweetness by adding balsamic vinegar to taste. Simmer, covered, 2 more minutes. Add the grouse pieces and any accumulated juices. Spoon sauce over grouse, cover and simmer for 2 more minutes.

Serves 4

Wine Suggestions: Girard Russian River Chardonnay or

Loredona Viognier

Pancetta-Wrapped Grouse Breast

This recipe can be varied, using different berries as they come into season, adding a little brown sugar if the berries are tart. It can also be used with other gamebird breasts, such as pheasant. With pheasant, a half breast would serve one person, and I would slit it in half horizontally to stuff it.

Ingredients

4 ruffed grouse breasts, deboned & halved
½ 5.2-ounce package of semi-soft cheese with herbs
4 slices pancetta

1 tablespoon olive oil
2 tablespoons brandy
⅔ cup chicken or gamebird stock
⅓ cup balsamic vinegar, or to taste
½ cup pitted dates, chopped

Preparation

DIVIDE the cheese into four equal sections. Place cheese in the middle of 4 grouse breasts. Top with the other half of the breasts. Wrap a slice of pancetta around each breast, tucking the ends underneath.

HEAT oven to 300 degrees. In a large skillet, heat oil over medium-high heat. Place the grouse breasts in the skillet with the edges of the pancetta on the down side. Sear for about 2 minutes, and turn. Sear about another 3 minutes and remove to a serving platter. Cover with foil and place in warmed oven.

ADD the brandy to the skillet and swirl to scrape up any brown bits. Add stock, balsamic vinegar, and dates and stir to combine. Continue cooking the mixture for about 5 minutes or until dates are softened.

TO SERVE, drizzle some of the sauce and the dates over the grouse. Serve the rest of the sauce in a gravy boat.

Serves 4

Wine Suggestions: Volteo Garnacha
or
Noble Vines 667 Pinot Noir

GROUSE A LA JEZORIO

Noted writer, Frank Jezorio, and his wife, Beverly, have a favorite recipe for ruffed grouse that they enjoy sharing with family and friends. Frank is the Director for the Department of Natural Resources in West Virginia, which gives him the perfect excuse to "check out" the ruffed grouse population in his beautiful state.

Ingredients

2 to 4 *ruffed grouse*
¾ *cup red wine – not too dry*
1 *teaspoon garlic powder*

¼ *teaspoon black pepper*
1 *tablespoon butter, melted*
¼ *cup Dale's Steak Sauce*

Preparation

REMOVE the breast meat from the bone and place the medallions in a glass baking dish along with the legs. Pour the wine over the meat, so that it covers it. Use more if needed. Sprinkle the garlic powder and pepper over all. You may use a dash of salt, but the steak sauce that you will use later has plenty of salt in it. Cover the dish with cling wrap and refrigerate for 24 to 30 hours.

PREHEAT grill. Mix the melted butter with the Dale's Steak Sauce. Remove the grouse from the wine marinade and place meat on the grill. Brush on a liberal coating of the butter and Dale's. In 2 minutes, turn and coat the other side with the basting mixture. After 2 minutes turn the meat over again, baste, and repeat until done to your taste.

THE KEY here is not to overcook. The whole cooking process will take only about 5 to 6 minutes, depending upon the heat of your grill. Cook only until there is a hint of pink at the middle. Think of cooking brook trout and how little cooking time it actually takes. Add wild rice or a baked potato with a crisp green salad and you have the King of Game Birds fit for a king.

Serves 2 – 4

Wine Suggestions: Ramón Bilbao Crianza
or
Noble Vines 446 Chardonnay

STEVE SMITH'S GRILLED WOODCOCK

Steve Smith is the editor of the Pointing Dog Journal and the Retriever Journal, two great hunting dog magazines. Steve is also one of the most knowledgeable people about woodcock. He wrote several books on the subject. Steve graciously shared his favorite woodcock recipes with us.

Because woodcock are becoming scarce in many parts of the country we have included only one recipe. Most hunters limit their take of woodcock to only a few birds each year. Any of the recipes for Hungarian partridge or chukar can also be used with woodcock.

Ingredients

woodcock – 2 per person

For the Breasts

½ *cup brandy*
½ *cup Italian dressing*
1 *garlic clove, chopped*

½ *bay leaf*
1 *small sweet onion or scallion*
   bacon strips

For the Legs

2 *tablespoons butter - melted*
1 *garlic clove, chopped*

Preparation

SKIN the birds whole, fillet off the breast halves, and cut off the legs and thighs, discarding the feet. Set legs and thighs aside.

MARINATE the breast halves in the brandy, Italian dressing, garlic clove, and bay leaf. Place in covered dish in fridge overnight.

CUBE a small sweet onion or use a scallion. Attach a cube of onion to the breast piece and wrap in bacon. Secure with several small toothpicks.

GET the barbecue grill medium-hot and cook until woodcock breasts are rare – do not overcook. Even if you are not a fan of rare beef, you will love this. A good indicator is when the bacon starts to sizzle, the toothpick ends are singed black, and the onion becomes soft, but not browned.

MEANWHILE, place the legs and thighs in a pan or small skillet with 2 tablespoons melted butter and 1 chopped garlic clove. Cook in pan on the grill. These cook quickly, so watch them – 3 to 4 minutes is plenty.

REMOVE breasts from grill, remove and discard bacon – or feed it to the dog under the table like I do – and distribute breast and legs/thighs on wild rice.

Wine Suggestions: Gnarly Head Zinfandel

or Villa Pozzi Pinot Grigio

Turkey

Brined and Grilled Wild Turkey Breast

Sometimes that great big exciting gobbler really gets the hunter enthused, but he may not be so tasty on the table. Just like any meat, the younger birds usually make more flavorful and tender dishes. However, don't give up if your partner chose the trophy over the tender. Brining does absolute wonders with old birds. The amount of salt in the recipe may be a put-off for those of us who use it in small amounts. However, it will not make the final product overly salty, but will help tenderize an old bird. This brine will work equally well for any older game bird.

Ingredients

- 1 wild turkey breast, neck and back removed (save neck and back for a stock)
- 3 tablespoons butter
- ¼ cup sherry

For the Brine

- 1½ cups kosher salt
- ¾ cup brown sugar
- 1 orange, cut in ¼-inch slices
- 1 teaspoon ground ginger
- 2 tablespoons white Worcestershire sauce
- 4 cups apple cider
- 4 quarts water

Early Preparation

COMBINE all the brine ingredients in a large stockpot. Place the turkey breast in the pot. Mixture should just cover the breast. If not, add more water and cider in equal amounts to cover. Cover the pot and place in the refrigerator for 24 to 48 hours. The older the turkey, the longer you need to keep it in the brine. Turn it a couple of times, if possible, or stir the mixture to be sure that the breast is evenly saturated with the brine.

Final Preparation

REMOVE the turkey breast from the marinade at least 1 hour before grilling. Discard the marinade. Rinse the turkey breast in cold water. Pat dry and let it sit to warm to room temperature, so that the interior and exterior will cook more evenly.

MELT the butter in small saucepan and add the sherry. Use this to baste the breast each time you turn it on the grill. If desired, soak wood chips in water and sherry for about 10 minutes. Add to smoking tray in grill if available.

WHEN the grill reaches about 400 degrees, put the breast on the grill with one side of the breast down. Turn and baste using the following times and temperatures:

5 minutes	first side down	400 degrees
5 minutes	second side down	400 degrees
3 minutes	cavity down	400 degrees

REDUCE heat by removing some coals or turning gas fire down

| 10 minutes | first side down | 300 degrees |
| 10 minutes | second side down | 300 degrees |

REMOVE turkey from grill and place on a serving platter. If you have any basting sauce left over, pour this over the breast. Put the turkey in a 300-degree oven while you finish the rest of the dinner, approximately 10 minutes.

Serves 4 to 8, depending on size of the turkey breast

Wine Suggestions: George Duboeuf Saint-Amour or Loredona Riesling

Spring gobbler

CURRIED TURKEY VELOUTE

If you have leftover wild or domestic turkey, this is a great use for it. It makes a fine meal served over wild rice, with crusty bread and a green salad. It also freezes well.

Ingredients

1 medium onion, finely chopped	1 spice ball, filled with 2 teaspoons
3 tablespoons butter	bouquet garni, 1 tablespoon parsley,
3 tablespoons flour	and ½ bay leaf
1 tablespoon curry	1 cup half and half cream
1 quart game bird or chicken stock	2-3 cups cooked turkey
½ cup Madeira wine	1½ cups mushrooms, sliced

Preparation

MELT butter in large pot. Add onion and sauté over medium-high heat, stirring frequently, until translucent. This should take about 5 minutes. Keep the onions from browning. Stir in the flour and curry, continuing to cook over medium-high heat, stirring constantly. This may take a few minutes. You want the roux to become a light golden brown.

TURN the heat down to low. Slowly add the stock, whisking to keep from getting lumpy. Then add the Madeira and the spice ball. Simmer for about 20 minutes, uncovered, and stirring occasionally. Remove the spice ball and add the mushrooms. Simmer for 5 minutes. Slowly stir in the cream and then add the cooked turkey. Continue to simmer gently for another 2 minutes to heat through. Taste and adjust seasonings if necessary, or add a splash of Madeira.

About 8 servings

Wine Suggestions: Gnarly Head Sauvignon Blanc or Joseph Carr Dijon Clone Chardonnay

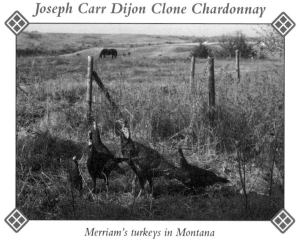

Merriam's turkeys in Montana

GRILLED WILD TURKEY BREAST

Ingredients

1 wild turkey breast, split in half
1 tablespoon liquid smoke (optional)

dash of thyme and tarragon (optional)

For the Marinade

½ cup peanut oil
½ cup sherry
4 tablespoons lemon juice
4 tablespoons soy sauce
4 tablespoons white Worcestershire sauce

½ teaspoon allspice
1 teaspoon thyme
2 teaspoons tarragon
2 tablespoons Dijon mustard

Preparation

COMBINE all the marinade ingredients in a bowl. Put the turkey breast in a large (jumbo) ziplock bag. Pour marinade into the bag and seal, pushing all air out to that turkey breast is surrounded by the marinade. Place in bowl in the refrigerator for at least 6 hours. Take out of the refrigerator and bring to room temperature before grilling.

IF YOUR grill allows, put a pan in the center with the coals around it, or the burners on the side. Put a little water in the pan along with the liquid smoke and the herbs.

WHEN the fire is very hot, remove the turkey breast from the marinade and place on the grill skin side down, over the pan. Close the lid and grill for 15 minutes. Meanwhile, bring the marinade to a boil, and boil for 5 minutes. Then you can use this to baste the turkey breasts each time you turn them. After 15 minutes, open grill, baste with marinade, turn, baste again and close grill for another 15 minutes.

NOW the timing is going to be up to the size of the turkey breast and the heat of your grill. Check the center of the breast right near the breastbone. If it is only slightly pink, it is done. If not, turn the breasts, baste, and grill for another few minutes skin side down, with the grill open and the heat reduced. Check again. If it still needs some more time, turn, baste, and finish skin side up.

Serves 6 to 8

Wine Suggestions: Llai Llai Pinot Noir
or
Twisted Riesling

WILD TURKEY OSSO BUCO

The legs on a wild turkey are longer and tougher than on a domestic bird. No wonder! They rely on their legs more than their wings to escape predators. But there's still great flavor on the meat, it just needs to cook slowly like a veal shank.

Ingredients

2 turkey legs, thighs and drumsticks separated
1 tablespoon butter
1 tablespoon olive oil
1 carrot, chopped
1 celery stalk, chopped
1 small parsnip, chopped
1 medium yellow onion, chopped
1 cup mushrooms, chopped

2 garlic cloves, minced
¼ cup brandy
1 bay leaf
1 teaspoon dried tarragon
¼ teaspoon thyme
2 tablespoons tomato paste
½ cup cream sherry
11/4 cup gamebird stock or chicken stock

Preparation

HEAT oven to 350 degrees. Pat turkey legs dry and season with salt and pepper. Heat butter and oil in a braising pan or Dutch oven on medium-high. Brown legs, two pieces at a time, for 2 minutes per side. Remove and set aside.

ADD carrot, celery, parsnip, onion, and mushrooms to the pan and sauté over medium heat until onion is soft and translucent. When onion is just about done, add garlic, stirring to combine. Add brandy and stir to loosen brown bits in bottom of pan. Continue cooking until brandy is absorbed. Turn heat to low and add bay leaf, tarragon, thyme, and tomato paste, stirring to combine. Pour in sherry, stirring to combine. Place turkey legs on top of vegetables and press them down, so they are surrounded by the vegetables. Pour stock over all and spoon some of the vegetables and stock over top of the turkey.

COVER and place in oven to braise until tender. Time will depend on size and age of the bird, but braise for at least 2 hours before checking. If needed, add more stock.

YOU can serve this dish "rustic" – just as it comes out of the oven. Or, you can pull the meat from the bones and discard the bones. Place the vegetable/stock mixture in a food processor and purée until smooth. Then return the meat to the mixture and reheat.

Serves 4 – 6
Wine Suggestions: George Duboeuf Brouilly
or Massimo Rioja

GRILL-ROASTED TURKEY BREAST

This is a great brine to use when you want to make two separate dishes with your wild turkey. Use it to grill the turkey breast, and then save the legs for Wild Turkey Osso Buco.

Ingredients

1 wild turkey breast – about 3½ to 4½ pounds
2 quarts water
½ cup kosher salt
¼ cup low-sodium soy sauce
½ cup brown sugar
¼ cup white sugar
¼ cup apple cider vinegar

½ cup spiced dark rum
½ teaspoon ground allspice
½ teaspoon onion powder
1 teaspoon chipotle smoked Tabasco sauce
½ cup sherry
butter, melted for basting

Preparation

COMBINE everything except the turkey breast, the sherry, and the melted butter in a large bowl. Place the turkey breast in a 1 ½ gallon self-sealing bag and pour the brine over the meat. Seal the bag, pushing as much air out of it as you can, so that the brine covers the meat. Brine the turkey in the refrigerator for 6 to 8 hours.

REMOVE from the refrigerator at least one hour before cooking. Thoroughly rinse and pat dry the breast two times.

HEAT grill to 350 degrees. Pour the sherry into the container in the base of a vertical roaster. Place the breast on the vertical roaster and place on covered grill. Baste with the melted butter until the meat is just barely pink in the center and the juices run clear. Finish in a 300-degree oven with the last of the melted butter.

Serves 6 – 8

Wine Suggestions: Twisted Moscato
or
Barone Fini Pinot Grigio

GRANDMA'S TURKEY DRESSING

Ingredients

1 pound pork sausage
2 large onions
2 cloves of garlic – minced
12 ounces fresh mushrooms – chopped
5 stalks celery – chopped (about 3 cups)
2 springs of celery tops (with leaves) chopped
6 tablespoons fresh parsley – chopped
2 8-ounce cans sliced water chestnuts – drained

1 large loaf of whole wheat or white bread – dried & crumbled fine
1 egg – well-beaten
2 tablespoons butter or margarine
1 14-ounce can chicken broth
sherry or white wine (optional)
dried sage – to taste
salt & pepper – to taste

Preparation

NOTE ON BREAD: You need to dry the bread a couple of days ahead, if possible. Lay the pieces in your roasting pan or use cookie sheets and let them air dry. If that's impossible (cat, young children, etc.), you can place the pans in the oven on very low temperature (150 degrees) for several hours, turning at least once. The only thing you need to worry about with this method is that you don't accidentally turn the heat up. That causes the bread to become TOAST, which you don't want!

BROWN the sausage thoroughly in a large skillet, until crumbly. Put sausage in colander or strainer over a bowl to let grease drain. Pour off grease from skillet.

MELT 1 tablespoon butter in the skillet. Sauté the celery and onions until limp. Do not brown. Add minced garlic and stir. Put mixture into large stockpot.

MELT 1 tablespoon butter in skillet, and add the mushrooms. Sauté until limp, adding sherry, wine, or chicken broth to keep moist. Scrape skillet with mushrooms into stockpot.

COMBINE the drained sausage, parsley, and water chestnuts with the mixture in the stockpot. Then add the well-beaten egg. Stir to combine well.

CRUMBLE the dried bread slices. (Put several in a zip lock bag without sealing completely, and roll a pie dough roller over the bag, until the pieces are very small.) Add each crumbled batch to the stockpot, stirring each time. As you add, judge the dryness of the mixture, and add chicken broth to keep somewhat moist. Dressing should be moist, but not soggy.

FINALLY, add salt, pepper, and sage to taste. I probably use at least 2 tablespoons of sage to start, and then taste.

KEEP dressing cool, if you are not ready to roast turkey. Let it warm up a little bit before stuffing into neck and body cavity.

THIS stuffs a 20-pound domestic turkey or a 12-pound wild turkey. If you have any left over, put it in a small casserole dish, drizzle some extra chicken stock on top and put it back in the same oven as the turkey. It can always be frozen and used to stuff smaller birds.

Dove

DOVE GUMBO

I asked my good friend Bill Maxwell to share his great dove recipes with us. Bill and I have hunted together for over twenty years. We have both moved from the Midwest, but Bill and I keep in contact. Texas is one of the best states for dove hunting. Bill always prepared doves for me whenever I visited him there. Here are six of his recipes I am sure you will enjoy.

Ingredients

12 dove breast, whole	1 teaspoon marjoram
½ cup oil	2 teaspoons liquid crab boil
½ cup flour	¼ teaspoon cayenne pepper (more if you
1 cup onion, chopped	like it very hot)
1 cup celery, chopped	salt and pepper to taste
1 pound fresh or frozen okra – see note	1 cup tomatoes, diced – see note
1 teaspoon thyme	

Preparation

COVER birds generously with water. Simmer in covered pot for 1 hour.

WHILE birds are cooking, make your roux, using the flour and oil in an iron skillet. You have to stir this constantly on very low heat until brown. The darker the roux (without burning), the better the gumbo. This requires patience and takes at least 45 minutes.

WHEN you have the roux the correct color, add the onion and celery, continuing to cook and stir until vegetables are soft. Remove from heat and set aside.

REMOVE the doves from the pot, reserving the liquid. Remove the meat from the bone. Combine the roux, meat, and stock with the rest of the ingredients in a heavy, non-stick pot. Add more water if needed. Cover and cook over low heat for about 1 hour, until okra disintegrates.

SERVE over rice.

NOTE: Okra can be cooked in advance in 2 or 3 tablespoons of oil to remove the slick texture. Cook slowly over a low heat until dry. You can also add 1 cup diced tomatoes to this recipe for color and texture.

Serves 4

Wine Suggestions: Twisted Zinfandel
or Josh Cellars Chardonnay

Dove Stroganoff

Ingredients

12 dove breasts, whole
 1 medium onion, diced
 1 can cream of celery soup
 1 can mushrooms
 ½ cup sauterne or Chablis

¼ teaspoon oregano
    pinch of rosemary
    salt and pepper to taste
 1 cup sour cream

Preparation

PLACE birds in large baking dish. Mix all the ingredients, except the sour cream, and pour over the birds. Cover lightly with foil, and bake at 375 degrees for one hour, turning occasionally.

REMOVE from oven and add the sour cream, stirring to blend.

SERVE over wild rice or noodles.

Serves 2 to 3
Wine Suggestions: Kunde Estate Reserve Chardonnay or
Noble Vines 667 Pinot Noir

Smothered Dove

Ingredients

12 dove breasts, whole
 1 cup flour
    salt and pepper to taste
 ¾ cup olive oil

 2 cloves garlic, halved
1½ cups red wine
 1 pound mushrooms (optional)

Preparation

COAT dove breasts with flour that has been seasoned with salt and pepper. Lightly brown breasts in a heavy skillet with the oil and garlic. When birds are browned, remove the garlic. Add the wine and enough water to just barely cover the birds. Simmer for 11/2 hours or until tender. Mushrooms can be added in the last 15 minutes of cooking if desired. Thicken pan juices with a small amount of seasoned flour.

SERVE over rice or pasta.

Serves 2 to 3
Wine Suggestions: Handcraft Chardonnay or Hob Nob Pinot Noir

GRILLED DOVE KABOBS

Ingredients

12 dove breasts (cut into 24 fillets)
2 green bell peppers, cut into big pieces
1 large onion, cut into big pieces
24 small mushrooms

12 cherry tomatoes, halved
Italian salad dressing
salt and pepper to taste
12 bacon slices, halved

Preparation

REMOVE fillets from dove breasts. Combine fillets, bell peppers, mushrooms, and tomatoes in non-reactive container. Cover with Italian dressing and marinate overnight in refrigerator.

WHEN ready to cook, wrap dove fillets with bacon and alternate on skewers with vegetables. Salt and pepper to taste.

GRILL over a low fire, basting with the marinade.

Serves 2 to 3
Wine Suggestions: Barone Fini Pinot Grigio or Handcraft Petite Sirah

FRIED DOVE

All of Bill's recipes call for twelve dove. That is the daily limit in Texas and is the amount that fits in a freezer package. Twelve will usually serve four as an appetizer or two to three as a main course. All birds are breasted. Bill uses a vacuum seal process to store. Freezing in water, as you would fish, gives a good shelf life with a minimum of freezer burn. Thaw in water to remove most of the blood.

Ingredients

12 dove breasts (24 fillets)
1 egg
1 cup milk

vegetable oil
salt, pepper, cayenne pepper
2 cups pancake flour

Preparation

FILLET meat from each side of breast. Mix egg and milk. Season fillets with salt and peppers. Soak in mixture while heating oil to 375 degrees in deep fryer.

REMOVE birds from milk and egg mixture. Roll them in the pancake flour and drop them in the hot oil. They will float to the top when they are done.

Serves 2 to 3
Wine Suggestions: Massimo Sauvignon Blanc or Sauvion Vouvray

SAUTÉED DOVE

Ingredients

12 dove breasts, whole
2 tablespoons butter
2 tablespoons olive oil
1 bunch green onions, chopped fine

1 pound mushrooms, sliced
2 ounces dry sherry wine
1 ounce brandy
salt and pepper to taste

Preparation

SAUTÉ the birds in a skillet with olive oil and butter until brown on both sides. Add green onions. Sauté 2 minutes, and add mushrooms. Cook 4 more minutes on high heat. Remove skillet from stove and add sherry. Put lid on and simmer 2 to 4 minutes.

WHEN serving, remove from heat; add brandy and flame. Serve with wild rice.

Serves 2 to 3
Wine Suggestions: Hob Nob Chardonnay or Gnarly Head Pinot Noir

JALAPENO STUFFED DOVE

Ingredients

12 dove breasts
6 bacon stripes, halved
dry fajita seasoning, such as Fiesta

jalapeno strips, fresh or pickled
olive oil

Optional (See note)

sliced water chestnuts
onion slices
cream cheese

Preparation

FILLET meat from each side of breast. In each piece, make a slice, forming a pocket. Rub each with olive oil and sprinkle lightly with the fajita seasoning. Place slice of jalapeno in each pocket and wrap with bacon. Secure with a toothpick.

COVER with plastic wrap and leave in refrigerator for 2 to 4 hours.

GRILL or broil until bacon strips are done. Do not over cook.

NOTE: Slices of water chestnuts, onion slices, or cream cheese can be added for variety. The cream cheese is wonderful.

Serves 2 to 3 for dinner or 4 for an appetizer
Wine Suggestions: Twisted Moscato or Yellow Tail Bubbles

Belle retrieving a wood duck.

~WATERFOWL~

Duck
&
Goose

BRAISED DUCK BREASTS

Ingredients

3 ducks, breasted – save legs for stock
    flour, salt, & pepper, mixed in ziplock
    bag
3 slices bacon, chopped
1 large onion, chopped

2 cloves garlic, minced
½ cup red wine
½ cup orange marmalade
2 tablespoons brown sugar
2 teaspoons cinnamon

Preparation

IN A large fry pan, cook bacon pieces until crisp. Remove and drain on paper towel. Drain bacon fat, leaving about 2 tablespoons in pan.

SAUTÉ onion and garlic in bacon fat until soft. Remove and set aside.

PLACE the 6 duck breast halves in the ziplock bag with the flour and seasonings to dredge. Remove and place breasts in the hot pan and sear quickly over high heat. Turn down heat to a simmer, and return the bacon, onions, and garlic to the pan. Add the wine and scrape up any brown bits in the pan. Mix in the marmalade, brown sugar, and cinnamon. Cover pan and simmer on low heat for about 12 minutes. Duck breasts should be pink in the middle.

Serves 3 to 4
Wine Suggestions: Sonoma Coast Vineyards Freestone Hills Pinot Noir
or Brazin Rock Pile Zinfandel

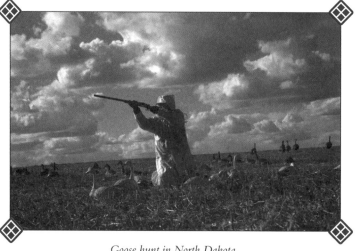

Goose hunt in North Dakota.

Brett Smith's Cajun Smothered Duck

Brett Smith has become a good friend of ours over the years. His artwork has been featured in several of the books that we have published, including this one. Brett spends his time between Louisiana, his original home, and his cabin in northwest Montana. Along with fly fishing, he is an avid duck hunter. He has spent many days in the Louisiana delta pursuing one of his favorite sports. He offered us this recipe for ducks cooked in a Cajun manner. The hot sauce amount is up to you!

Ingredients

4-6 *large ducks such as mallards, pintails, gadwalls or,*
6-8 *small ducks such as teal, scaup*
½-¾ *cup oil*
2 *cups onions, chopped*
½ *cup parsley, chopped*
2 *bunches shallots, chopped*

1 *cup green peppers, chopped*
1 *small package fresh mushrooms, sliced*
1 *pound smoked or hot sausage, sliced*
salt and pepper to taste
hot sauce
enough water to cover ducks

Preparation

TRADITIONALLY, this recipe is cooked in a large black iron pot or Dutch oven. Clean the ducks and cut them into pieces. Salt and pepper to taste. Pour oil into pot and cook ducks in oil until well browned. Sausage can also be browned at this time. Remove ducks and sausage and pour off most of the oil from the pot. Brown onions and shallots in remaining oil until transparent and well browned.

RETURN ducks and sausage to the pot with the onions and add enough water to cover the pieces. Bring to a boil over high heat. After the water starts to boil, turn the heat down to a medium high fire. Cover pot and cook for 2½ to 3 hours or until meat pulls easily from the bone. The gravy will thicken as it cooks down, so add water as needed.

ADD salt and pepper and hot sauce to taste as the gravy cooks down. During the last half hour of cooking, add the green peppers, parsley and mushrooms to the pot.

SERVE over cooked white rice.

Serves 8 to 10

Wine Suggestions: Massimo Malbec or Ramón Bilbao Valiñas Albariño

BRAISED GOOSE LEGS WITH FIGS AND SQUASH

Slow braising takes the toughness out of the leg meat of wild birds and the sweetness of the figs complements the rich goose meat perfectly. Add the squash toward the end of the cooking time. You want the cubes to remain a little firm for their texture as well as for the presentation of the dish. Adding the small amount of vinegar just before serving will brighten the flavors of the dish.

Ingredients

½ pound dried figs, sliced thin
¼ cup brandy
4 goose legs, skinned
1 tablespoon olive oil
1 onion, chopped
2 large carrots, chopped
2 celery stalks, chopped
6 garlic cloves, minced
¾ teaspoon Chinese five-spice powder

4 sprigs fresh thyme, or 1/2 teaspoon
   dried thyme
4 – 5 cups chicken broth
1 cup cream sherry
1½ pounds squash, peeled, seeded, and
   cut into 2-inch cubes
1 tablespoon Champagne vinegar
2 tablespoons flat leaf parsley, chopped

Preparation

PLACE figs in a small bowl and cover with brandy. Let soak for 30 minutes.

HEAT oven to 350 degrees. Season goose legs with salt and pepper. Over medium-high heat, heat oil in Dutch oven or large heavy pot and sear goose legs in two batches, about 3 minutes per side. Remove from pot and set aside. Lower heat to medium and add onion, carrot, and celery and sauté for 3 - 4 minutes, until onion is translucent. Add garlic and sauté for another minute. Stir in the figs and brandy, thyme, and five-spice powder. Add 4 cups broth and the sherry. Return goose legs to mix and bury them in the liquid and vegetables.

COVER mixture with parchment and then Dutch oven lid. Place in heated oven and cook for 2 - 3 hours. About 30 minutes before the meat is done, lift lid and parchment and stir mixture. Check liquid level and add more broth if necessary. Parchment cover should keep the liquid from evaporating. Add squash cubes, and replace parchment and lid. Continue cooking until meat is ready to fall off the bone.

REMOVE pot from oven and let rest for 15 - 20 minutes. Just before serving, stir in Champagne vinegar and sprinkle with parsley.

Serves 4
Wine Suggestions: Volteo Garnacha or Loredona Viognier

Mushroom Blackberry Duck

Ingredients

1 mallard, quartered
¼ cup flour, seasoned with salt, pepper,
  and ¼ teaspoon ground thyme
1 tablespoon butter
1 tablespoon olive oil
6 green onions or 3 shallots, chopped
1 cup shiitake mushrooms, sliced
¼ cup brandy

¾ cup game bird or chicken stock
1 cup sweet Marsala, plus 1–2
  tablespoons extra
1 bay leaf
¼ teaspoon ground thyme
½ teaspoon tarragon
½ pint fresh blackberries (frozen can also
  be used)

Preparation

HEAT skillet to medium-high, and add the butter and olive oil. Dredge the duck quarters in the seasoned flour and sear them quickly, about 1 minute per side. Turn the heat off and remove them to a covered dish in a 250-degree oven.

IN THE same skillet over medium heat, sauté the green onions or shallots for about 1 minute. Add the mushrooms and sauté for another minute, stirring constantly. Deglaze the skillet with the brandy, and add the stock, Marsala wine, and the herbs, stirring to blend. Simmer for about 15 minutes.

JUST before serving, add the blackberries and simmer 3 to 4 minutes. Return the duck quarters to the skillet. Pour 1 to 2 tablespoons of Marsala wine into the dish that held the duck and stir to combine with the duck juices. Add this to the skillet, and combine with the sauce.

PLACE the duck quarters on a serving platter and pour the sauce all around. Serve with asparagus and a risotto cooked with green onions and Parmesan cheese.

Serves 2

Wine Suggestions: Ruta 22 Malbec
or
Loredona Pinot Grigio

GRILLED DUCK BREAST WITH CHERRY/MARNIER SAUCE

Ingredients

> 6 wild duck breasts, split in half

For the Marinade

> ½ cup olive oil
> ½ cup peanut oil
> 2 tablespoons lemon or lime juice

> 2 tablespoons soy sauce
> 2 tablespoons sherry
> 1 large garlic clove, minced

For the Sauce

> ½ cup orange juice
> 1 cup dried Bing cherries
> 4 tablespoons Grand Marnier, or Cherry Marnier
> 1 cup dry red wine
>   dash of tarragon

> 1½ cups game bird or chicken stock
> 1 cinnamon stick, broken in half
> 1 tablespoon balsamic vinegar
> 1 tablespoon arrowroot
> 2-3 tablespoons butter, cubed and chilled

Preparation

MARINATE duck breasts for at least 2 hours.

IN A medium saucepan, soak the cherries in the orange juice and 2 tablespoons of the Grand Marnier for at least 20 minutes. Add red wine, tarragon, stock, and cinnamon stick pieces. Bring to a boil and reduce by half. Turn heat down to a simmer. Remove the cinnamon sticks and add 1 tablespoon balsamic vinegar. Simmer for 3 to 5 minutes. Add remaining Grand Marnier.

PUT arrowroot into a small bowl and add some of the sauce to dissolve the arrowroot. Combine with the wine mixture to thicken. Turn down heat, and keep warm until duck breasts are finished.

REMOVE the duck breasts from the marinade and grill over very hot coals for about 3 minutes per side. Put on platter and keep in a warm oven while you finish the sauce.

INCREASE the heat for the sauce. When it is just about at a simmer, slowly swirl in the butter in small chunks until you achieve the desired consistency. You do not have to use all the butter if you prefer a leaner sauce.

BEFORE serving, pour a small amount of the sauce over the duck breasts, and then serve the rest of the sauce in a sauceboat.

SERVE with wild rice mixed with toasted pecans.

Serves 6
Wine Suggestions: Noble Hills 667 Pinot Noir or George Duboeuf Pouilly Fuisse

GRILLED DUCK BREAST

Ingredients

4 wild ducks, breasted and skinned (save
   the carcasses for stock)
1 cup olive oil
  juice of 1 lemon

2 tablespoons soy sauce
1 tablespoon Worcestershire sauce
⅓ cup red wine
½ cup chopped parsley

Preparation

COMBINE the ingredients and marinate duck breasts for 1 to 2 hours. Remove breasts from marinade and put marinade in a saucepan. Bring to a boil, and then lower to a simmer. Cook for about 10 minutes. Remove from heat.

WHEN the barbecue is very hot, place breasts on grill and cook 3 to 5 minutes per side, depending on the size of the breasts. Baste with the warm marinade while cooking. Watch the breasts carefully, so they don't overcook. Duck tastes best when cooked rare.

Serves 4
Wine Suggestions: Ramón Bilbao Reserva or Handcraft Chardonnay

©Brett Smith

GRILLED DUCK WITH RASPBERRY SAUCE

Ingredients

>   2 wild ducks, quartered

For the Marinade

>   ½ cup peanut oil
>   2 tablespoons lemon juice
>   2 tablespoons soy sauce
>   1 tablespoon Worcestershire sauce

>   1 inch fresh ginger, peeled and thinly
>   sliced lengthwise
>   ¼ teaspoon ground star anise
>   dash of ground thyme

For the Raspberry Sauce

>   4 green onions, sliced, with green tops
>   1 tablespoon butter, plus 2 tablespoons
>   chilled, to finish
>   1 tablespoon brandy

>   ¾ cup raspberry jam
>   2 tablespoons Grand Marnier
>   2 tablespoons balsamic vinegar
>   ½ cup fresh raspberries

Preparation

COMBINE the marinade ingredients, and marinate ducks for at least 2 hours. They can also be marinated as long as overnight.

WHILE the grill is heating, make the sauce. Heat a medium saucepan and add 1 tablespoon of butter. As soon as it melts, add the green onion and sauté over medium-high heat for 2 minutes. Add the brandy, jam, and Grand Marnier, stirring to combine. Turn heat down to a simmer and add the balsamic vinegar. Keep warm until duck is about finished.

WHEN the grill is fiery hot, remove the duck pieces and place on grill. Grill the pieces for 3 minutes per side, depending on size. Remove to a warm oven while you finish the sauce.

TURN the heat back up on the sauce until it starts to slowly simmer again. Swirl in the 2 tablespoons of butter to thicken the sauce. You can use less if you prefer. Add the fresh raspberries and stir gently. Continue heating until the raspberries are warmed through.

SPOON a small amount of the sauce over the duck on the serving platter, and serve the rest on the side, so that diners can use to individual preference.

Serves 4
Wine Suggestions: Noble Vines 446 Chardonnay or
Castello di Monastero Chianti Classico

Duck Fajitas

Our friend, Chris Francis, not only loves to hunt waterfowl, he also enjoys finding new ways to enjoy his harvest. The duck marinade in this recipe is from him. He claims that it's important to cut the breast meat of the duck cross-wise across the breast, instead of slicing it with the grain of the meat. This thin slice creates a tender piece of meat. And, as always, keep your duck meat rare!

Ingredients

¼ cup hot sauce
¼ cup A-1 Sauce
12 ounces Sprite, or other lemon-lime
    soda (not diet)
    salt
4 duck breasts, skinned & filleted
1 small red onion, cut in half and sliced
    thin

1 red bell pepper, sliced thin
1 green bell pepper, sliced thin
    olive oil
    warm tortillas
    fajita accompaniments

Preparation

IN A small bowl, combine the two sauces and the Sprite and lightly salt. Slice each duck breast across the grain into thin slices. Add to marinade and cover. Refrigerate and marinate for several hours, turning occasionally.

WHEN ready to cook, remove duck breasts from marinade and pat dry. Put a small amount of oil in a hot skillet and add the sliced onion and peppers. Sear the mixture until the onion and peppers just start to soften. Remove from skillet and keep warm in a serving bowl. Add duck slices to skillet and sear for just a couple of minutes. You want the duck meat to be rare. Remove to serving bowl.

TO SERVE, place the bowl with the onion-pepper mixture and the bowl with the duck on the table along with a bowl of warmed tortillas. Allow guests to serve themselves by placing a portion of duck and onion-pepper mixture in the center of the tortilla and then add fajita accompaniments as desired. Some favorite accompaniments are shredded lettuce, grated cheese, sour cream, sliced green onions, sliced black olives, chopped tomatoes, and salsa.

Serves 4

Wine Suggestions: Volteo Verdejo Sauvignon Blanc
or
Loredona Riesling

SMOKED DUCK BREAST WITH PLUM WINE REDUCTION

Japanese plum wine works wonders with duck breasts. This recipe works equally well with the red meat of the prairie grouse: sharptails and sage hens. In this recipe, we used a special seasoning blend produced by Penzey's Spices. It's great for seasoning so many dishes, or just sprinkled over a baked potato. If you don't have it, you can substitute a combination of shallots, chives, garlic, green peppercorns, and a little salt.

The recipe calls for smoking the duck breasts, which adds an extra layer of flavor. However, you could just as easily grill the duck breasts for just 3 minutes per side and serve with the reduction for a quicker meal.

Ingredients

> 3 *mallard duck breasts, split in half*

For the Marinade

> 1½ *cups Japanese plum wine*
> 6 *fresh sage leaves, or 1 teaspoon dried sage*
>
> 1 *teaspoon nutmeg*
> 2 *tablespoons Penzey's Sunny Paris Seasoning*

For the Plum Wine Reduction

> 2 *cups Japanese plum wine*
> 1 *tablespoon butter, cut in small chunks*

Preparation

COMBINE the marinade ingredients and pour over the duck breasts. Marinate for at least 4 hours, or overnight in the refrigerator. Remove the duck and marinade from the refrigerator at least 1 hour prior to cooking.

SOAK some hickory chips in water and place in your smoker. When the coals are ready, remove the duck breasts from the marinade and place in the smoker. Smoke them for 3 hours.

ABOUT 30 minutes before the duck breasts are done, bring 2 cups of plum wine to a boil in a small saucepan. Lower the heat to a gentle boil, and reduce the wine to about ⅓ cup. Slowly swirl in the chunks of butter. Keep warm.

WHEN breasts are done, remove them to a serving platter. Drizzle the plum wine reduction over the breasts, and serve.

Serves 4
Wine Suggestions: Barone Fini Merlot
or Black Stallion Chardonnay

BRINED GOOSE BREAST

Ingredients

1 breast of Canada goose, filleted and
    halved
2 cups apple cider
½ cup kosher salt
½ cup brown sugar
1 bay leaf

1 cinnamon stick, broken in half
1 teaspoon juniper berries
1½ teaspoons mix of green and black
    peppercorns, crushed
4 cups dark beer

Preparation

IN A large saucepan, combine the cider, salt and brown sugar. Cook over low heat until the salt and sugar are dissolved. Add the rest of the ingredients and cool to room temperature.

PUT the goose breast in a large ziplock bag. Pour the marinade over the goose and seal the bag, squeezing out all the air. Place bag in a large bowl and marinate in the refrigerator for 24 hours.

REMOVE the goose and the marinade from the refrigerator at least one hour before cooking.

GRILL the breasts over very hot coals for 6 to 7 minutes per side. Do not over cook. Breasts should still have a pink tinge to them.

Serves 4 to 6
Wine Suggestions: Noble Vines 446 Chardonnay or
Castello di Monastero Chianti Classico Reserva

©Brett Smith

SMOKED GOOSE

Ingredients

1 5- to 6-pound goose, skinned strips of bacon

3 oranges, one cut in thin slices and two quartered
apple wood chips, soaked for 1 to 2 hours

For the Brine

1 cup kosher salt
¾ cup brown sugar

2 cups apple cider
1 gallon water

For the Basting Sauce

1 cup chicken broth
2 oranges
6 large sage leaves, chopped

1½ cups triple sec or other orange liqueur
6 black peppercorns, crushed

Preparation

THE DAY before serving, combine the brine ingredients in a container large enough to hold the goose. Place the goose in the brine, adding more water if necessary, to cover. Cover pot and brine overnight in refrigerator.

REMOVE goose from brine and rinse thoroughly. Pat dry and then rinse and pat dry again. Place the quartered oranges in the breast cavity. Attach bacon strips to breast and legs with toothpicks.

DRAIN the water from the applewood chips and combine with the orange slices. Then place them in smoking tray of outdoor grill. Light grill and heat to about 250 degrees with cover closed. Place bacon-wrapped goose on grill, lower cover, and cook slowly for 4 to 4½ hours.

IN A saucepan, add the chicken broth, sage, triple sec, and peppercorns. Zest the oranges and add to pan. Cut oranges into quarters and squeeze juice into pan. Bring to a simmer and reduce liquid by half. Place half the sauce in a separate bowl, and keep the remaining sauce warm in the pan.

AFTER the first half hour of cooking the goose, turn it a quarter turn and baste with the sauce in the bowl. Cover again and continue cooking, basting and turning the goose about every half hour.

WHEN ready to bring goose in from grill, heat oven to 350 degrees. Finish goose in oven until meat in breast is still pink – about 20 minutes. Remove from oven, remove bacon strips, and discard. Let rest about 5 minutes. Serve with the heated sauce.

Serves 6 – 8

Wine Suggestions:Chateau Bonnet Rose or Irony Chardonnay

Duck Breast a L'Orange

Fruit-based chipotle sauces are often found in grocery stores, but you can also check online for them. See our Culinary Sources section in the back of the book for some of our favorites.

Ingredients

- *4 duck breasts, with bone in*
- *2 cups orange juice*
- *½ cup Drambuie*

- *5 strips of orange peel*
- *1 tablespoon mango chipotle sauce or raspberry chipotle sauce*

Preparation

COMBINE juice, Drambuie, orange peel, and mango chipotle sauce. Sprinkle duck breasts with salt and pepper and place in marinade for 4 to 8 hours.

HEAT grill to 450 degrees. Remove duck breasts from marinade and pat dry. Grill breasts quickly on grill, about 2 minutes per side. Apply a liberal amount of raspberry chipotle sauce and grill for 1½ minutes per side. Meat should be rare for best taste. Remove and place in warm oven (250 degrees) to rest meat before serving.

Serves 4

Wine Suggestions: Loredona Riesling
or
Sauvion Vouvray

Grilled Goose Breast – Hot and Cold

We split our geese into two parts when we freeze them, since we usually braise the legs slowly and grill or pan-sear the breast meat quickly. This recipe combines two ways to serve goose breast for two meals or a meal and an appetizer. The idea for this dish came from our good friends and hunting companions, Katie and Bill Kluchko. Katie and Bill have taken many geese with their wirehaired pointing Griffons, Bucky and Fritz.

Ingredients

2 goose breast halves
3 tablespoons kosher salt
1 cup apple cider
1 cup olive oil
½ cup brandy, plus 1 tablespoon
3 large sage leaves, julienned

Raspberry Game Sauce or Prairie Grouse Sauce (see recipes in Sauce Section)
⅓ cup Dijon mustard
⅓ cup sour cream

Preparation

PLACE goose breasts in a container just big enough to fit. Sprinkle kosher salt over meat and pour in apple cider. Pour in just enough water to cover the meat. Refrigerate for a couple of hours.

MAKE a marinade by combining the olive oil, the ½ cup brandy, and the sage leaves. Remove the breasts from the brine and rinse thoroughly. Pat dry and place in the marinade. Refrigerate for 4 to 6 hours. Before cooking, remove marinade from refrigerator for about an hour to bring to room temperature.

HEAT grill to 375 degrees. Remove meat from marinade and pat dry. With a sharp knife, score the top of each breast with "X"s. Season to taste with freshly ground salt and pepper. Grill for 8 minutes on each side. Place on a platter and hold in a warm oven for about 5 minutes to let the meat rest. To serve, slice thin across the narrow side and serve with a fruit-based sauce such as Raspberry Game Sauce or Prairie Grouse Sauce.

ANY leftover meat can be chilled and served as an appetizer or a cold meal on a hot day with a mustard sauce made of Dijon mustard, sour cream, and 1 tablespoon of brandy.

Serves 2 as a meal per breast half

Wine Suggestions: Hob Nob Wicked Red
or Gnarly Head Pinot Grigio

CALVADOS-MARINATED DUCK BREASTS

Grilling is one of the best ways to bring out the rich flavor of duck. The key is to make sure that you do not cook the duck more than medium-rare – and preferably keeping it rare. While overcooked duck tastes and feels like shoe leather, duck cooked rare tastes remarkably like rich beef.

Ingredients

4 full duck breasts, skinned
¼ cup olive oil
2 tablespoons soy sauce
1 teaspoon lemon juice

4 cloves garlic, minced
½ cup Calvados brandy
salt and pepper to taste
4 strips bacon, cut in half

Preparation

PLACE all liquids and the garlic in a bowl and whisk to combine. Add duck breasts and marinate in the refrigerator for 5 hours to overnight. Remove from refrigerator at least 1 hour before grilling.

BRING grill to 425 degrees. Place 2 pieces of bacon on each duck breast and secure with toothpicks. Place duck breasts on grill with bacon side up. Grill for 3 minutes, then turn and grill for 2 minutes. Turn back to bacon side up for 1 more minute and remove from grill. Finish in a warm oven for 4 minutes to let the meat relax.

Serves 4

Wine Suggestions: Loredona Viognier
or
Ramón Bilbao Crianza

Pan-seared Duck Breast with Fig Sauce

The key to this recipe is to sear the duck breasts quickly over high heat to achieve a rich, slightly crusty outside and a juicy, rare inside.

Ingredients

10 figs, halved
½ cup port
2 duck breasts, split in half
2 tablespoons butter, 1 chopped into small pieces and chilled

¼ teaspoon Chinese 5-spice powder
1 cup red wine
1 tablespoon Dijon mustard
toasted sesame seeds, for garnish

Preparation

THIRTY minutes before cooking the duck breasts, place the figs in a small bowl and pour the port over them to soak.

PAT duck breasts completely dry and season with salt and pepper. In a large sauté pan, heat 1 tablespoon of the butter over medium-high heat. Add the duck breasts and sear them 2 to 3 minutes, depending on the thickness of the meat. Turn breasts over and sprinkle with Chinese 5-spice powder and sear another 2 to 3 minutes. Remove to a warm plate.

ADD the red wine to the pan and stir in the mustard. Add the figs and port to this mixture and simmer for about 5 to 7 minutes, reducing the liquid and making it syrupy. Remove from heat and whisk in the chilled tablespoon of butter. Return the pan to the medium-low heat and put the duck breasts and any accumulated juices into the pan, stirring the liquid and spooning it over the breasts. Continue cooking until the breasts are warmed through.

WHEN serving, spoon the fig sauce onto the plate, place a duck breast on top, drizzle a little of the liquid over top, and sprinkle with the toasted sesame seeds.

Serves 2 to 4, depending on the size of the duck breasts

Wine Suggestions: Ruta 22 Malbec
or
Noble Vines 667 Pinot Noir

GOOSE BREAST EN BRIOCHE

This is a great way to serve waterfowl that is older and tougher since it's shredded in a food processor. The recipe can be made in an infinite variety of ways, using all types of wild game and adding extras like chopped dried cherries. It can be served as an entrée, but it can also be sliced and served as an appetizer.

Ingredients

½ goose breast (about 1 pound), cut into small chunks
6 ounces pork sausage
1 tablespoon Dijon mustard
2 teaspoons Worcestershire sauce
¼ teaspoon dried thyme

3 green onions, chopped
17 ounces puff pastry – 2 sheets
1 egg, beaten with 1 tablespoon water
specialty mustard or fruit chutney

Preparation

PREHEAT oven to 400 degrees. Place goose meat in food processor and pulse until meat is shredded. Place in a bowl and add pork sausage, mixing gently to combine. Add mustard, Worcestershire sauce, thyme, and onions. Add salt and pepper to taste, stirring to combine flavors. Do this gently by using your hands. Divide into four balls.

UNROLL pastry and cut each sheet in half. Form each ball of meat into a long sausage roll and place one on each pastry sheet, leaving enough pastry on each side to be able to roll up. Brush both sides of pastry with beaten egg mixture and roll pastry over to seal. Glaze the outside of the pastry with the egg wash.

LINE a large cookie sheet with parchment paper and place goose breast rolls on it. Bake in oven for 15 - 20 minutes, until pastry is golden brown. Cut each roll in half and place on a plate in a V formation. In the crook of the V place a condiment, such as a specialty mustard or chutney.

Serves 4 as an entrée

Wine Suggestions: Irony Pinot Noir
or
Sauvion Chinon

Mallard Duck Rotisserie

As with any duck, do not overcook the meat or it will taste like liver. Better to have the meat on the rare side when you take it off the grill. You can always finish it in a warm oven to the desired degree. You can find the huckleberry chipotle sauce in the Culinary Sources section of this book. It's absolutely great with most wild game.

Ingredients

2 mallard ducks, skinned
4-6 strips bacon
1 orange, halved

1 orange, juiced
¼ cup olive oil
    huckleberry chipotle sauce

Preparations

HEAT the grill to 400 degrees. Combine the orange juice and the olive oil in a small bowl. Place half an orange in each duck and tie the legs together with twine to hold it in the cavity. Secure the bacon strips to the ducks with toothpicks.

BASTE the ducks with the orange juice and oil combination, and put ducks breast side down on the grill and close the lid. Cook for 4 minutes. Lower the heat and raise the lid. Cook for 2 more minutes with the lid open, basting again with the juice and oil.

REMOVE the ducks from the grill, remove the bacon and discard it. Drizzle some of the huckleberry chipotle sauce over the ducks and set in a warm oven for 5 minutes or until done.

Serves 4

Wine Suggestions: George Duboeuf Morgon
or
Gnarly Head Pinot Noir

~BIG GAME~

Deer

GRILLED MEDITERRANEAN VENISON ROAST
with Mushroom and Sun-dried Tomato Sauce

Ingredients

3-4 *pound venison roast, shoulder or sirloin tip*
3-4 *strips bacon*

For the Marinade

½ *cup soy sauce*
½ *cup dry red wine, such as a Merlot or Zinfandel*
½ *cup sherry*
¼ *cup olive oil*
5–6 *garlic cloves, minced*

½ *cup fresh oregano leaves, chopped or 1 tablespoon dried oregano*
2 *tablespoons fresh rosemary, crushed or 1 tablespoon dried rosemary ground pepper and salt*

For the Sauce

1 *tablespoon butter, plus extra for finishing if desired*
1 *tablespoon olive oil*
2 *cups fresh mushrooms – any mix of shiitake, oyster, crimini, portobello*
6 *green onions with green tops, sliced finely*

⅓ *cup sun-dried tomatoes marinated in oil, drained and chopped*
½ *cup game stock or beef broth*
¼ *cup Marsala wine*
½ *teaspoon dried thyme*

Preparation

COMBINE the marinade ingredients and marinate the elk roast for 4 to 24 hours, turning occasionally. The longer you leave the roast in the marinade, the tastier it will be.

AT LEAST 2 hours before cooking time, remove roast from refrigerator so that it can come to room temperature. Then remove the roast from the marinade and pat dry. Wrap the roast with the bacon, using toothpicks to secure. Grill the roast for approximately 35 to 40 minutes, turning every 10 to 12 minutes. If you like, you can baste the roast with the marinade. Just be sure that you gently boil the marinade for at least 10 minutes before using. Check the roast with a meat thermometer. Do not overcook. It is done when the thermometer registers medium rare for beef. When done, remove the bacon strips and discard. Place the roast in a warm oven while finishing the rest of the dinner.

WHILE the roast is grilling, melt the butter with the olive oil in a large saucepan. Sauté the green onions over medium-high heat until the onions are soft, but not browned. Add the sun-dried tomatoes, and sauté for another 2 minutes. Then add the mushrooms, stirring frequently for 2 more minutes. Add the Marsala wine, the stock and the thyme, stirring to combine. Cover and let simmer, stirring occasionally, for 10 to 15 minutes. Keep warm until roast is done and has had a few minutes to set in the oven. Then add any juices that have seeped from the roast to the sauce. Stir them in and slowly add little pieces of butter to the sauce if you want it thicker and richer.

TO SERVE, you can place some of the mushroom mixture around the roast on the serving platter and serve the rest in a gravy bowl. This is luscious with boiled red potatoes with butter and chives.

Serves 6 to 8
Wine Suggestions: Château de Rochemorin Rouge
or Noble Vines 337 Cabernet Sauvignon

Alternate Cooking Method:

You can also roast the venison in the oven. After wrapping with bacon, spray a roasting pan lightly with oil or butter. Place in a 450 degree oven for 15 minutes, then turn the heat down to 325 degrees, and continue roasting at about 15 minutes per pound.

Blanche with her Pennsylvania white-tail.

GRILLED ROUND STEAK WITH CHILI-RED PEPPER TOPPING

The cheese helps mellow the kick from the puréed chilies. You can also vary the amount of puréed chilies to individual tastes. It is best to serve the steak within 5 minutes of putting the grilled steaks in the warming oven. Otherwise, you may end up with puddles of melted cheese on the platter.

Ingredients

2 pounds venison round steaks, cut into 4 total pieces
1 dried ancho chili, seeds removed
1 dried chipotle, seeds removed
1 clove garlic, halved

1 cup roasted red peppers in olive oil, drained
4 slices Monterey Jack or Jarlsburg cheese

For the Marinade

¼ cup olive oil
¼ cup red wine
1 tablespoon Worcestershire sauce

1 garlic clove, minced
salt and pepper

Preparation

COMBINE the marinade ingredients and marinate the steaks for 1 to 2 hours.

SOAK the chilies in water until soft. Put the chilies in a blender along with the red pepper and garlic clove. Add 3 tablespoons of the water in which the chilies had been soaked. Purée the mixture, adding more water if it is too thick, but don't make it runny.

GRILL the steaks over hot coals for about 3 minutes per side for medium rare. For the last minute, add a cheese slice to the top of each steak.

PUT in a warm oven and put a spoonful of the chili purée on top of the cheese. Serve within a couple of minutes so the cheese doesn't melt too much.

Serves 4

Wine Suggestions: Black Stallion Cabernet Sauvignon
or
Girard Old Vine Zinfandel

VENISON MEDALLIONS NAPOLEON

Why I named this "Napoleon" has been lost over the years. It may have been because of the use of brandy and Dijon mustard, or it might be simply because Napoleon is one of Chuck's heroes, along with John Wayne; and "Venison Medallions John Wayne" just didn't seem to flow well.

Ingredients

4 small medallions of venison, or 2 large
   medallions
1 tablespoon olive oil
2 large garlic cloves, peeled and minced
1 cup mushrooms, sliced
¼ cup brandy
½ cup port wine

1 cup game stock or beef broth
1½ tablespoons Dijon mustard
2 tablespoons currant jelly
¼ teaspoon ground thyme
½ cup sour cream (optional)
   arrowroot to thicken

Preparations

HEAT skillet over medium-high heat and brown medallions in olive oil, approximately 1 to 1½ minutes per side, depending on thickness. Remove to a covered dish and keep in warm oven.

LOWER heat in skillet and sauté garlic and mushrooms in remaining oil. For 1 to 2 minutes. Add brandy, scraping up any browned bits. Add rest of ingredients except sour cream and arrowroot. Stir occasionally while simmering over low heat for about 10 minutes.

TASTE to determine if you want to add the sour cream. The sauce is lighter and "meatier" without it, but has a rich creamy taste if it is added. A touch of arrowroot can added to either version if you prefer a thicker sauce.

RETURN medallions, and any juices, to the skillet for about another minute. Serve with wild rice.

Serves 2

Wine Suggestions: Girard Artistry
or
Brazin Old Vine Zinfandel

Roast Sirloin Tip with Cherries and Port

This recipe works just as well with elk and antelope. All three are lean meats and cook in just about the same time.

Ingredients

3 pounds venison sirloin tip
2 large carrots, peeled and quartered

2 medium parsnips, peeled and quartered

For the Marinade

¼ cup dried cherries
¼ cup port, plus ½ cup
1 shallot, chopped fine
1 carrot, peeled and chopped fine
6 sprigs of thyme

½ teaspoon allspice
1 tablespoon tomato paste
¼ cup olive oil
1 tablespoon balsamic vinegar

For the Sauce

¾ cup dried cherries
1 cup Marsala wine
2 tablespoons butter
3 large portobello mushrooms, sliced

1 shallot, thinly sliced
1 cup game stock or beef broth
1 tablespoon currant jelly
1-2 teaspoons arrowroot

Early Preparation

SOAK the cherries in the 1/4 cup of port for at least 20 minutes in a small bowl. Process the mix in a blender or food processor to break the cherries into small pieces. Put the mixture into a medium saucepan and turn heat to medium-high. Add the rest of the marinade ingredients, and simmer gently for 5 minutes to blend the flavors. Cool to room temperature.

PLACE the roast in the marinade and refrigerate for at least 4 hours, but preferabley overnight.

Final Preparation

SOAK the dried cherries and the Marsala wine for at least 20 minutes.

REMOVE the roast and marinade from the refrigerator at least 1 hour before roasting. Preheat oven to 450 degrees. Lightly oil a roasting pan and place the carrot and parsnip pieces on the bottom of the pan. Remove the roast from the marinade and pat dry. Place it on top of the root vegetables and add salt and pepper to taste. Place in oven at 450 degrees for 15 minutes. Turn heat down to 325 degrees and roast another 40 minutes. Check for doneness and continue cooking at 325 degrees if it is too rare, but don't overcook. As with steaks, big game roasts taste much better if they are cooked medium-rare to rare.

MEANWHILE, add the butter to a medium saucepan over medium-high heat, and sauté the shallot and mushrooms for 3 minutes. Add the soaked cherries and Marsala to the pan, scraping any browned bits up. Add the stock and the jelly, and simmer for about 15 minutes. Add a little arrowroot to the mixture if you want the sauce to be thickened. Turn down heat and keep warm.

WHEN roast is done, remove to serving platter and place vegetables around. Let sit a few minutes. Serve with the cherry sauce on the side.

Serves 6

Wine Suggestions: Black Stallion Chardonnay
or
Windsor Sonoma Cabernet Sauvignon

©Brett Smith

Venison Round Steak with Italian Seasonings

Ingredients

2 ½-inch thick cuts of venison round steak, seasoned with salt, cracked pepper, and garlic powder
2 tablespoons olive oil
3 large garlic cloves, peeled and split in half
3 large green onions, chopped
1 portobello mushroom, cut in large chunks
1 cup oyster or shiitake mushrooms, cut in large chunks

2 tablespoons brandy
½ cup game stock or beef broth
¼ cup dry red wine, such as Zinfandel
½ teaspoon basil
½ teaspoon oregano
¼ teaspoon thyme
1 tablespoon currant jelly
½ cup roasted red pepper in olive oil, drained and cut in strips
1 teaspoon arrowroot (optional)

Preparation

PLACE olive oil in skillet and add the garlic slices. Turn the heat on low and let garlic infuse the oil as it heats up. Do not let it sizzle or burn. With a fork or spatula, lightly crush the cloves to speed the process. This takes about 10 minutes. Remove the garlic cloves and set aside.

TURN the heat up to medium-high and sauté the seasoned steaks 1 to 2 minutes per side. Remove to a covered dish and put in a warm oven.

TURN the heat down in the skillet and sauté the green onions for about a minute. Add the mushrooms and sauté another 1 to 2 minutes. Add brandy to deglaze the pan. Add the stock, wine, herbs, currant jelly, and the garlic cloves. Stir to combine and then add the red pepper strips. Cover and simmer gently for 10 to 15 minutes. If you wish the sauce to be a little thicker, sprinkle the arrowroot on the sauce and stir to combine. Simmer another minute or two to thicken.

DRAIN any of the accumulated juices from the steaks and combine with the sauce.

PLACE the sauce on the serving dish and top with the steaks.

Serves 2

Wine Suggestions: Coldisole Brunnelo di Montalcino
or Massimo Rioja

Venison Steaks with Huckleberry Shallot Sauce

Huckleberries and venison just seem to go together. If you don't have huckleberries available (since they are only harvested in the wild and tend to be expensive) you can substitute blueberries, fresh or frozen. If you can find the frozen wild blueberries at your grocery, they probably mimic the huckleberry the best, since they tend to be a little smaller and a little more tart than the regular ones.

Ingredients

4 *venison steaks*
flour seasoned with salt, pepper, and garlic powder
1 *tablespoon olive oil*
3 *shallots, sliced thin*
2 *cups mushrooms, sliced*
½ *cup port wine*

1 *cup game stock or beef broth*
1 *teaspoon thyme*
¾ *cup huckleberries, or blueberries*
⅔ *cup cream*
brown sugar to taste
balsamic vinegar to taste

Preparation

HEAT a large skillet over medium-high heat. Add olive oil. Dredge steaks in seasoned flour and brown in skillet, about 1 to 2 minutes per side, depending on thickness. Remove to covered dish in 300-degree oven.

ADD the shallots and mushrooms to the skillet and sauté for 3 to 4 minutes, stirring frequently. Add port wine, and deglaze the pan. Add stock and thyme, stirring to combine. Now add the huckleberries and cream, stirring to combine. Simmer gently until the liquid is reduced by half.

SEASON to taste, adding a little brown sugar and balsamic vinegar to balance the sweetness of the port with the tartness of the huckleberries. Return steaks to pan along with any juices, and gently simmer for 1 or 2 minutes.

THIS combination works perfectly with wild rice.

Serves 4

Wine Suggestions: Bota Box Malbec
or
Vidal Fleury Chateauneuf du Pape

VENISON POT ROAST

This recipe works equally well for any type of venison – deer, elk, antelope. It's best to use a shoulder chuck roast but, like any game meat, you will need to add some fat laced into the roast to keep it moist like a beef chuck roast. It's also best to tie the roast to hold its shape.

Ingredients

2-3 pounds venison chuck roast
4 slices bacon, chopped
2 garlic cloves, diced fine
¼ cup flour, seasoned with salt and pepper
1 tablespoon peanut oil
1 small onion, chopped
2 small to medium turnips, chopped
2 carrots, chopped
1 small parsnip, chopped
¼ cup brandy

1 ½ cups beef broth or game stock
1 beer, such as Killian's Red
1-2 teaspoons chopped fresh thyme, or 1/2 teaspoon dried
1-2 teaspoons chopped fresh sage, or 1/4 teaspoon dried
1 bay leaf
1 tablespoon tomato paste
2 tablespoons butter, softened
2 tablespoons flour

Preparation

HEAT oven to 300 degrees. Lay the roast out flat on a table. Insert a small knife blade into what will be the interior of the roast, and then push a small piece of garlic into the hole. Follow it with a piece or two of the chopped bacon. Fold the roast over. Cut 3 or 4 pieces of kitchen twine and lay them out on a platter. Place the folded roast over the twine. Tie each piece of kitchen twine firmly around the roast. Cut 2 longer pieces of twine and place them under the roast lengthwise. Tie these also. Make some slits on the outside of the roast and repeat the process with the garlic and bacon. If you have some garlic left over, set it aside. You will have at least half of the bacon.

PLACE the remaining bacon in a skillet and heat it until crisp. Remove the bacon and drain on paper towels. Add the peanut oil to the skillet. Dredge the roast in the seasoned flour, pressing down to push it into the roast. Over medium heat, brown the roast on all sides. Remove it and place it in a Dutch oven or ovenproof pot.

ADD the chopped vegetables to the skillet and sauté for about 5 minutes, sitting occasionally. Transfer the mixture to the Dutch oven, arranging them around the roast. Add the brandy to the skillet, scraping up any brown bits. Reduce liquid to about a tablespoon and add the beer and beef broth. Add the crisped bacon, thyme, sage, and bay leaf, the rest of the diced garlic, and the tomato paste, stirring to combine. Bring this mixture to a high simmer and reduce by half. Pour over the roast and vegetables.

CUT a piece of parchment paper that is at least 1/3 bigger than the surface of the pot. Place this paper over the roast, pressing down to remove any air pockets. Let the balance of the paper come up the sides of the pot. Place in heated oven and cook until tender, about 2 to 2-1/2 hours.

WHEN the roast is tender, mix the butter and flour together in a small bowl. Remove the pot from the oven and turn off the heat. Place roast on a serving platter and remove the twine. Slice the roast into ¼- to ½-inch slices. With a slotted spoon, transfer the vegetables to the platter, arranging them around the sliced roast. Cover all with foil and place back in the still-warm oven.

SET the pot on the stove and remove any surface fat. Bring the liquid to a simmer. Transfer several tablespoons of the liquid to the bowl containing the butter-flour mixture, whisking to combine. When smooth, gradually add to the simmering liquid, whisking to combine. Simmer on low until the liquid thickens into gravy. Place in a gravy boat and serve with the roast.

Serves 6 – 8

Wine Suggestions:Yellow Tail Merlot
or
Gnarly Head Pinot Grigio

GRILLED VENISON SIRLOIN TIP ROAST
with Mushroom-Bell Pepper Sauce

There are several types of naturally smoked salt available in some grocery stores and on the Internet. See the Culinary Sources section of this book to find the salt used in this recipe if you can't find it locally. It's really great with grilled meats and especially grilled salmon. The smoky flavor adds a special touch to this recipe, but if you can't find it, you'll still enjoy this roast.

Ingredients

1   1 - 2 pound venison sirloin tip roast
¼   cup olive oil
¾   cup sherry
1   teaspoon nutmeg
½   teaspoon ground ginger
1   garlic clove, cut in thin slivers
2   small shallots, thinly sliced
2   large brown mushrooms, halved and
      thinly sliced

4   thin slices red bell pepper
4   thin slices yellow bell pepper
      alderwood smoked salt (optional)
      freshly ground pepper
½   cup dry Marsala wine
¾   cup venison stock or beef broth
2   tablespoons chilled butter

Preparation

COMBINE olive oil, sherry, nutmeg, and ginger in a bowl. Pat the roast dry and insert the garlic slivers evenly into the meat. Place in marinade, making sure all sides of the roast are coated. Cover and marinate in refrigerator for 2 to 4 hours.

HEAT grill to 400 degrees. Grill meat turning to cook all four sides: 6 minutes on the first side, 6 minutes on the second, 3 minutes on the third, and 3 minutes on the last side. Place in a 300-degree oven to finish.

WHILE the meat is grilling, put a small amount of olive oil in a sauté pan over medium heat and sauté the shallots until soft. Add the pepper slices and sauté a couple more minutes, and then add the mushrooms. Sprinkle the mixture with smoked salt and ground pepper and sauté 2 more minutes. Add wine and deglaze pan. Add stock, cover, and slowly simmer for about 15 minutes. Keep warm. When ready to serve, cut the butter in small pieces. Remove the sauce from the heat and swirl in the butter a little at a time.

Serves 4 – 6

Wine Suggestions: Irony Chardonnay
or
Hob Nob Cabernet Sauvignon

VENISON STEAKS
with Roasted Garlic Blackberry Compound Butter

Compound butters can be made ahead, and even frozen for later use. They're great with any simple grilled game meat, both birds and big game.

Ingredients

2 venison steaks
½ cup olive oil
4 cloves garlic, minced
¼ teaspoon ground ginger

1 cup tawny port
Roasted Garlic Blackberry Compound
Butter (recipe follows)

Preparation

SEASON steaks with salt and pepper. Combine the marinade ingredients and marinate the steaks for 6 hours to overnight.

HEAT grill to 400 degrees. Grill steaks 3 to 4 minutes per side, depending on thickness. Place on platter and let rest in a warm oven for 3 to 5 minutes. Just before serving, place a pat of the compound butter on the top of each steak.

Serves 2

Wine Suggestions: Girard Petite Sirah
or Black Stallion Chardonnay

For the Roast Garlic Blackberry Compound Butter

1 head garlic
olive oil
¼ pound (1 stick) butter, room
temperature

½ cup blackberries, smashed
blackberry preserves, as needed

HEAT oven to 400 degrees. Remove the top of the garlic head and some of the outer papery skin. Place on a small plate or in a garlic roaster and generously drizzle olive oil over garlic. Roast in oven until garlic is tender, about 30 to 40 minutes. Remove from oven and let cool. Squeeze garlic out of each clove and mash. Stir into butter along with mashed blackberries. Depending on the sweetness of the blackberries, add a little blackberry preserves. Roll compound butter into a log and wrap in cling wrap. Chill in refrigerator until ready to use, or freeze for later use.

Deer

VENISON CHUCK ROAST WITH CHERRIES AND CHOCOLATE

Ingredients

1 3½ to 4-pound venison chuck roast	1 leek, top removed, split and rinsed,
2 tablespoons smoked paprika	then diced
1 tablespoon sweet paprika	2 garlic cloves, minced
1 teaspoon turmeric (optional)	¼ cup brandy
3 tablespoons brown sugar	1 tablespoon unsweetened cocoa powder
3 tablespoons kosher salt	1 tablespoon Worcestershire sauce
1½ tablespoons garlic powder	1 cup cherry preserves
1½ teaspoons ground cinnamon	2 cups gamestock or beef broth
¾ teaspoon ground cardamom	1 cup port
1 teaspoons ground black pepper	2 large mushroom, sliced
4 thick bacon slices, chopped	lemon juice or balsamic vinegar
olive oil	flour or cornstarch for thickening, if
1 red onion, chopped	necessary
1 stalk celery, diced	
1 carrot, diced	

Preparation

THE DAY before cooking, mix the spices together and rub into the roast that has been patted dry. Put in a large zip-lock bag, seal and refrigerate overnight.

HEAT oven to 300 degrees. In a Dutch oven or large pot over medium heat, brown bacon pieces until crisp. Drain on paper towels. Discard all but a tablespoon of the bacon fat. Lightly brush the rub off the roast, leaving a little on it. Brown roast on all sides in hot bacon fat. Remove from pot and set aside.

ADD a little olive oil to the pot and sauté the onion, celery, carrot, and leek until the onion is translucent. Add the garlic and pour in the brandy to deglaze. Now add the cocoa powder, Worcestershire sauce, and preserves, stirring to combine. Pour in the stock and port, and then stir in the mushrooms. Place the roast in the middle of the pot, spooning the sauce over top. Cover with parchment paper, and then lid. Place in the oven until meat is very tender, about 4 to 5 hours. Check on roast a couple of times, turning it and adding extra liquid if necessary.

JUST before finishing, taste and adjust with lemon juice or balsamic vinegar, if too sweet. If thicker gravy is desired, mix some flour or cornstarch with a little water and stir into the sauce. Keep cooking until thickened.

Serves 6 – 8

Wine Suggestions: Gnarly Head Cabernet Sauvignon
or Kunde Estate Reserve Cabernet Sauvignon

VENISON SIRLOIN ROAST
with Mushroom Port Sauce

There are lots of brands of chipotle fruit sauce in the stores today. They add a piquant zip to marinades and sauces. You can find several sources online also. See the Culinary Sources in the back of this book for a few that we have enjoyed.

Ingredients

1   *1½ to 2-pound venison sirloin roast*
¼   *cup olive oil*
2   *tablespoons lemon juice*
½   *cup apricot chipotle sauce*
½   *cup orange brandy*

1   *thick slice fresh or canned pineapple, cut into small pieces*
dash of cinnamon
salt and pepper

Preparation

COMBINE marinade ingredients well and pour into zip-lock bag. Place roast in bag and seal, eliminating as much air as possible. Place bag in a bowl and refrigerate for 6 hours or overnight.

REMOVE roast from refrigerator an hour before cooking. Heat grill to 400 degrees. Grill roast about 6 minutes on each side. Place on platter and check doneness. If too rare, place in 300-degree oven until done. Serve with Mushroom Port Sauce. Roasted yam wedges pair well with this dinner.

Serves 4
Wine Suggestions: Flirt Red Blend or Irony Merlot

For the Mushroom Port Sauce:

2   *tablespoons butter, 1 cut into pieces and chilled*
1   *tablespoon olive oil*
2   *shallots, halved and sliced thin*
8   *porcini mushroom caps, halved and sliced*

½   *cup port*
¼   *teaspoon dried tarragon*
1   *cup gamestock or beef broth*
1   *tablespoon currant jelly*
2   *teaspoons cornstarch*

MELT 1 tablespoon butter with the olive oil in a sauté pan over medium heat. Add shallot slices and sauté until tender, 2 to 3 minutes. Stir in mushrooms and sauté another 2 to 3 minutes. Add half of the port and deglaze the pan, simmering for another couple of minutes. Season with tarragon, salt, and pepper. Add rest of port, stock, and jelly, whisking in the jelly. Simmer to reduce slightly. Mix cornstarch with a little water and then add some of the hot sauce to it. Stir this mixture into the sauce and continue simmering until thickened. Keep warm until serving. Just before serving, swirl in the tablespoon of chilled butter.

VENISON NECK ROAST BRAISED IN BEER

If you're not lucky enough to have a butcher that will give you the neck roast, you can use any roast or cut of meat that should be braised. You can do without the parchment covering, but you will find that the liquid evaporates quickly, and you will have to keep adding to it.

Ingredients

1 2-pound venison neck roast
  flour seasoned with salt, pepper, garlic powder, and onion powder
1 tablespoon olive or canola oil
1 tablespoon butter
3 medium carrots, cut in ½-inch chunks
2 onions, chopped
1 celery stalk, chopped
¼ cup brandy
5 garlic cloves, halved
2 cups fresh tomatoes, chopped

2 bay leaves
1 ancho chile, cut open and seeds removed
1 tablespoon coriander seeds, cracked
4 large fresh sage leaves (or 1/2 teaspoon dried sage)
4 sprigs fresh thyme (or 1/2 teaspoon dried thyme)
1½ cups beef broth or game stock
1 1-pint, 9-ounce bottle dark beer

Preparation

HEAT oven to 350 degrees. Dust roast with seasoned flour. Heat oil and butter in a Dutch oven or large pot and brown roast on all sides over medium heat. Remove and set on a plate. Place carrots, onions, and celery in pot and sauté over medium heat until onions are translucent. Stir in brandy to deglaze. Let brandy cook down and then add garlic, tomatoes, along with the spices and herbs and the liquids. Stir well and return the neck roast to the pot, along with any juices. Spoon some of the liquid and vegetables over the roast. Cover with parchment, then the lid, and place in oven until roast is tender and falling off the bone, about 4 - 5 hours. Check halfway through, turning roast, and adding more liquid (stock or water) if needed.

WHEN roast is tender, remove from oven and place on stove. Remove roast to platter, cool, and pull meat from bones. Remove bay leaves. Check liquid, and simmer to reduce if you have too much. Spoon vegetables into food processor and process until smooth. Return to liquid along with meat and reheat.

Serves 4 – 6

Wine Suggestions: Black Stallion Cabernet Sauvignon
or
The Calling Cabernet Sauvignon

Venison Shoulder Roast
with Cherries and Mushrooms

We enjoy the slightly smoky taste that smoked salt adds to this recipe, but it is still great if you use just regular salt. The one caution that needs to be followed is to not get carried away with adding smoked salt to a dish to get a really smoky flavor and forget that you are also adding salt! It needs to be used in moderation. If you want a strong smoky flavor in a dish, there are other ways to add it – such as using a smoke flavoring in liquid form.

Ingredients

1   3-pound blade shoulder roast
   smoked salt
   freshly ground pepper
2   strips thick bacon, chopped
1   red onion, chopped
2   carrots, chopped
¼   cup brandy
1   cup port

2   cups big game stock or beef broth
2   bay leaves
1   cup dried cherries
2   cups mushrooms, sliced
2   tablespoons butter
½   lemon, juiced
⅓   cup fresh parsley, chopped

Preparation

PAT roast dry and sprinkle with smoked salt and freshly ground pepper. Place bacon in skillet over medium heat and fry until crisp. Remove bacon and drain on paper towel. Brown roast on all side in the bacon fat. Place browned roast in a large crockpot.

SAUTÉ onion and carrots in skillet until lightly caramelized – about 5 minutes. Add brandy and deglaze skillet. Pour over roast. Add port, stock, bay leaves, and cherries to the crockpot, making sure the cherries are covered in the liquid. Cover and cook on low for 6 hours.

WHEN there is just 1 hour left to go, sauté the mushrooms in butter and sprinkle a small amount of smoked salt and pepper over them. Add this mixture to the crockpot and continue cooking on low for 45 to 50 minutes more.

JUST before serving, remove the meat from the crockpot and cut into serving-sized pieces. Return to crockpot and stir in the lemon juice and parsley. This is great served over buttered noodles or wild rice.

Serves 4 – 6

Wine Suggestions: Sonoma Coast Vineyards Freestone Hills Pinot Noir
or
Noble Vines 667 Pinot Noir

BRAISED VENISON SHOULDER ROAST WITH CRANBERRIES

If you don't butcher your own deer, elk, or antelope, you might try talking your butcher into leaving the bone in the shoulder roast. The bones add an amazing amount of flavor to braised dishes, as well as to soups and stews. This roast is braised in moist heat until the meat falls off the bone, so carving is not a problem.

Ingredients

1 3- to 4-pound venison shoulder roast	¼ cup brandy
2 tablespoons flour	8 -10 mushrooms, stems removed and
2 tablespoons brown sugar	chopped
½ teaspoon sweet paprika	¼ teaspoon ground ginger
pepper to taste	¼ teaspoon ground cloves
2 tablespoons butter	¾ cup port
1 tablespoon canola oil	2 cups gamestock or beef broth
2 small parsnips, chopped	12 ounces cranberries
2 large carrots, chopped	brown sugar or balsamic vinegar to
1 onion, chopped	taste

Preparation

HEAT oven to 350 degrees. Remove as much of the silver skin as you can from the roast. Pat meat dry. Combine flour, brown sugar, paprika, and pepper and roll roast in the mixture, and then rub it into the meat.

Place butter and oil in a Dutch oven or large pot and heat over medium heat. Slowly brown roast on all sides and remove from pot. Place all chopped vegetables, except mushrooms, in pot and sauté until just starting to soften. Pour in brandy and continue cooking until liquid is almost absorbed, stirring occasionally. Add mushrooms, ginger, cloves, and port and simmer for 2 minutes, then add stock. Bring back to a boil and return roast to the pot, burying it in the middle of the vegetables and liquid.

PLACE parchment over the roast and liquid, cover with lid, and place in oven. Cook for about 3½ hours, or until meat is almost ready to fall off the bone. Rinse cranberries and add to the sauce, stirring to combine. Cook about 20 more minutes, until cranberries pop open.

TASTE sauce and adjust seasonings if necessary. If too tart, add a small amount of brown sugar. If too sweet, add a little balsamic vinegar.

Serves 6 – 8
Wine Suggestions: Massimo Rioja
or
Castello di Monastero Chianti Classico

MUSHROOM VENISON WITH LASAGNA NOODLES

This makes a quick weeknight dinner that tastes like it was braised all day. The term venison is used here to describe any type of large wild ungulate – deer, antelope, or elk. Any noodles or pasta can be used, but the rich gravy seems to stick so well to the wide lasagna noodles. A nice optional addition to this dish is to add 2 cups fresh kale that has been cut in strips to the venison about 3 minutes before adding the noodles.

Ingredients

12 ounces venison, cut in bite-sized
    pieces
2½ tablespoons flour, seasoned with salt
    and pepper
1 tablespoon olive oil
½ cup port
2 cups (1 pint) grape tomatoes, halved

4 garlic cloves, minced
5 ounces mushrooms, stems removed
    and sliced thin
10 ounces game stock or beef broth
4–5 ounces whole grain lasagna noodles
    (6 strips) each broken into 3 pieces
    Parmigiano Reggiano, freshly grated

Preparation

PAT venison with paper towels to make them as dry as possible. Dust the pieces with the seasoned flour.

PLACE oil in a skillet and heat over medium-high heat. Place the venison in the heated oil and sear on all sides for about 3 to 4 minutes. Turn heat down and remove venison from skillet. Add half of the port to the skillet and deglaze, scraping up the brown bits. Add tomatoes, garlic, and leftover flour, stirring to combine, and then adding the rest of the port. Sauté the mixture for about 3 to 4 minutes. Add the mushroom slices and simmer for about 5 minutes, adding a little of the stock if the skillet gets too dry. Add the stock, stir, and let simmer gently for another 5 minutes.

MEANWHILE, cook pasta according to directions. Drain and put in a bowl. Toss with a little olive oil to keep from sticking. When the venison is ready, add lasagna noodles and toss to coat.

SERVE with the grated cheese and a green salad or vegetable.

Serves 4

Wine Suggestions: Girard Artistry
or
Gnarly Head Authentic Red

VENISON CHOPS WITH SMOKED PAPRIKA–SAGE RUB

This is an easy and quick way to cook any type of venison steaks or chops. We like to use the wonderful variety of spicy fruit-based sauces – like Grandma Hoot's Huckleberry Chipotle Sauce – that you can order online. Check out our Culinary Sources section in the back of the book for online sources. You can also find a variety of sauces in better grocery stores.

Ingredients

2 large venison chops
2 tablespoons Spanish smoked paprika
6 large sage leaves, chopped

⅓ cup olive oil
1 cup port or red wine
    commercial spicy fruit-based sauce

Preparation

Combine the paprika and sage and rub generously over the venison. Combine the olive oil and port and place the chops in the marinade. Place in refrigerator and marinate for 4 hours to overnight. Remove from refrigerator about an hour before cooking.

Heat grill to 400 degrees and cook venison for about 3 to 4 minutes per side, depending on thickness. Place on a platter and drizzle the sauce over all. Place in a warm oven to rest for a few minutes before serving.

Serves 2

Wine Suggestions: Massimo Rioja
or
Ruta 22 Malbec

Antelope

ANTELOPE CHOPS WITH BALSAMIC VINEGAR AND CAPERS

Ingredients

2 thick antelope chops
1½ tablespoons olive oil
1 large garlic clove, peeled and sliced in
   half and sliced in half again
1 cup sliced mushrooms
2 tablespoons brandy
½ cup game stock or chicken broth

¼ cup sherry
3 sprigs of fresh thyme, or ½ teaspoon
   dried thyme
2 tablespoons capers, drained
1 tablespoon balsamic vinegar
   dash of brown sugar (optional)
   salt and pepper to taste

Preparation

HEAT oven to 300 degrees. Place the olive oil in a cold skillet and place the garlic slices in the oil. Turn the heat on medium-low to let the garlic infuse the oil. Do not let the garlic burn. After it has started heating up, press down on the garlic pieces with a spoon or spatula to increase the infusion. This may take 5 to 10 minutes. Remove garlic pieces and place in the stock.

TURN the heat up to medium-high. Lightly salt and pepper the chops and sear them in the oil for about 2 minutes per side, depending on thickness. Remove to a covered dish in a 300-degree oven.

TURN heat down to medium and sauté the mushrooms for 1 minute. Add the brandy and deglaze the pan. Add the sherry, the stock with the garlic cloves, and the thyme, stirring to combine. Cover and simmer slowly for 10 minutes. Then add the capers and balsamic vinegar, stirring to blend. At this time, taste the mixture for its acidity. If necessary, add a small touch of brown sugar if the vinegar is too strong. The better the quality of balsamic vinegar you use, the less likely that you will need to add any sugar.

RETURN the chops to the skillet, along with any accumulated juices. Cover and simmer for 2 to 3 minutes, just until the flavors blended and the chops are done to desired finish.

Serves 2

Wine Suggestions: Loredona Pinot Grigio
or
George Duboeuf Regnie

Antelope Chops with Cranberry-Mustard Sauce

Ingredients

2	thick-cut antelope chops	1	cup whole berry cranberry sauce
½	teaspoon vegetable oil	1½	tablespoon Dijon mustard
6	green onions with green tops, chopped	1	tablespoon balsamic or raspberry vinegar
2	tablespoons brandy		
¼	cup sherry		salt and pepper to taste
¼	cup game stock or beef broth		

Preparation

HEAT oven to 300 degrees. Lightly salt and pepper the antelope chops. In a skillet over medium-high heat, add the oil, and as soon as it is hot, sear the chops for about 2 minutes per side. Remove to a covered dish in the warmed oven.

TURN the heat down to medium, and sauté the green onions in the skillet for about 2 minutes. Add the brandy and deglaze the pan. Add the rest of the ingredient, stirring to combine. Cover and simmer gently for 10 minutes. Remove cover and add any accumulated juices from the chops, stirring to combine. Return the chops to the skillet, cover with some of the sauce and let if simmer on low for a minute or two.

SERVE in the skillet if it is made for the table, or pour the sauce into a shallow casserole dish and place the chops on top, garnishing with a little extra chopped green onion. This goes well with orzo tossed with a little garlic-infused olive oil, Parmesan cheese, and chopped parsley.

Serves 2

Wine Suggestions: Windsor Sonoma Dry Creek Zinfandel
or
Noble Vines 446 Chardonnay

ANTELOPE STEAK
with Oyster Mushrooms and Red Pepper Coulis

Red pepper coulis is a superb accompaniment to big game dishes. I like to use roasted peppers that are packed in olive oil to shorten the process, but you can also roast your own by roasting them in the oven or grilling them on the grill. While still hot, place them in a paper bag to cool. After cooling, you can peel off the charred outer layer, and then proceed with the recipe.

Portobello mushrooms can be substituted for the oyster mushrooms, and will give the sauce a "beefier" taste. But, if you like that taste of red peppers, the oyster mushrooms have a lighter taste, letting the roasted peppers shine through.

Ingredients

4 antelope steaks
2 tablespoons olive oil
3 large garlic cloves, peeled and sliced
   thin
1 cup roasted red peppers, drained
3 green onions, chopped
1½ cups oyster mushrooms, trunks
   removed

4 sprigs fresh thyme, or ½ teaspoon
   dried
½ cup dry Marsala wine
½ cup game stock or beef broth
1 tablespoon brown sugar
2-3 tablespoons butter, cut in small chunks
   & chilled
   toasted pine nuts for garnish

Preparation

HEAT oven to 300 degrees. Season steaks with salt and pepper, and keep refrigerated until ready to cook. Put the roasted red peppers and the chopped green onions in a blender, and purée.

ADD the olive oil to a cold skillet, and place the garlic slices evenly on the oil. Turn the heat on to low, and let the garlic infuse the olive oil for about 10 minutes. The heat should not be high enough to let the garlic sizzle or brown. Remove the garlic pieces and set aside.

TURN the heat to high and pan-fry the antelope steaks for just a couple of minutes, depending on their thickness. The desired result is to have the outside of the steak seared nicely, but the inside still very rare. Put the steaks in a covered dish and keep in the warm oven.

TURN the heat down to medium, and sauté the mushrooms for about 2 to 3 minutes, adding a little Marsala wine if the pan is too dry. Now add the rest of the Marsala wine and deglaze the pan. Add the stock, thyme, and the garlic slices, stirring to combine. Continue simmering on medium heat until the liquid is reduced by half. Add the red pepper/onion purée, stir to combine, and simmer on low another 5 to 10 minutes.

REMOVE the dish with the steaks from the oven and add any accumulated juices from the dish to the skillet, stirring to combine. Now slowly add the chunks of butter, swirling after each addition. Simmer for about 2 more minutes to thicken slightly.

POUR the sauce onto the serving platter, place the steaks on top and sprinkle some toasted pine nuts around the outside on top of the sauce.

Serves 4

Wine Suggestions: Black Stallion Chardonnay
or
Joseph Carr Merlot

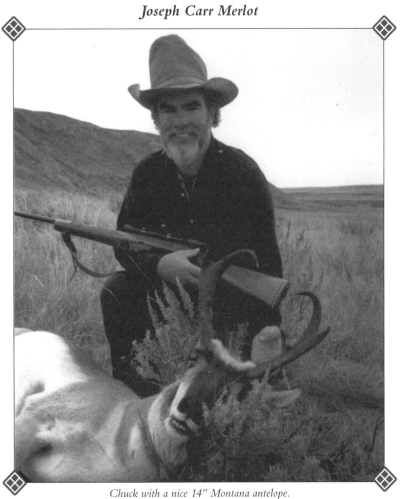

Chuck with a nice 14" Montana antelope.

Antelope

ANTELOPE TENDERLOIN WITH MARSALA-BRANDY SAUCE

Ingredients

4 6-ounce antelope tenderloins, butterflied
1 tablespoon olive oil

2 large or 4 medium portobello mushrooms, sliced in 1-inch thickness

For the Marinade

½ cup olive oil
2 teaspoons thyme
2 teaspoons rosemary, crushed

1 teaspoon green peppercorns, crushed
2 large garlic cloves, peeled and minced

For the Sauce

2 shallots, peeled and sliced thinly
2 tablespoons brandy
½ cup game stock or beef broth
1 teaspoon green peppercorns, crushed

1 tablespoon tomato paste, or chopped sun-dried tomato
1 teaspoon dried tarragon
¾ cup Marsala
1 tablespoon currant jelly

Preparation

COMBINE the marinade ingredients and marinate the tenderloins for 2 hours.

HEAT a skillet to medium-high and add 1 tablespoon olive oil. Remove the tenderloins from the marinade. Do not pat dry; leave any herbs or spices on the meat.

SEAR the tenderloins in the skillet for 1½ minutes per side – no longer. Remove to a covered dish and place in a warm oven.

SAUTÉ the shallots in the remaining oil for 1 minute. Add the mushroom slices, and sauté another 2 to 3 minutes. Add the brandy and deglaze the pan. Add the game stock, stirring to combine. Now remove the mushroom slices and place them in the covered dish with the antelope.

ADD the rest of the ingredients to the skillet and stir to combine. Cover and simmer for 10 to 15 minutes. Return the mushrooms to the skillet, along with any accumulated juices, cover and simmer for 3 minutes. Add the antelope to the pan, spooning some of the sauce over the tenderloins, and simmer gently for another minute. Serve immediately with wild rice.

Serve 4

Wine Suggestions: Kunde Estate Syrah
or
Handcraft Malbec

Grilled Antelope Roast with Mustard Sauce

Ingredients

> 2-3 pound antelope roast

For the Marinade

12 ounces dark beer	2 tablespoons brown sugar
¼ cup peanut oil	3 cloves garlic, minced
1 tablespoon soy sauce	1 1-inch piece of fresh ginger, peeled
¼ cup lime juice	and sliced thin

For the Mustard Sauce

8 tablespoons mayonnaise	½ teaspoon dried tarragon
3 tablespoons Dijon mustard	2 tablespoons chopped parsley
2 tablespoons honey mustard	2 teaspoons horseradish

Preparation

COMBINE marinade ingredients and marinate antelope roast at least 4 hours, or preferably overnight in the refrigerator, turning occasionally.

THE ingredients for the mustard sauce can be combined at this time, also, so that they have time for the flavors to blend. Keep refrigerated.

REMOVE roast and marinade from the refrigerator at least an hour before grilling so that the roast can warm to room temperature.

FIRE the barbecue, and remove the roast from the marinade, patting it dry. Over hot coals, grill the roast for 4 minutes, turn roast and grill another 4 minutes, turn roast again and grill a third set of 4 minutes. Turn roast again and grill 2 minutes this time.

LOWER heat in barbecue by removing some charcoal from underneath roast or turning gas down. Grill another 12 minutes on lower heat, turning once.

CHECK roast. It is done if the inside of roast is still pink. Remove from grill and let roast stand in a warm oven for a few minutes.

SERVE with mustard sauce on the side.

Serves 6 to 8

Wine Suggestions: Massimo Malbec
or
Ramón Bilbao Gran Reserva Rioja

GRILLED ANTELOPE STEAKS
WITH GREEN PEPPERCORN SAUCE

Ingredients

4 antelope steaks, about 6 ounces each
2 tablespoons olive oil
6 large sage leaves, 3 kept whole and 3 cut in strips
1 tablespoon sweet paprika
1 teaspoon ground cinnamon

4 tablespoons cream sherry
3 cups big game stock or beef broth
1 cup chicken stock
1½ cups cream sherry
1 bay leaf
2 garlic cloves, minced
16 dried green peppercorns

Preparation

COMBINE the olive oil, sage leaf strips, paprika, cinnamon, and sherry in a bowl or plastic bag. Place steaks in marinade and cover bowl or seal bag. Place in refrigerator for 6 hours to overnight. Remove from refrigerator an hour before cooking.

IN A saucepan, bring to a simmer the stocks, sherry, whole sage leaves, bay leaf, garlic, and peppercorns. Season to taste with salt and pepper. Continue to simmer mixture until it has reduced to a little more than half. Strain liquid and discard solids. Pour about a cup of the liquid in a separate bowl. Keep the remaining liquid in the covered saucepan and keep warm.

HEAT grill to 400 degrees. Remove the antelope steaks from the marinade and cook on the grill for about 3½ to 4 minutes per side, basting with the liquid in the bowl.

SERVE steaks with wild rice and the peppercorn gravy.

Serves 4

Wine Suggestions: Cruz de Alba Crianza
or
Gnarly Head Old Vine Zinfandel

ANTELOPE STEAKS MARINATED IN COFFEE AND BRANDY

Ingredients

4 antelope steaks, about 6 ounces each
¼ cup olive oil
⅓ cup regular black coffee

⅓ cup brandy
5-7 fresh sage leaves, chopped
2 teaspoons lemon juice

Preparation

PAT steaks dry and season with salt and pepper.

COMBINE all other ingredients in a nonreactive bowl. Place steaks in marinade, cover, and place in refrigerator. Marinate steaks for 2 to 4 hours. Remove from refrigerator an hour before cooking.

HEAT grill to 400 degrees. Remove steaks from marinade and grill for 3 minutes per side for medium rare. Spread a small amount of butter on steaks and let rest in a warm oven for a few minutes before serving.

Serves 4

Wine Suggestions: Chateau Bonnet Rouge
or
Black Stallion Cabernet Sauvignon

GRILLED ANTELOPE ROAST

Ingredients

2-3 pound antelope roast
3-4 bacon strips
¼ cup olive oil
¼ cup sweet vermouth
¼ cup brandy
1 tablespoon soy sauce

1 tablespoon Worcestershire sauce
1 tablespoon green peppercorns, crushed
½ teaspoon ground sage
1 teaspoon tarragon
3-4 sprigs fresh thyme or ½ teaspoon dried thyme

Preparation

COMBINE all ingredients except the bacon, and marinate the roast overnight, turning occasionally.

REMOVE the marinade and roast from the refrigerator about 2 hours before grilling, so that it can come to room temperature.

WRAP the bacon slices around the roast, securing them with toothpicks.

HEAT the barbecue grill to high. Place the roast on the grill and grill for 7 minutes. Turn and grill on the other side for another 7 minutes. Turn again and grill for 2 more minutes. Check for doneness by inserting a meat thermometer or making a small cut into the center of the roast. It should still be quite pink in the middle for medium rare. Do not overcook. Like most wild game, it is better to err on the rare side if you want a good tasting cut.

Serves 4 to 6

Wine Suggestions: Windsor Sonoma Pinot Noir
or
Gnarly Head Zinfandel

Roast Antelope Sirloin Tip with Root Vegetables

Ingredients

2 pounds sirloin tip antelope roast
2 parsnips, peeled and split in half
2 carrots, peeled and split in half
1 turnip, peeled and quartered

1 onion, peeled and quartered
8 large garlic cloves, peeled
   olive oil
1½ teaspoons sugar

For the Marinade

¼ cup olive oil
¼ cup dry red wine
2 tablespoons soy sauce
2 tablespoons Dijon mustard

fresh chopped sage leaves
fresh thyme sprigs
cracked peppercorns

Preparation

COMBINE the marinade ingredients and marinate the roast 6 hours to overnight, turning occasionally.

REMOVE the marinade and the roast from the refrigerator at least 2 hours before roasting.

PREHEAT oven to 400 degrees. Put the vegetables in a large bowl and drizzle a little olive oil over them. Sprinkle the sugar and a little salt, and grind some fresh black pepper over the vegetables. Toss to coat all the vegetables equally. Place the vegetables in a shallow roasting pan, spread out in a single layer. Roast for about 20 minutes.

BEFORE placing the roast in the pan, push the vegetables to the center of the pan and turn the heat up to 450 degrees. Close the oven and wait until it reaches 450 degrees. Then add the roast, placing it on top of the vegetables.

ROAST for 15 minutes, then turn the oven down to 325 degrees and continue roasting for about 30 minutes. Check for doneness, and continue roasting a few more minutes if it is still too rare.

WHEN done, remove to a serving platter, and surround the antelope with the roasted vegetables.

IF YOU want a little gravy, you can add a little red wine or brandy and some game stock to the roasting pan, scraping up any brown bits from the vegetables. Reduce the liquid for a few minutes and serve on the side.

Serves 3 to 4
Wine Suggestions: Noble Vines 446 Chardonnay
or Château la Louvière Rouge

The Duel.

Elk

BRAISED ELK SHANKS

Although butchering your own big game is a lot of work, it definitely has its benefits. Most wild game butchers today, with the short time they have to butcher wild game, will not honor requests to cut bones into rib pieces, short ribs, and shanks, or crack the bone joints for soups and stocks. So, all that great eating ends up in the garbage pile. Butcher your own, and keep your options open.

Just like shanks in domestic meats, braising is the desired method. This slow cooking in liquid aids in breaking down the tough connective tissues around the shank bones. If you are used to cooking beef or lamb shanks, you will be amazed at the lack of grease that comes to the top after the cooking process. You will also find that you will need to cook the shanks longer to achieve the same tenderness.

Ingredients

3 pounds elk shanks	¼ cup brandy
olive oil	½ teaspoon thyme
1 large carrot, finely chopped	¾ cup red wine or port
2 large celery stalks, finely chopped	½ cup water
1 small parsnip, finely chopped.	salt and pepper to taste
8 large cloves garlic, peeled	2-3 tablespoons butter, cut in small chunks
1 small onion, finely chopped	& chilled (optional)

Preparation

SALT and pepper the shanks. On medium-low heat, slowly brown the shanks in a couple of tablespoons of olive oil in an ovenproof skillet or Dutch oven. Don't rush the process; take about 15 minutes per side. Add a little more oil if needed to keep the meat from burning. The browned pieces that stick to the pan will add a great flavor to the gravy.

REMOVE the shanks to a plate. Add the vegetables and sauté slowly until limp. Deglaze the pan with the brandy. Stir in the thyme. Return the shanks to the pan, mixing them in with the vegetables. Pour the red wine and water over all. Cover and gently simmer for about 3 hours, or until tender. Stir several times to be sure that nothing is burning on the bottom of the pan. Add more water if it becomes too dry.

WHEN shanks are tender, remove them from the pan. Working in batches, puree liquid and vegetables on low in a blender. Return to pan along with the shanks. Turn heat to low to keep hot until ready to serve. You can also make a day ahead and reheat. The longer this sits, the better the flavors blend.

Serves 2 to 4, depending on the amount of meat on the bones

*Wine Suggestions: Kunde Estate Reserve Cabernet Sauvignon
or Noble Vines 337 Cabernet Sauvignon*

Braised Elk Short Rib Style

This recipe works wonders with any game meat that comes from an older animal. You can use round steak or any type of roast that is not too tender. The slow roasting breaks down the muscles just like it does the connective tissues in short ribs.

Ingredients

2-3 pounds elk meat, cut in large chunks
3-4 strips bacon, chopped
  2 onions, chopped
  2 carrots, grated
  2 cloves garlic, minced
  ¼ cup brandy
  ½ cup red wine or port
  2 teaspoons horseradish
  1 teaspoon paprika

  2 tablespoons lemon juice
  1 10½-ounce can of consommé
  1 can beef broth
  ¼ cup flour
  ½ cup water
  1 teaspoon white sugar
  2 teaspoons dill
     salt and pepper to taste
  1 cup frozen peas, not thawed (optional)

Preparation

PREHEAT the oven to 350 degrees. Brown the bacon pieces in a large ovenproof skillet or Dutch oven. When crisp, remove the pieces and drain on a paper towel. Pour off all but about 1 tablespoon of the bacon fat. Working in batches, so that you don't crowd the pieces, brown the elk in the bacon fat over medium heat. As they are browned remove them to a plate.

AFTER browning the elk, turn the heat down to medium and add the carrots and onions to the pan. Sauté until the onions are translucent and soft. Add the minced garlic toward the end of this process so that they don't brown and turn bitter. Add the brandy to the pan and deglaze. The crusty brown bits will add a lot of flavor to the gravy. Add the next 6 ingredients (wine to beef broth), and return the bacon pieces, stirring to combine.

PUT the browned elk back in the skillet in a single layer if possible, moving the carrot-onion mixture to the side to let the elk touch the bottom of the pan. The liquid should just cover the elk. If a chunk is too big, cut it in half so that it can be submerged in the liquid. This will help to keep the elk from drying out during the cooking. Cover, and put in the 350-degree oven for at least 3 hours. Check a couple of times to be sure the meat is covered. Add water if liquid gets too low.

REMOVE pan from oven. Remove meat from pan and skim off any grease. Measure liquid, adding water if needed, to make approximately 2½ cups. Pour liquid back in pan. Combine the flour and water, whisking to avoid lumps. Add to pan along with sugar and dill. Slice meat into thin slices and return to pan, covering slices with gravy. Add the frozen peas and stir. Return to a boil, cover, and return to oven for another 30 minutes.

Serves 6 to 8
Wine Suggestions: Brazin Dry Creek Zinfandel
or Yellow Tail Reserve Cabernet Sauvignon

Brandied Elk Medallions with Hunter Sauce

I always keep a couple of packages of Knorr or McCormick sauces in my cupboard for quick gourmet meals. When you are in a hurry, or are cooking in a hunting camp, they can really be a handy asset. For extra flavor, I often substitute a little wine for part of the water called for in the package directions. Since packaged sauces tend to have more salt than needed, eliminate any salt in the seasoned flour mixture below, and don't add any to the recipe.

Ingredients

*4 elk tenderloins, butterflied
flour seasoned with pepper, and a little
garlic powder*
3 tablespoons butter
2 shallots, peeled and sliced thin

*2 cups shiitake (or brown) mushrooms,
sliced thin*
¼ cup cognac or brandy
1 package Hunter Sauce
¼ cup port wine
3 tablespoons sour cream

Preparation

HEAT oven to 300 degrees. In a small saucepan, prepare the Hunter Sauce according to package directions, but substitute ¼ cup of port for ¼ cup of the water. Keep warm.

DUST the elk medallions with the seasoned flour. In a skillet over medium-high heat, melt 2 tablespoons butter and brown the medallions for 1½ minutes per side. Remove to covered dish and keep in a 300-degree oven.

ADD the remaining tablespoon of butter to the skillet, lower the heat to medium and sauté the shallots until they start to get soft. Add the mushrooms and sauté them for about 2 minutes. Add the cognac to the skillet and deglaze the pan, scraping up any brown bits. Add the prepared sauce, stirring to combine. Add the sour cream and stir again. Return the medallions and any accumulated juices to the skillet. Spoon some of the sauce over the medallions, and simmer until medallions are done to desired temperature.

Serves 4

Wine Suggestions: Girard Petite Sirah
or
Black Stallion Cabernet Sauvignon

ELK CHOPS WITH PORTOBELLO MUSHROOMS

Ingredients

4 elk chops, 1 inch thick
2 tablespoons olive oil
5 garlic cloves, peeled and sliced
   lengthwise
6-8 green onions, the white and half of the
   green part chopped
2-3 large portobello mushrooms, cut in
   half and sliced

3 tablespoons brandy
¼ cup sherry
½ cup game stock or beef broth
3-4 sprigs of thyme
5-6 sprigs of parsley, chopped

Preparation

PUT olive oil in cold skillet and place garlic slices evenly on oil. Turn heat to medium-low and let garlic infuse the olive oil as it heats. Do not let the garlic sizzle or brown. After about 10 minutes, remove the garlic and set aside. Salt and pepper the elk chops. Turn the heat to medium-high, and brown the chops about 2 minutes per side. Remove to a covered dish and place in a warm oven.

LOWER the heat to medium-low and sauté the green onions for about 1 minute. Add the mushrooms and keep stirring for about 1 more minute. Add brandy to deglaze the pan, stirring to scrape up any brown bits. Add the sherry, stock, thyme, and garlic slices. Cover and simmer on low for 10 minutes.

RETURN the elk chops and any accumulated juices to the pan, spooning some of the sauce over the chops. Sprinkle the parsley over all. Cover and simmer on low for a couple of minutes, making sure the chops do not overcook. To check, cut into a chop near the bone. It should still be pink.

Serves 4

Wine Suggestions: Black Stallion Chardonnay
or
Cruz de Alba Crianza

ELK STEAK WITH PEAR, MUSHROOMS AND HAZELNUTS

Contrary to the usual instructions to serve a big-bodied red wine with big game, this recipe actually goes equally well with a rich shiraz. It must be the combination with the pears and hazelnuts. We've also tried this recipe with filleted breasts of sharptail, and it's great.

Ingredients

¾–1 *pound of elk steak (enough for 2)*
1 *tablespoon + 1½ tablespoons butter*
1 *slightly ripe pear, peeled and sliced – core removed*
3 *tablespoons brandy or cognac*
4 *large mushrooms, cut in half and sliced*

½ *cup tawny port*
½ *cup game stock or chicken broth*
3 *whole cloves*
1 *teaspoon arrowroot, mixed with a little water to dissolve*
½ *cup hazelnuts, chopped and toasted*

Preparation

MELT 1 tablespoon of butter in a skillet, and sauté pear slices over medium-high heat until slightly browned but not too soft. Remove to a plate and keep warm.

ADD 1½ tablespoons butter to the skillet and brown the elk steak for a couple of minutes; just enough to sear the outside but leave the inside rare. Remove to a covered dish and place in 300-degree oven. Sauté mushrooms for a couple of minutes, then add brandy to the skillet and deglaze.

ADD the port, stock, and cloves to the skillet, stirring to combine. Bring to a simmer and reduce liquid by half. Add arrowroot mixture, stir, and simmer another minute or so to thicken sauce. Return pear slices to the skillet and simmer another couple of minutes. Then add elk steak along with any accumulated juices and one half of the hazelnuts. Spoon some of the sauce over the steak, and simmer for another minute or two, just to bring steak to its serving temperature.

TRANSFER to steak to serving platter and place pears in a circle around the steak. Pour the rest of the mushroom sauce over the top of the steak, and sprinkle the pear slices with the rest of the toasted hazelnuts.

Serves 2

Wine Suggestions: Yellow Tail Reserve Shiraz
or
Gnarly Head Zinfandel

Sirloin Tip Roast of Elk on Vegetable Rack

with Mushroom Gravy

Root vegetables make a delicious roasting rack for game roasts, just as they do for beef. The bacon wrapped around the roast helps baste the lean elk meat so that it doesn't dry out, and as the bacon fat melts, it drips down onto the vegetables along with the roast drippings.

Ingredients

2½-3 pounds sirloin tip roast of elk
3-4 strips of bacon
2 parsnips, peeled and quartered
2 large carrots, peeled and quartered

2 leeks, cut in half and rinsed to remove dirt
1 onion, peeled and quartered
½ cup Marsala wine

For the Marinade

¼ cup olive oil
1 tablespoon soy sauce
1 tablespoon Worcestershire sauce
1 shallot, sliced thin

2 garlic cloves, minced
½ cup red wine
½ teaspoon dried thyme
½ teaspoon dried tarragon

For the Mushroom Gravy

1½ tablespoons olive oil
2 shallots, peeled and sliced
6-7 large mushrooms, sliced
½ cup Marsala wine

½ cup game stock or beef broth
dash of thyme
dash of tarragon

Preparation

COMBINE the marinade ingredients. Rinse and pat the roast dry. Put it into a large ziplock bag, and pour in the marinade. Seal the bag, squeezing all the air out, and place in a bowl in the refrigerator. Marinate the roast for at least 6 hours, but preferably overnight, turning occasionally to be sure the entire roast is covered with the marinade.

REMOVE the roast from the refrigerator about 2 hours before roasting so that it can warm to room temperature.

PREHEAT oven to 450 degrees. In a large pot, bring water to a boil and add the parsnips and carrots. Parboil for about 5 minutes, adding the leeks for the last 2 minutes. Remove and drain. Lightly oil a shallow roasting pan. Place parboiled vegetables in the center of the pan, along with the onion quarters. Remove the roast from the marinade and pat dry. Wrap the roast with the bacon strips, securing it with toothpicks. Place on the rack of vegetables.

ROAST in 450-degree oven for 20 minutes. Turn the heat down to 350 degrees and continue roasting for 50 minutes more. About half way through the roasting time, pour the Marsala wine over the roast. Roast is done when interior meat is still pink.

Sirloin Tip Roast of Elk on Vegetable Rack
CONTINUED

WHILE elk is roasting, heat a medium saucepan over medium-high heat. Add the olive oil and sauté the shallots for a couple of minutes until they are slightly soft. Add the mushrooms, and sauté them for a couple of minutes. Turn down the heat and add the wine and stock along with the herbs, stirring to combine. Cover and simmer slowly for at least 15 minutes, then keep warm.

WHEN roast is done, remove it to a serving platter and surround it with the roast vegetables. Scrape the drippings in the pan into the sauce, and simmer for a couple more minutes, while the roast sits. Serve the gravy on the side.

Serves 6 to 8
Wine Suggestions: Gnarly Head Chardonnay
or
Sonoma Coast Vineyards Freestone Hills Pinot Noir

GRILLED ELK ROAST
with Sautéed Mushrooms in Marsala & Brandy Sauce

Ingredients

2   pounds rolled sirloin tip roast of elk
3   strips of bacon

For the Marinade

1   large shallot – cut in half & thinly sliced
1   carrot – peeled, quartered & finely chopped
1   tablespoon tomato paste

¼   cup olive oil
1   tablespoon balsamic vinegar
½   cup port wine
½   cup dry red wine
1   teaspoon thyme

For the Mushroom Sauce

1   tablespoon olive oil
1   tablespoon butter
4   garlic cloves – peeled & halved
2   cups mushrooms – sliced (mushrooms can be button, but adding some portobello or shiitake adds extra flavor

½   cup brandy
½   cup game stock (beef broth may be substituted)
½   cup dry Marsala wine
1   tablespoon currant jelly
½   teaspoon tarragon
1   teaspoon arrowroot

Preparation

COMBINE the marinade ingredients in a non-reactive bowl. Put the elk roast in the marinade, making sure to coat all sides. Cover and refrigerate for at least 6 hours or overnight. Turn the roast several times.

REMOVE the roast & marinade from the refrigerator at least one hour before roasting, so that it can come to room temperature. Weave the 3 strips of bacon through the strings on the rolled roast, or secure with toothpicks.

PREHEAT gas grill for 5 minutes. Roast meat on grill with high heat for 6 minutes, then turn and roast for 6 more minutes. Turn heat down slightly, and roast another 12 minutes, turning the roast every 3 minutes. Roast should be done to medium rare.

WHILE roast is grilling, melt the olive oil and butter in a large saucepan on medium heat. Add the garlic cloves and let them infuse the oils slowly. Press on the garlic pieces to help them release their flavor; then remove them from the oil. Save to add back in to sauce in next step.

TURN heat up to medium-high and add the mushrooms, sautéing for 2 minutes. Add the brandy, stirring constantly until most of the brandy has evaporated. Add the Marsala and game stock, finishing up with the currant jelly, tarragon, and the garlic cloves. Stir to combine. Simmer until mushrooms are tender, and starting to give up their juices. Cover and keep warm until close to serving time.

REMOVE roast from grill when done and let sit in warm oven for 5 minutes. Combine the arrowroot with a small amount of water. Add some of the mushroom liquid and reintroduce to the mushroom sauce, stirring as the sauce thickens.

BEFORE serving, add any juices that have released from the roast to the mushroom sauce, and stir to combine.

Serves 4

Wine Suggestions: Joseph Carr Cabernet Sauvignon
or
Black Stallion Chardonnay

BRAISED ELK NECK ROAST WITH CRANBERRIES

The best part of butchering your own game is the special cuts that you can have, that most professional butchers won't take the time cut for you. The neck is a perfect example. The neck meat on any four-footed animal is especially flavorful. It just needs to be cooked slowly to achieve tenderness. Even if you aren't lucky enough to have an elk neck roast, you can still make this with any of the tougher cuts of elk or deer that need slow roasting or braising.

Ingredients

2 strips thick bacon, chopped	2 garlic cloves, chopped
1 tablespoon olive oil or butter	2½ cups beef broth or game stock
1 3-pound elk neck roast, or other braising-type roast	1½ cups port
2 cups chopped onion	1 teaspoon ground ginger
1 leek, top removed, split in half, rinsed & sliced thin	1 teaspoon orange zest
1 carrot, finely chopped	¼ cup brown sugar
2 cups fresh mushrooms, sliced	3 tablespoons flour
	2 tablespoons balsamic vinegar
	12 ounces fresh or frozen cranberries

Preparation

HEAT oven to 250 degrees. In a Dutch oven, cook bacon over medium heat until crisp. Remove and drain on paper towel. Add the oil or butter to the bacon fat.

SEASON the neck roast with salt and pepper, and brown on all sides in the fat over medium heat. Remove neck and set aside.

ADD onion to pot and sauté until just soft. Add leek and carrot and sauté about 5 minutes. You can add a little broth or port if bottom of pan gets too dry. You don't want the brown bits from the neck roast to burn, since they will add great flavor to the sauce. Now add mushrooms and garlic, stirring to combine. Then add broth, port, ginger, and orange zest, swirling and scraping up the browned bits stuck to the pot. Return neck, and any accumulated juices, to pot. Cover with parchment paper (which will keep the liquid from evaporating) topped with the lid, and braise in oven for 5 hours, or until meat is about ready to fall off the bone.

REMOVE the neck to a platter and cover with foil to keep warm. Combine the brown sugar and flour and stir into the liquid in the Dutch oven, followed by the vinegar and cranberries. Stir all to combine, and bring to a simmer. Cook for about 20 minutes, or until the cranberries pop open. Taste the sauce and correct with either a little more brown sugar or vinegar if needed.

MEANWHILE, pull the meat from the neck bones and cut into bite-sized pieces. Add back into the sauce to reheat.

Serves 2

Wine Suggestions: Windsor Sonoma Alexander Valley Cabernet Sauvignon or Noble Vines 446 Chardonnay

ELK CHOPS WITH DRAMBUIE-MUSTARD SAUCE

Ingredients

- 4 elk chops
- ¼ cup olive oil
- 3 garlic cloves, minced
- 1¼ teaspoon rosemary, divided
- 1 large shallot, halved and thinly sliced
- 2 large brown mushrooms

- ¼ cup Drambuie, plus 2 tablespoons
- 1 tablespoon Dijon mustard
- ¾ cup venison stock
- ¼ teaspoon thyme
- ¼ cup half and half or heavy cream

Preparation

COMBINE olive oil, garlic, and 1 teaspoon of the rosemary. Rub over the chops, cover, and refrigerate for a couple of hours. Remove from refrigerator about an hour before cooking.

OVER medium heat, sauté shallot slices in a little olive oil for about 4 minutes. Stir in mushrooms and sauté another minute. Add the 2 tablespoons of Drambuie and continue cooking until liquid has almost evaporated. Stir in mustard, stock, thyme, and remaining ¼ teaspoon rosemary. Bring back to a simmer, and continue on a slow simmer for 5 to 6 more minutes. Remove from heat and add a small amount of the sauce to the cream to warm up the cream. Then stir mixture into the sauce and return to low heat until sauce thickens. Cover and keep warm until ready to serve.

HEAT grill to 400 degrees. Season chops with salt and pepper. Place chops on grill and cook for 6 minutes on each side for medium rare. Baste liberally with the ¼ cup Drambuie.

HEAT oven to 350 degrees. Remove chops from grill, place on serving platter, and place in oven for 4 to 6 minutes to finish. Serve with the Drambuie-Mustard Sauce.

Serves 2

Wine Suggestions: Noble Vines 446 Chardonnay or Hob Nob Pinot Noir

ELK LOIN STEAKS WITH HUCKLEBERRY-GARLIC COMPOUND BUTTER

Ingredients

4 8-ounce elk loin steaks
½ cup olive oil
2 tablespoons lemon juice
1 fresh basil leaf, shredded
1 cup red wine

1-2 dashes ground chipotle
       pepper, to taste
       zest of 1 orange
       Huckleberry-Garlic Compound Butter
       (recipe follows)

Preparation

COMBINE oil, lemon juice, basil, wine, chipotle pepper, and orange zest in a bowl. Pat steaks dry, season with salt and pepper and place in marinade for about 6 hours. Remove from refrigerator an hour before cooking.

HEAT grill to 400 degrees. Remove steaks from marinade and grill for 2½ to 3 minutes per side for medium rare. Place a tablespoon of the chilled compound butter on each steak and let rest in a warm oven for a few minutes.

Serves 4

Wine Suggestions: Girard Old Vine Zinfandel
or
Noble Vines 446 Chardonnay

For the Huckleberry-Garlic Compound Butter

1 head garlic
    olive oil
8 tablespoons butter (1 stick), warmed to room temperature
2 tablespoons huckleberry jam

HEAT oven to 400 degrees. Remove some of the papery skin on the garlic head and cut off of the pointy end of the garlic. Place on an oven-proof plate and drizzle olive oil over top. Roast in oven until garlic is tender – about 30 to 40 minutes. Remove from oven and let cool. Place softened butter in a bowl and blend in the huckleberry jam. When cool, squeeze garlic out of each clove and add to butter. Continue to blend until garlic and jam are evenly combined with butter. Lay out a piece of cling wrap. Shape butter into a log on the wrap, toward the edge. Gently roll wrap around butter and chill in refrigerator. This can last in refrigerator for at least a week, or freeze any extra.

ELK CHOPS WITH CHERRY-ALMOND SAUCE

The sauce for this dish can be prepared a day ahead, but make it at least an hour before serving so that the flavors can blend.

Ingredients

4 thick elk chops
¾ cup dried cherries, divided
4 tablespoons olive oil, divided
3 tablespoons lemon juice
½ teaspoon ground cinnamon
¼ - ½ teaspoon almond extract
2½ cups port, divided

2 shallots, thinly sliced
4 medium mushrooms, halved and thinly sliced
½ teaspoon dried tarragon
1 cup venison stock or beef broth
½ cup sliced almonds, toasted
1 tablespoon butter, chilled

Preparation

IN A bowl, combine ¼ cup of the cherries with 3 tablespoons of the olive oil and lemon juice, cinnamon, almond extract, and 1½ cups of the port. Pour into a gallon self-sealing bag and add the elk chops. Place in a bowl and seal the bag, squeezing out as much air as possible. Place in refrigerator and marinate for 4 hours up to overnight, turning the bag occasionally.

TO MAKE the sauce, soak the remaining ½ cup of the cherries in the remaining cup of port for 15 minutes. Heat the last tablespoon of olive oil in a saucepan over medium-high heat until oil begins to sizzle if you add a couple of drops of water. Turn heat down to medium and add the shallots, sautéing for about 2 minutes. Add mushrooms and sauté mixture for another 2 minutes. Season to taste with salt and pepper. Turn heat down and add the port-cherry mixture and tarragon. Stir to combine and simmer for 3 minutes. Add venison stock and most of the toasted almonds, saving the rest for garnish. Bring to a slow simmer, cover, and simmer for 20 minutes. Let sit until ready to serve.

HEAT grill to 400 degrees. Remove chops from marinade and pat dry. Season with salt and pepper and grill 4 to 5 minutes per side for medium rare, depending on thickness. Remove to a warm oven and let rest before serving.

JUST before serving, make sure sauce is hot and stir in butter. Drizzle a little of the sauce over the chops and garnish with the remaining toasted almonds. Serve the rest of the sauce in a gravy boat.

Serves 4

*Wine Suggestions: Black Stallion Chardonnay
or Kunde Estate Cabernet Sauvignon*

Bison

BISON TENDERLOIN WITH MUSHROOM SAUCE

Ingredients

4 2-inch thick bison tenderloins,
butterflied and seasoned with salt and
cracked pepper

2 tablespoons top quality virgin olive oil

6 cloves garlic, sliced

3 large portobello mushrooms, sliced in
about ½-inch pieces

3 tablespoons brandy

1 cup game stock or beef broth

½ cup tawny port

3-4 sprigs fresh thyme, or ½ teaspoon
dried

1 tablespoon currant jelly

2 teaspoons cornstarch, mixed with
water

Preparation

PUT olive oil in a cold skillet and place garlic slices evenly throughout the oil. Turn the heat to medium-low, and let the garlic slowly infuse the oil. Turn the heat down if the garlic starts to sizzle or brown, or it will become bitter. Remove the garlic and set aside.

TURN heat up to medium-high and brown the tenderloins in the oil for about 2 minutes per side. Remove to a covered dish and keep in 300-degree oven.

TURN the heat down to medium and sauté the mushrooms in the oil, adding a little stock if they get too dry. After about 2 minutes, deglaze the pan with the brandy and simmer until the liquor is absorbed.

ADD the stock, port, and thyme. Simmer over high heat to reduce the liquid by half. Lower the heat and add the currant jelly, simmering gently until the jelly is dissolved. Add the cornstarch and water mixture and continue simmering until the sauce thickens. Return the bison tenderloins to the pan and simmer just until the steaks reach their desired temperature. Serve with a side of creamy horseradish sauce.

Serves 4

Wine Suggestions: Massimo Malbec
or
Girard Cabernet Sauvignon

GRILLED BISON STEAKS WITH BLACKBERRY SAUCE

At this point, there may be some debate as to whether buffalo (actually, bison) should be considered wild game. Many grocery stores now carry some cuts of bison, or at least ground bison meat. There are many ranchers that are now raising bison as a lean but tasty alternative to beef. There are also several places where you can "hunt" bison, but don't expect the usual thrill of the hunt. Taking a bison is basically driving out to the herd, having the rancher or guide point out the animal you can take, and pulling the trigger. However, the result is a freezer full of delicious meat and a great bison rug. Just be sure to have a big freezer, or lots of friends with which to share the harvest!

Ingredients

2 bison steaks
    marinade made of 2 parts dark
    molasses to 1 part water
1 tablespoon butter
3 large shallots, sliced thin

1½ cups dry red wine, such as Zinfandel
    or Cabernet
2 tablespoons balsamic vinegar
1 tablespoon Chambord or blackberry
    brandy
1 cup blackberries, fresh or frozen

Preparation

MARINATE bison steaks in molasses and water for at least 1 hour. In a small saucepan, caramelize the shallots in the butter over medium-high heat. Remove from the heat, and add the wine and vinegar to the pan, stirring to combine. Return to heat and reduce to about ½ cup by simmering gently for about 15 minutes. Add the Chambord or blackberry brandy and simmer another minute. Keep warm.

REMOVE the steaks from the marinade and pat dry. Grill over hot coals until medium rare, or desired temperature. Just like wild game, buffalo tastes better when it is rare or medium rare. This should take only about 3 minutes per side, depending on the thickness of the steaks.

WHILE steaks are cooking, turn the heat up under the sauce and add the blackberries, stirring carefully to coat with the sauce but not breaking up the berries. Heat the berries through, and serve on the side.

Serves 2

Wine Suggestions: Castello di Monastero Infinito
or
Bota Box Redvolution

GRILLED BISON STEAKS WITH PORT-BRANDY REDUCTION

Ingredients

2 bison steaks
3 tablespoons olive oil
1 tablespoon Worcestershire sauce

1 tablespoon orange juice
1 tablespoon lemon juice
   salt and cracked pepper

For the Sauce

¼ cup brandy
⅓ cup port
½ cup game bird stock or chicken broth

2 teaspoons green peppercorns, drained
2 tablespoons butter, cut in small chunks
   & chilled

Preparation

ABOUT an hour before grilling the steaks, combine the olive oil, Worcestershire sauce, orange juice and lemon juice on a dinner plate. Pat the bison steaks dry and season them with salt and cracked pepper, pressing the mixture into the steak. Place them on the dinner plate. Using a fork and spoon, ladle some of the marinade on top of the steak and pierce the steak several times, drawing the marinade into the steak. Repeat with the other steak, then turn them over and repeat the process on the other side. Let the steaks sit in the marinade until you are ready to grill them.

MEANWHILE, put the brandy and port in a small saucepan, bring to a simmer and reduce to about 2 tablespoons of liquid. Add the stock and the green peppercorns and reduce until it thickens slightly. Keep warm. When you are about ready to serve, slowly whisk in the butter and simmer very gently for a minute.

WHEN the coals are very hot, remove the steaks from the marinade and grill for about 3 to 4 minutes per side, depending on thickness.

LADLE half of the sauce onto each plate and place the grilled steak on top.

Serves 2

Wine Suggestions: Black Stallion Cabernet Sauvignon
or
Kunde Estate Reserve Century Vine Zinfandel

ROAST BISON WITH MUSHROOM AU JUS

Ingredients

1 3-pound bison roast	dash of garlic powder
4 strips bacon	dash of thyme
1 jar pearl onions, drained	1 cup game stock or beef broth
¾ cup port, divided into ¼ and ½ cups	1 teaspoon arrowroot, mixed with a little
1½ tablespoons butter	water (optional)
4-6 large mushrooms, sliced	

Preparation

PREHEAT oven to 450 degrees. Remove roast from refrigerator at least 1 hour before roasting. Generously salt and pepper the roast, then wrap the strips of bacon around the roast, securing with toothpicks.

SPRAY or lightly oil a shallow roasting pan. Place roast in center of the pan and arrange the pearl onions around the roast. Place in 450-degree oven for 15 minutes. Turn the temperature down and keep roasting for about 48 more minutes, or 16 minutes per pound of roast. Halfway through the total roasting time, pour the ½ cup of port over the center of the roast. With a spoon, turn the onions and baste them with the drippings.

WHILE the roast is cooking, sauté the mushrooms in the butter in a medium saucepan over medium heat. Sprinkle the mixture with a dash of garlic powder and thyme. Add pepper to taste. If using commercial beef broth, do not add any extra salt. Add the stock or beef broth and the ¼ cup port to the mixture and simmer gently for about 10 minutes. Keep warm.

WHEN the roast is done, transfer it and the pearl onions to a serving platter. Remove the bacon and discard. Remove any fat in the roasting pan, leaving the juices in the pan. Put a splash of port in the roasting pan, and scrape up any browned bits that have stuck to the pan. With a spatula, transfer the mixture to the mushroom mixture, scraping the bottom of the pan to be sure you get all the goodies out of it. Stir to combine the liquids, and simmer gently for a couple more minutes. If desired, you can thicken the mixture with the arrowroot and water by simmering and stirring for another minute or two.

SERVE the roast with the au jus on the side, along with some horseradish.

Serves 6 to 8
Wine Suggestions: Windsor Sonoma Pinot Noir
or Noble Vines 181 Merlot

POTTED BISON

If you like to have a large roast, even if the original dinner is just for two, this is a great way to enjoy the rest of the roast as a true comfort food. Take your time browning the onions – you want to achieve a rich caramelization. This dish is lovely served over mashed potatoes or noodles and accompanied by a nice crisp salad.

Ingredients

2 pounds cooked bison roast, cut in 1-inch cubes	1 cup full-bodied red wine
5-6 slices bacon, chopped	1 10.5-ounce can beef consommé or leftover gravy
2 tablespoons olive oil	1 cup beef broth or game stock
¼ cup butter	2 bay leaves
5 cups onion, chopped	1 teaspoon thyme
4 garlic cloves, minced	1 tablespoon orange zest
1 cup flour, seasoned with pepper, garlic powder, and sweet paprika	1 tablespoon sweet paprika
¼ cup brandy	¼ teaspoon ground allspice

Preparation

IN A stockpot or Dutch oven, render fat from bacon. When bacon is crisp, remove and drain on a paper towel. Pour off all but 1 tablespoon of fat, and add the olive oil and butter. Heat until it just starts to smoke. Add onions and slowly brown them over medium heat until they are well caramelized, stirring frequently. Add the garlic for the last couple of minutes.

PLACE seasoned flour in a plastic bag and add meat cubes, shaking to coat the cubes evenly. Remove the caramelized onions from the pot and set aside. Add the meat cubes to the pot and brown evenly, stirring frequently. When brown, deglaze the pot with the brandy. Cook until brandy has evaporated. Return onions to pot and add rest of ingredients, adding freshly ground pepper to taste. Before adding salt, taste to be sure it is needed, since certain beef broths and consommés already contain a lot of salt.

COVER and simmer on low for 12 hours. You can remove to the refrigerator at night and finish the next day.

Serves 6 – 8

Wine Suggestions: Gnarly Head Chardonnay
or
Joseph Carr Cabernet Sauvignon

~Small Game~

Squirrel and Rabbit

GRILLED SQUIRREL
with Honey-Mustard Basting Sauce

Ingredients

2 squirrels, cut into 6 pieces each
4 tablespoons honey

4 tablespoons Dijon mustard

For the Marinade

4 tablespoons olive oil
4 tablespoons Dijon mustard
1 tablespoon fresh sage or ½ teaspoon
dried

1 teaspoon ground chipotle pepper or
red cayenne
1 teaspoon Tabasco
3 cloves garlic, smashed
4 tablespoons brandy

Preparation

COMBINE the ingredients for the marinade. Cut the squirrels into 6 pieces per squirrel: 2 hind legs, 2 front legs, upper back and ribs, and lower back with the loin. Put the pieces in the marinade and marinate for 2 to 6 hours.

IN A small saucepan, slowly heat the honey until it thins. Add the mustard and stir to combine. Keep warm while the grill is heating up. Remove the squirrel pieces from the marinade and grill over a hot fire for about 3 minutes per side, basting with the honey-mustard mixture.

SERVE immediately with steamed green vegetables and wild rice mixed with sautéed mushrooms and toasted pine nuts.

Serves 3 to 4

Wine Suggestions: Gnarly Head Pinot Noir
or
Josh Cellars Cabernet Sauvignon

Braised Rabbit with Sherry and Italian Sausage

Ingredients

1 rabbit, cut into serving pieces
1 tablespoon olive oil
2 links of Italian sausage, casings removed
6 garlic cloves, crushed

6 sprigs of fresh rosemary, or ½ teaspoon dried
6 sprigs of fresh tarragon, or 1 teaspoon dried
2 cups sherry
salt and pepper to taste

Preparation

PREHEAT oven to 375 degrees. In skillet or Dutch oven, brown the rabbit pieces in the olive oil over medium-high heat for 2 to 3 minutes per side. Remove and set aside. Break up the sausage and add to the skillet, browning the meat. Drain off most of the fat. Put the rabbit back in the pan. Sprinkle the garlic, rosemary, and tarragon over the mixture. Pour the sherry over all. Cover the skillet and place in 375-degree oven for 45 minutes.

REMOVE skillet from oven and add salt and pepper to taste. This is great served with grits cooked with a little cheese.

Serves 2 to 3
Wine Suggestions: Poggio alle Sughure Sangiovese or Massimo Rioja

Rabbit in Almond Sauce

Ingredients

1 rabbit, cut into 6 pieces
2 tablespoons olive oil
1 onion, chopped
6 cloves of garlic, peeled
12 whole peppercorns
24 blanched whole almonds

¼ teaspoon cinnamon
2 tablespoons fresh parsley, chopped
1 tablespoon chopped fresh sage, or ½ teaspoon dried
3 bay leaves
1 cup red wine

Preparation

CRUSH the peppercorns and one garlic clove and set aside. Heat olive oil in skillet and cook onion and the other 5 garlic cloves until the onion just starts to brown. Remove from pan. Turn heat to medium-high and brown the rabbit pieces in the skillet. Add the rest of the ingredients to the skillet, stirring to combine. Cover and simmer gently for 30 to 40 minutes. Add water as needed, if mixture gets too dry.

Serves 2 to 3
Wine Suggestions: Gnarly Head Pinot Grigio or George Duboeuf St. Veran

FRIED RABBIT

Ingredients

1 rabbit, cut into serving pieces
4 strips bacon, chopped
2 tablespoons unsalted butter, or
1 egg
¼ cup milk
1 teaspoon white Worcestershire
⅓ cup flour

½ teaspoon ground cloves
½ teaspoon ground ginger
½ teaspoon dried mustard
salt and pepper
Crisco®butter flavor shortening
Calvados apple brandy (optional)

Preparation

IN A large skillet, fry the bacon pieces until they are crisp. Remove and save for other use. On a dinner plate beat the egg with a small whisk, and add the milk and Worcestershire sauce, whisking to combine. On another dinner plate, combine the flour with the spices and the salt and pepper. Place both plates on the counter next to the skillet.

ON medium-high, add the Crisco or unsalted butter to the skillet. Working with the thicker rabbit pieces first, place them in the egg and milk mixture to coat, and then dredge them in the flour mixture. Place immediately in skillet to start frying. As soon as the first to pieces go into the skillet, start timing 2½ minutes. When the time is over, turn the larger pieces first, and then the small ones. After 2 more minutes, turn the heat down to low. Cover and cook another 3 to 4 minutes. If most of the fat has been absorbed in the pan, you can add a little water or Calvados when you cover the skillet.

UNCOVER and check the thickest piece. It should be just barely pink at its thickest part. If not, turn up the heat and continue cooking another minute or two.

SERVE with redskin potatoes that have roasted in the oven with a little olive oil, salt and pepper. Sprinkle them with a little fresh chopped parsley and the bacon bits.

Serves 2

Wine Suggestions: Vidal-Fleury Côtes du Rhône Blanc
or
Gnarly Head Merlot

Rabbit Putanesca

Ingredients

2 wild rabbits, cut into 8 pieces each
flour, seasoned with salt, pepper, and paprika
5 slices bacon, chopped
olive oil, if needed
1 medium yellow onion, halved and then sliced thin
5 garlic cloves, sliced thin
1 large carrot, diced
2 stalks celery, diced
¼ cup brandy
2 cups shiitake mushrooms, sliced

2 cups Roma tomatoes, chopped
¼ cup sun-dried tomatoes in olive oil, drained and chopped
1½ cups red wine
2 cups game stock or chicken broth
½ teaspoon thyme
½ teaspoon sage
1 tablespoon basil
¼ cup fresh parsley, stems removed and chopped
arrowroot, mixed with a little water (optional)

Preparation

CUT the rabbits into serving pieces: 4 legs, upper back and ribs cut in two, and lower back and loins cut in two. In a large skillet or Dutch oven, heat the chopped bacon until it renders its fat and the pieces are crisp. Remove the bacon and let it drain.

DUST the rabbit pieces with the seasoned flour, and brown in the bacon fat over medium-high heat. Remove the rabbit to a covered dish and keep warm in the oven.

SAUTÉ the onion, celery, carrots, and garlic in the skillet over medium heat, adding a little olive oil if necessary. Do not let the garlic burn. When the onions are transparent, push the vegetables to the sides of the skillet, and pour the brandy in the middle. As it simmers, scrape the bottom of the skillet to loosen any brown bits. Add the mushrooms and continue cooking over medium heat for another 2 minutes. Add the rest of the ingredients except the parsley and arrowroot, stirring to combine. Cover and simmer for about 40 minutes, stirring occasionally. At this point, you can add a teaspoon or 2 of arrowroot mixed with a little water if you wish to thicken the sauce. If so, stir to combine and simmer for another 5 minutes.

RETURN the rabbits to the skillet, along with any accumulated juices. Stir the juices into the sauce and spoon some of the sauce over the rabbit pieces. Sprinkle the parsley over all. Cover and simmer gently for another 5 to 10 minutes until rabbit pieces are no longer pink inside. Don't cook too long after the pieces lose their pinkness, or the meat will start to toughen.

SERVE over fettuccini that has been tossed with a little olive oil and garlic. Sprinkle freshly grated Parmesan cheese over all.

Serves 4 to 6
*Wine Suggestions: Gnarly Head Authentic Red
or Mar de Frades Albariño*

HASENPFEFFER–STYLE RABBIT

You can increase your servings by just adding an extra rabbit and increasing the Calvados and the stock by a small amount to increase the final volume of the sauce. You do not need to increase any of the ingredients in the marinade.

Ingredients

1 rabbit, cut in serving pieces
flour, seasoned with salt, pepper, and paprika
¼ pound bacon, chopped
1 tablespoon olive oil
½ cup Calvados apple brandy

1 cup game bird or chicken stock
½ cup sour cream, mixed with 3 teaspoons arrowroot (optional)
¼ cup Calvados (optional)
brown sugar (optional)

For the Marinade

3 cups dark beer, preferably German
2 shallots, sliced thin
2 cloves of garlic, minced
2 bay leaves
2 onions, sliced thin
1 carrot, sliced thin
2 small parsnips, sliced thin

⅛ teaspoon powdered cloves
⅛ teaspoon powdered ginger
⅛ teaspoon nutmeg
⅛ teaspoon ground allspice
1 cinnamon stick, broken in half
¼ teaspoon thyme
1 tablespoon Worcestershire sauce

Preparation

THE day before, combine the ingredients for the marinade and add the rabbit, stirring to make sure the marinade covers all of the rabbit pieces. Refrigerate overnight, stirring occasionally.

WHEN ready to start cooking, remove the rabbit pieces from the marinade and pat them dry. Fry the chopped bacon in a skillet until crisp. Remove and set aside. Drain off all but 2 tablespoons of the bacon fat. Add a tablespoon of olive oil to the skillet. Dust the rabbit pieces with the seasoned flour, and brown in the skillet over medium-high heat, about 3 minutes per side. Remove rabbit to a covered dish and keep in a warm oven.

REMOVE the 2 pieces of cinnamon stick from the marinade. Scoop the vegetables out of the marinade and sauté them in the skillet over medium heat for about 10 minutes. Add about one cup of the marinade liquid to the skillet, along with ½ cup of Calvados, the stock, and the bacon. Stir to combine and then return the rabbit pieces to the skillet, spooning some of the mixture over the meat. Cover and simmer for 30 minutes, stirring occasionally.

REMOVE the bay leaves from the skillet and check the sauce. Here's where you can tailor this recipe to your own tastes. The three optional ingredients can be added or deleted as you wish. If the sauce tastes a little too bitter from the dark beer, you can add a small amount of brown sugar. We like to add ¼ cup of the Calvados at the end of the cooking time to refresh the apple taste in the sauce. Sometimes, we enjoy a little thicker and creamier sauce. Then we add the sour cream with the arrowroot. Whichever way you want to finish this dish, just be sure to gently simmer the mixture a couple of more minutes to blend the flavors.

Serves 2 to 3

Wine Suggestions: Hob Nob Malbec or Gnarly Head Pinot Grigio

GRILLED RABBIT CALVADOS

Ingredients

1 rabbit, cut into serving pieces	1 tablespoon ground chipotle pepper, or red cayenne
⅓ cup olive oil	
2 teaspoons lemon juice	1 cup Calvados apple brandy
2 tablespoons soy sauce	1 cloves garlic, minced
1 tablespoon chopped fresh sage, or ½ teaspoon dried	

Preparation

COMBINE all ingredients, add rabbit and marinate for 6 hours or overnight in the refrigerator. At least 1 hour before cooking, remove rabbit and marinade from refrigerator.

PREHEAT barbecue grill to about 350 degrees. Remove the rabbit from the marinade and pat dry. Pour marinade into a saucepan and simmer for at least 10 minutes.

GRILL the rabbit pieces for 2 to 4 minutes per side, depending on the size of the rabbit. Baste with the hot marinade. It will be done when the pieces are still slightly pink in the thickest parts.

JUST before serving, top of the rest of the marinade with a little more Calvados, simmer for a minute or two and serve on the side.

Serves 2 to 3

Wine Suggestions: Gnarly Head Merlot or Sauvion Vouvray

Rabbit Paella

Paella is a time-consuming dish to prepare, but well worth the effort. Traditional paella usually includes some seafood, which we have not added to this dish, but could be easily incorporated. Also, traditional paella is cooked in a wide paella pan over a large fire that heats the whole width of the pan. The problem with the ranges of today is that a wide braising pan on a small fire tends to cook the rice unevenly. The heat bubbles up in the center of the pan, causing the rice in the center to cook on time, but leaving the rice at the edges hard and under-done. We've come up with two different ways to solve this problem:

RICE SOLUTION #1: When ready to add rice, move all ingredients to the outer circle of the pan. Pour rice in center and distribute evenly over center, moving ingredients in and over the top of the rice.

RICE SOLUTION #2: Pre-cook the rice with some of the stock for about 10 to 15 minutes before adding to rest of ingredients.

Ingredients

6 cups chicken stock
1 teaspoon saffron threads
1½ pounds Roma tomatoes
1 large rabbit, cut in small pieces – about 12 to 14
2 tablespoons olive oil
½ medium green pepper, diced
½ medium red pepper, diced
1 small yellow onion, diced

4 garlic cloves, minced
2 Andouille sausages, cut in bite-sized pieces
2 garlic sausages, cut in bite-sized pieces
¼ cup pancetta, diced
1 teaspoon smoked paprika
1 cup frozen peas
2 cups short- or medium-grain rice

Preparation

IN A large saucepan, heat chicken stock with saffron threads and keep warm. Make a small "x" in the bottom of each tomato and blanch in a 3-quart saucepan of boiling water for 10 seconds. Remove to an ice bath. When cool, peel tomatoes and discard seeds. Chop fine, and set aside.

SEASON rabbit with salt and freshly ground pepper. Heat oil in a paella pan or wide braising pan on medium-low heat and sauté rabbit pieces for 10 to 15 minutes. It is very important to use low heat. If you sear the meat on high, it will shrivel up and be very dry. Remove from pan and set aside.

ADD peppers and onion to pan and sauté for about 10 minutes. Add garlic and sauté until you smell the garlic aroma. Add tomatoes and cook, stirring, until tomatoes release their juice and the mixture begins to thicken a bit – about 7 minutes. Now add the sausages and pancetta and continue cooking for 5 minutes. Add smoked paprika, stirring to combine. Add frozen peas and return rabbit to pan and combine.

ADD rice – using one of the methods described above – and 3/4 of the saffron-chicken broth, keeping the rest warm. Mix all together – keeping meats and vegetables to side if using first method – and keep rice at an even depth. Add half of remaining broth. Cook until rice is tender, adding extra broth if needed. Remove from heat and rest about 10 minutes before serving.

Serves 4

Wine Suggestions: Ramón Bilbao Valiñas Albariño
or
Loredona Viognier

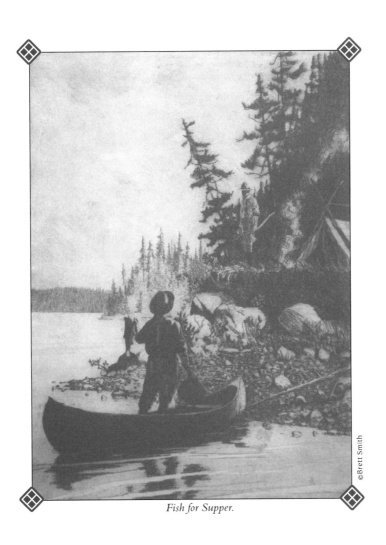

Fish for Supper.

Squirrel and Rabbit

CLAY POT RABBIT WITH ROOT VEGETABLES AND APPLE

Ingredients

1 rabbit, but in 8 pieces
 olive oil
1 chipotle pepper, seeds removed and
 minced
2 tablespoons smoked paprika
2 carrots, chopped
2 small parsnips, chopped
4 medium red potatoes, quartered
1 teaspoon ground cinnamon

5 sage leaves, chopped
1 onion, chopped
½ cup tawny port
½ cup Marsala wine
1 cup chicken broth
1 Granny Smith apple, cored and cut in
 8 pieces
 brown sugar, if needed

Preparation

RUB rabbit pieces with paprika and chipotle pepper. Cover and place in refrigerator for 4 to 5 hours.

SOAK clay pot in cool water for 20 minutes. Bring a large pot of water to a boil and cook the carrots, parsnips, and potatoes for 10 minutes. Remove and drain.

REMOVE clay pot from water and place apple slices in the bottom. Lightly sprinkle with cinnamon and scatter sage over all.

BROWN the rabbit in olive oil in a skillet for a couple of minutes per side. Remove rabbit and set aside. Add the drained carrots, parsnips, and potatoes to the skillet along with the onion and sauté for about 5 minutes. Add a little wine or broth if skillet becomes too dry. Remove half of the mixture from the skillet and place on top of the apples in the clay pot. Place rabbit pieces on top of this mixture and spread remaining vegetables over the rabbit. Pour wines and broth over all, cover, and place in cold oven. Turn the oven to 400 degrees and bake for 40 minutes, or until rabbit is tender and juices are clear.

REMOVE from oven and let sit for about 10 minutes. If the chipotle seasoning is too strong, stir in a little brown sugar.

Serves 2 – 3

Wine Suggestions: Vidal-Fleury Côtes du Rhône Blanc
or
Foghead Sauvignon Blanc

Mustard Crusted Rabbit

Ingredients

1 rabbit, cut into 6 pieces
½ cup Dijon mustard
¼ cup butter, melted
1 cup panko bread crumbs

2 teaspoons chipotle pepper
¼ cup fresh thyme leaves, chopped
   olive oil, to be sprayed

Preparation

HEAT oven to 500 degrees. Season rabbit pieces with salt and freshly ground pepper. In a small bowl, combine mustard and melted butter. On a plate, combine the panko, chipotle pepper, and thyme leaves. Spray a small amount of olive oil on this mixture and stir.

BASTE rabbit pieces with the mustard-butter mixture, and then dip them in the panko mixture, coating pieces well. Place pieces in a small roasting pan that has been lightly sprayed with olive oil. Place in pre-heated oven and bake for 15 minutes at 500 degrees. Check the meat for doneness after 15 minutes. Meat should be just slightly pink. Depending on the size of the rabbit, you may need to continue baking a little longer. If so, reduce oven temperature to 350 degrees and continue baking until done – usually only a few minutes longer.

SERVE with a crisp green salad, yellow grits, and cornbread.

Serves 2

Wine Suggestions: Gnarly Head Pinot Grigio
or
Sauvion Vouvray

CLAY POT RABBIT WITH SWEET PAPRIKA AND CINNAMON

Ingredients

1 rabbit, cut into 6 pieces	2 garlic cloves, chopped
5 tablespoons olive oil, divided	16 dried green peppercorns, cracked
6 large sage leaves, divided	2 red potatoes, quartered
1 tablespoon sweet paprika	½ yellow onion, chopped
1 teaspoon ground cinnamon	1 red bell pepper, chopped
1¾ cup cream sherry, divided	16 grape tomatoes
1 cup game stock of chicken stock	½ pound lamb sausage
1 bay leaf	

Preparation

MAKE a marinade by combining 3 tablespoons of the olive oil, 3 of the sage leaves, paprika, cinnamon, 4 tablespoons of the sherry and a dash of salt and freshly ground pepper. Pat rabbit pieces dry and place in a self-sealing plastic bag. Pour marinade in and seal, pushing most of the air out of the bag so the liquid coats all of the rabbit. Place in refrigerator for 6 hours to overnight.

FILL sink with cold water and place clay pot in water to soak for 20 minutes.

IN A saucepan, combine the stock, remaining sherry, remaining sage leaves, bay leaf, garlic, and cracked peppercorns. Heat mixture over low heat until flavors start to blend and then remove from heat and set aside.

HEAT a pan of water to a boil and boil potatoes for 5 minutes. Drain and set aside. Heat remaining 2 tablespoons of olive oil in a skillet and brown the rabbit for 3 minutes each side. Remove from skillet and add onions and peppers and sauté for about 5 minutes over medium heat. Place rabbit, onion, peppers, and potatoes in the clay pot and pour the braising liquid over all. Place clay pot in cold oven and set temperature to 325 degrees. Cook for 30 minutes.

MEANWHILE, cut up lamb sausage and brown in skillet. Keep warm. Carefully remove clay pot from oven after the 45 minutes. Pot will be quite hot, so carefully remove the top and set on a heat resistant surface. Add the browned sausage and tomatoes, recover and cook in oven for another 30 minutes.

REMOVE from oven and let rest for 5 to 10 minutes before serving.

Serves 4
Wine Suggestions: Joseph Carr Dijon Clone Chardonnay
or
Noble Vines 181 Merlot

Rabbit from the Moors

This recipe uses single malt Scotch in the basting sauce and works best with what is called a "peaty" Scotch. This term refers to Scotch that uses malted barley that has been dried over peat fires, giving the liquid a smoky flavor. Peat is created from decayed vegetation in wetland bogs – especially prevalent on the moors of Scotland. This matter is harvested, dried, and used as a source of fuel. One of the most famous of the peaty Scotches is Laphroaig. If you want help with this, go to a liquor store that has a wide variety of single malt Scotches and ask for the ones with a peaty flavor.

Ingredients

1 rabbit
6 tablespoons butter
4 tablespoons Dijon mustard
2 tablespoons peaty Scotch
4 tablespoons honey
½ cup Calvados apple brandy

1 teaspoon fresh rosemary, chopped fine
2 teaspoons fresh tarragon, chopped fine
2 tablespoons fresh sage, chopped fine

Preparation

SEASON rabbit inside and out with salt and pepper. In a small saucepan place the rest of the ingredients and heat until combined. Brush some of this on the rabbit and let rest for about 30 minutes.

HEAT the grill to 350 to 400 degrees. Secure rabbit on rotisserie. Cook rabbit on the rotisserie for about 16 minutes, depending on size of rabbit. Baste the rabbit with the mustard-Scotch mixture every 4 minutes. Meat should be slightly pink, and juices should run clear when done.

Serves 2

Wine Suggestions: Loredona Pinot Grigio
or
Yellow Tail Bubbles

RABBIT IN RED WINE SAUCE

This recipe works best if you marinate the rabbit for about 24 hours, so plan ahead.

Ingredients

2 rabbits, cut in pieces	½ pound bacon, chopped
1½ bottles fruity red wine	2 onions, chopped
¼ cup brandy or cognac	¼ cup olive oil
2 lemons, juiced	12 small red potatoes
2 sprigs fresh thyme	2 carrots, chopped
4 sage leaves, chopped	2 tablespoons butter
4 garlic cloves, chopped	12 small brown mushrooms
2 bay leaves	1 cup pearl onions, frozen or canned
flour, seasoned with salt and pepper	1 tablespoon brown sugar

Preparation

COMBINE the wine, brandy, lemon juice, thyme, sage, garlic, and bay leaves in a container big enough to hold the rabbits. Add rabbit pieces and refrigerate for about 24 hours.

HEAT oven to 350 degrees. Remove the rabbit from the marinade and pat dry, reserving the marinade. Place rabbit in seasoned flour to coat all sides. Fry bacon in a Dutch oven or large cast iron skillet until crisp. Remove and drain on paper towels. Place rabbit in pan and brown on all sides. Remove and set aside. Add onion to pan and cook for about 5 minutes on medium heat. Return bacon and rabbit to pan and add carrots and potatoes. Pour marinade over all, cover, and place in oven for 2 hours, or until rabbit is tender.

ABOUT 45 minutes before the rabbit is finished, heat the butter in a skillet over medium heat and sauté the mushrooms and pearl onions for about 5 minutes. Add a little red wine or chicken broth if it gets too dry. Sprinkle brown sugar over all and stir to combine. Continue cooking for a couple of minutes. When there is about 30 minutes left of cooking time for the rabbit, add this mixture to the Dutch oven, stirring to combine, and cook the last 30 minutes.

REMOVE from oven and let sit for about 10 minutes before serving.

Serves 4 – 6

Wine Suggestions: Kunde Estate Chardonnay
or
Noble Vines 667 Pinot Noir

Comfort Foods

CHUKAR PIZZA

The low fat content of wild game meat makes it perfect for pizzas: it won't drip extra fat onto the pizza when it's cooking, and the short cooking time for pizzas is perfect for game meat that shouldn't be overcooked. Use your imagination to make delicious wild game pizzas, varying the toppings to suit the type of wild game you use.

Ingredients

1 fresh pizza shell
2 chukars, meat removed from bones and cut in ½-inch chunks
1½ tablespoons olive oil
½ medium green pepper, chopped
½ medium red pepper, chopped
½ onion, chopped
1½ cups mushrooms, chopped

¼ cup sherry, white wine, or chicken stock
smoked ham, ¾" thick, chopped
pizza sauce
spices to your taste: basil, oregano, thyme
1½ cups shredded Italian cheeses: Mozzarella, Parmesan, Romano, etc.

Preparation

PREHEAT oven to 450 degrees.

IN A skillet over medium-high heat, quickly brown the chukar pieces in the olive oil, about a total of 2 minutes. Remove the chukar and set aside. Add the peppers and onion to the skillet, reduce heat to medium, and sauté until the vegetables are starting to get limp. Add the mushrooms, and sauté for another minute or 2, stirring occasionally. Add the wine or stock and deglaze the pan. Stir in the ham, and add the pizza sauce, varying the amount to suit your own tastes. Turn the heat to medium-low and stir until all is heated through. Add the spices to your own taste. I usually sprinkle equal amounts of oregano and basil, with a smaller amount of thyme. Stir to combine and taste, adding more spice if necessary. Return the chukar pieces and the accumulated juices to the mixture and continue simmering for another minute.

LIGHTLY brush the pizza shell with olive oil. Sprinkle ½ cup of the cheese over the shell. Spoon the mixture in the skillet evenly over the shell, leaving a half-inch around the outside. Sprinkle the rest of the cheese evenly over the mixture.

PLACE pizza on the middle rack of the oven and bake for about 8 to 10 minutes. The baking time may vary, based on the type of pizza shell that you use. When done, remove from oven and let cool a couple of minutes to set the cheese before cutting. Cut into 8 pieces.

Serves 4

Wine Suggestions: George Duboeuf Beaujolais-Village, Handcraft Chardonnay, or Loredona Viognier

Big Game Pizza

This pizza is quick to whip up for an easy dinner or for snacks. Any big game meat can be used and the toppings can be changed to fit your whim. Try adding some chopped bell peppers that have been microwaved for a couple of minutes, or drain a can of black beans and sprinkle them on top.

Ingredients

¾–1 *pound ground elk, or other big game meat*
 2 *tablespoons olive oil*
 1 *cup sliced mushrooms*
 ½ *large onion, chopped*

 1 *11-ounce can corn*
 1 *cup prepared barbecue sauce*
 2 *cups shredded Italian cheese*
 1 *large pizza shell*

Preparation

PREHEAT oven to 425 degrees. In a large skillet, sauté the onions and mushrooms in 1 tablespoon of olive oil over medium heat until the onions are translucent. Remove and set aside. Turn the heat to medium-high and brown the ground elk in the other tablespoon of olive oil, stirring occasionally. Return the vegetables to the skillet and add the corn and the barbecue sauce, stirring to combine. Heat through.

LIGHTLY brush the pizza shell with olive oil and spoon the meat mixture onto the shell, spreading it evenly within about a half inch of the edge. Sprinkle the top with the cheese. Bake 12 to 15 minutes or until the cheese has melted.

REMOVE to a wire rack and let cool for 5 minutes. Cut into 8 wedges, or cut into 2-inch squares for appetizers.

Serves 4

Wine Suggestions: Massimo Malbec
or
Villa Pozzi Nero d'Avola

ELK AND BLACK BEAN MEDITERRANEAN CHILI

This recipe is enjoyed so much, it has become a staple in our freezer. It makes 20 to 22 servings, so that we have plenty to freeze for later use. It's always a hit in hunting camp, served with a fresh green salad and dark bread. The use of epazote is optional. This herb is used a lot in Mexican and South American cooking and can be found in Mexican grocery stores. You can also find it in Penzey's Spices catalog.

It seems like we usually make it with elk, because of the amount of meat you get from this huge animal, but it tastes equally as good made with any big game meat. It can be made with either ground big game meat or with the meat cut in small chunks. I sometimes forget to soak the beans the night before. If that happens to you, just rinse the beans, cover with water and bring to a boil. Remove from heat, cover, and let sit for an hour. Then drain and rinse the beans.

This is an all-day affair, but well worth it when you get those cheers.

Ingredients

1 pound dry black beans, rinsed and soaked overnight in cold water
3-4 pounds elk meat, ground or cut in small cubes
1 pound pork sausage
1 can beef broth
butter, as needed
2 large onions, chopped
5 shallots, chopped
3 stalks celery, chopped
3 garlic cloves, minced
2 jalapeno peppers, stem and seeds removed, minced
1 dried chipotle pepper, chopped fine
½ cup flour
4 large tomatoes, chopped

1 pound mushrooms, chopped
1 large red pepper, chopped
1 large green pepper, chopped
2 cans pitted black olives, sliced
1 1-pound can of your favorite baked beans, we like Bush's Original Recipe
½ cup red wine
1 bottle chili sauce
1 cup parsley leaves, chopped
1 tablespoon oregano
1 tablespoon coriander seeds, ground
2 teaspoons ground cumin
4 tablespoons chili powder
1 tablespoon epazote (optional)
salt and pepper to taste

Preparation

THE night before, rinse the black beans and put in a large pot. Fill the pot with cold water to about 2 inches above the beans. Let them sit overnight.

THE next morning, drain the water from the beans and return them to the same pot. Add the can of beef broth and enough water to cover the beans. Bring the pot to a boil, turn the heat to low and simmer the beans, covered, for about 1½ hours. Drain and reserve.

ALL chopped vegetables should be chopped in fairly large pieces, since they will be simmering for a long time and need to retain some of their original shape to make the chili look more interesting. Have all the vegetables chopped and ready to go before you start cooking.

IN A large skillet, preferably cast iron, place the pork sausage. Turn the heat to medium high and brown the sausage until it releases its fat. With a slotted spoon, scoop up the brown pork and put it in a strainer that has been placed over a bowl, so that the fat can drip off. Drain almost all of the fat from the skillet, and add 2 to 3 tablespoons butter. Add the onions, shallots, celery, garlic, jalapenos, and chipotle pepper to the skillet. Sauté the vegetables, stirring occasionally, until the onions are translucent and soft. Do not let the garlic burn. Put the mixture into a large stockpot and add the drained sausage. Sprinkle the flour over this mixture, and stir to combine. At this time, the stockpot is not over heat.

ADD another tablespoon of butter to the skillet and brown the elk in batches, adding the browned pieces to the stockpot. Now add the rest of the ingredients, including the drained black beans. Save the red wine and the chili sauce to add at the end. After emptying the chili sauce into the stockpot, pour the red wine into the empty bottle, put the lid back on, and shake the bottle to loosen any chili sauce that has not come out. Pour the contents into the stockpot.

BRING the mixture to a low boil, lower the heat, cover, and simmer for 2 hours, stirring every 10 minutes to keep the mixture on the bottom of the pot from burning. After about an hour and a half, taste the mixture and adjust the seasonings according to your preference for a hotter or milder chili. After 2 hours, remove from heat and let the chili sit, covered. This helps to blend the flavors. Skim off any fat that might form on the top.

LIKE any stew or chili, the flavor actually gets better as it blends. Serve in individual bowls with a dollop of sour cream in the middle.

Serves 20 to 22

Wine Suggestions: Ramón Bilbao Crianza
or
Noble Vines 337 Cabernet Sauvignon

MIXED BAG POT PIE

This recipe is a favorite of ours and is an adaptation of the King's Arms Tavern Colonial Game Pie from Colonial Williamsburg. We met when we were going to school in Washington, D.C., a wonderful area with so much history. We both loved to go down to Williamsburg whenever we had a weekend free. Shortly after we were married, we revisited Williamsburg together and ate at the King's Arms Tavern. At that time, I was new to hunting and was just learning to cook wild game. Chuck's love of wild game drew him to their Colonial Game Pie immediately. It was absolutely delicious, and I decided that I would learn to make this fabulous pie myself.

Although labor intensive, I still love making this pie. It is Chuck's favorite request for his birthday dinner. I have used many combinations of wild game over the years. I usually try to include big game, small game, and wild fowl in each rendition. However, if I have no rabbits or squirrels, the recipe is just as good with upland bird and waterfowl along with the big game meat. Smoked game birds are also fabulous in this dish, and add another layer of flavor. You can also cook the duck and the rabbit the day before. I make this in a large braising pan instead of a regular pie pan. My philosophy is that, if I'm going to go to all this work, I want to be able to share it with a lot of guests or have lots of leftovers for future meals.

Ingredients

2 mallard ducks
2 rabbits, quartered
2 pounds venison, round steak or sirloin, cut in cubes
½ cup flour, seasoned with salt and pepper
½ pound bacon, cut in small chunks + 3-4 strips
3 carrots, quartered
4 stalks celery, cut in half
½ medium onion, cut in half
1 cup sherry + ¼ cup olive oil, if needed

2 cups mushrooms, quartered
3 tablespoons butter
2 cups port wine
2 cloves garlic, minced
2 cups brown sauce (see recipe in Sauce Section)
1 tablespoon Worcestershire sauce
⅓ cup currant jelly
2 jars pearl onions, drained
1 cup frozen peas
   prepared pie crust, enough to cover a large braising pan or casserole
1 egg
2 tablespoons milk

Early Preparation

EITHER early in the day or the day before, cook the ducks and the rabbits.

PLACE the rabbit quarters in a large pot along with the carrots, celery, and onion. Pour the sherry over the rabbit and add water just to cover. Cover the pot and simmer the rabbit for about 1 hour, or until the rabbit pieces are tender. Remove the rabbits from the pot and place on a plate to cool.

WHILE the rabbit is cooking, preheat the oven to 425 degrees. Lightly oil a shallow roasting pan and place the ducks breast side up in the pan. Lay a strip or 2 of bacon across the ducks to keep the meat from drying out, especially if you have skinned the ducks. Bake the ducks for 15 minutes at 425 degrees, then turn the heat down to 325 degrees and continue baking for another 15 minutes, depending on the size of the ducks. The breast meat should still be rare. Remove the ducks from the oven and place them on a plate to cool, discarding any bacon that has been used. Drain any fat from the pan and add the ¼ cup sherry, scraping the bottom of the pan to loosen any brown bits. Save this liquid.

Final Preparation

PLACE the bacon chunks in a large braising pan and fry until the bacon pieces are crisp. With a slotted spoon, remove the bacon and place on a paper towel to drain. Drain all but about 2 tablespoons of bacon fat from the skillet. Dredge the venison cubes in the seasoned flour. Brown the venison cubes in bacon fat over medium-high heat. Do not crowd the skillet; work in batches, removing each batch to a plate. Add a little olive oil to the skillet if needed. After the last of the venison has been browned and removed from the skillet, pour in the port wine and the minced garlic. Simmer the wine for several minutes while scraping up any browned bits. Return the venison to the skillet and add the brown sauce. Cover and simmer the mixture for about 45 minutes. Add the Worcestershire sauce and the currant jelly, stirring to combine. Keep this mixture warm, just below a simmer.

PREHEAT the oven to 350 degrees. Meanwhile, cut the meat from the ducks and the rabbits into bite-sized pieces. Add these to the venison mixture, along with the pearl onions. In a small skillet, sauté the mushrooms in the butter for about 4 minutes. Add to the mixture, along with the peas.

SCRAPE down the sides of the braising pan, and wipe clean the area that will be above the pastry crust. Place the pie dough over the game mixture, piercing the dough in a circle as you would for a fruit pie. Whisk the egg and the milk together and brush the mixture over the top of the dough with a pastry brush.

BAKE in a 350-degree oven for 35 to 40 minutes, or until the crust is golden brown.

REMOVE from oven and let the pie sit for a few minutes before serving.

Serves 8 to 10

Wine Suggestions: Noble Vines 181 Merlot
or
Vidal-Fleury Côtes du Rhône Rouge

Quick and Easy Game Pot Pie

Many comfort foods take time in the kitchen to prepare. Once in a while, it's fun to serve comfort food that can be whipped up on a weeknight with ingredients that save a lot of time and still give you that warm feeling of home cooking. This recipe just uses one large skillet and one medium saucepan to make a complete meal. Today's supermarkets offer so many combinations of frozen vegetables that you can make many variations of this recipe. Our personal favorite is a combination of bell peppers and onions with some broccoli mixed in. If the frozen vegetables include potatoes, just delete the can of potatoes and include more frozen veggies. Since you are using a prepared gravy, there is no need to add any salt.

Ingredients

2 *pounds venison steak, or other big game meat, cut into small cubes*
1 *tablespoon olive oil*
½ *teaspoon thyme*
¼ *teaspoon garlic powder*
1 *package frozen mixed vegetables*

2 *tablespoons water, or 1 tablespoon brandy and 1 tablespoon water*
1 *can small potatoes, drained*
1 *jar prepared mushroom gravy pepper to taste*
1 *can refrigerated crescent rolls*

Preparation

PREHEAT oven to 375 degrees. Brown the venison cubes in a large ovenproof skillet over medium-high heat. This should only take a minute or two. Sprinkle with the thyme and garlic powder. Remove from heat.

IN A medium saucepan, combine the frozen vegetables, the water, and the brandy. Turn the heat to medium, cover and cook the vegetables for just a couple of minutes until they are defrosted. Add the vegetable mixture to the skillet along with the potatoes, stirring to combine. Stir in the gravy, and bring the mixture to a boil, stirring occasionally.

REMOVE from heat. Separate the crescent rolls into 8 triangles. Place the tip of the first triangle in the middle of the skillet and lay it down on the mixture with the wider end near the edge of the skillet. If the wider end overlaps the skillet, roll it up to fit. Do the same with another piece directly opposite the first one. These are your north and south points. Now lay another triangle each at the east and west points. Fill in the last four triangles between each of the first four. You will have gaps between them where the mixture can bubble up.

PLACE the skillet in the 375-degree oven and bake for 17 to 19 minutes, or until the crust turns a golden brown.

Serves 4 to 6

Wine Suggestions: Chateau Bonnet Rouge or Handcraft Petite Sirah

Sage Grouse Enchiladas

Just like waterfowl, sage grouse and sharptail grouse have dark red meat that is best when not overcooked. This type of meat is perfect for enchiladas. If you are substituting sharptail grouse for the sage grouse, use 2 sharptails since they are a much smaller bird. The use of canned enchilada sauce and refried beans makes this an easy recipe to whip up on a busy night. The epazote is optional in this recipe. It is an herb that is used in Mexican and South American cooking. Mexican grocers often carry it, or you can find it in Penzey's Spices catalog.

Ingredients

1   sage grouse, meat removed from the bones and cut in cubes
1   tablespoon canola oil
1   cup chopped onion
¾   cup chopped green pepper
4-5   mushrooms, halved and then sliced

1   teaspoon epazote (optional)
1   large can enchilada sauce
1   can refried beans, regular or low fat
2   cups shredded cheddar cheese
1   package corn tortillas

Preparation

PREHEAT the oven to 350 degrees.

IN A large skillet over medium-high heat, quickly brown the grouse cubes in the oil. Remove from the skillet and set aside. In the same skillet, sauté the onion and green pepper until the onion becomes translucent. Add the mushrooms and sauté for a couple more minutes. Sprinkle the epazote over the mixture and stir to combine. Turn the heat down to low and add half of the enchilada sauce, the refried beans, and 1 cup of the cheese, stirring to combine. Remove from heat and add the grouse and any accumulated juices, stirring just to mix.

LIGHTLY oil a shallow casserole or baking pan. Heat the tortillas in a microwave for a few seconds.

PLACE ¼ cup of the grouse mixture in the middle of a tortilla, roll up, and place seam side down in the pan. Continue with the rest of the tortillas, or as many as will fit in one layer in the pan. If any of the grouse mixture is left over, spoon it on top of the rolled tortillas. Spoon the rest of the enchilada sauce evenly over the tortillas, and then sprinkle the rest of the cheese on top. Bake in a 350-degree oven for 20 minutes.

SERVE with small bowls of sliced ripe olives, sliced green onions, chopped tomatoes, and sour cream.

Serves 4 to 6
Wine Suggestions: Handcraft Pinot Noir or Yellow Tail Pinot Grigio

Comfort Foods

197

SHARPTAIL POT PIE

Pot pies are such a delicious dinner on a cold winter night. Yes, they can be somewhat labor-intensive, but they are definitely worth the effort, and you've got an entire meal in one dish. Though these dishes are usually made with chicken or turkey, we have found that they are wonderful with all kinds of game. Sharptail grouse is a case in point. Many people have a prejudice against this bird, thinking that it just isn't worthy of a dinner. We have found that our guests often come back for seconds on this pie, and are surprised that the meat in it is from the "lowly" sharptail. The main thing to remember when using wild birds in a pot pie is that you don't want to continue cooking them with the entire mixture. They don't have enough fat to withstand that much cooking. Sear them quickly so they are still rare inside. Then add them back into the mixture just before you put it in the oven. This keeps the meat tender and tasty.

Note: This recipe works equally well with duck and goose meat.

Ingredients

2 sharptailed grouse, deboned and the meat cut in ½-inch cubes
2 tablespoons butter
1 tablespoon olive oil
2 ribs celery, chopped
2 garlic cloves, minced
2 cups frozen mixed vegetables, thawed
¼ cup port wine
3-4 tablespoons flour
3 cups game bird or chicken stock
1 teaspoon tarragon
¼ teaspoon thyme
¼ teaspoon nutmeg
1 jar pearl onions, drained
1 small can corn kernels, drained
1 small can sliced water chestnuts (optional, if you like a crunchy texture)
¼ cup chopped parsley leaves
½ cup half and half cream, or heavy cream if preferred
salt and pepper to taste
1 egg white
pastry dough for 1 large crust, rolled out to fit top of pan

Preparation

PREHEAT oven to 450 degrees.

HEAT a large braising pan or range-proof casserole dish over medium-high heat and add the butter and olive oil. Quickly brown the sharptail pieces in the skillet. Place in a covered dish and set aside. Add the celery, garlic, and mixed vegetables to the skillet and sauté for 3 to 4 minutes. Turn the heat down to low and add the port, stirring to scrape up any brown bits. Sprinkle the flour evenly over the mixture in the skillet. Stir for about 2 minutes, letting the flour brown slightly.

NOW slowly add the stock, stirring constantly. The mixture will start to thicken the stock as soon as it is added to the pan. Now add the spices, onions, corn, parsley, and water chestnuts (if used), stirring to combine. Simmer a few more minutes. Remove from heat and stir in the half and half cream. Return to heat and simmer until thickened. Now return the browned sharptail cubes and the juices to the pan, stirring to combine. If sauce is too thin, sprinkle a little more flour on top and stir in, letting the mixture simmer at least another minute. If too thick, add a little more stock or wine.

REMOVE the pan from the heat, and make sure that the sides of the pan are as clean as possible, so that the area above the crust doesn't end up with burned bits. Place the pastry dough gently on top of the mixture. Brush the dough generously with the egg mixture, and pierce the dough in a circle just as you would a fruit pie, so that some steam can escape.

PLACE the pan in the 450-degree oven for 15 minutes. Turn the heat down to 325 degrees, and continue cooking for another 10 minutes, or until the crust is browned. Remove from the oven and let it cook on a rack for about 15 minutes.

Serves 8

Wine Suggestions: The Crossings Pinot Noir or Gnarly Head Chardonnay

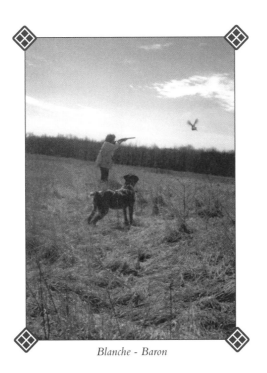

Blanche - Baron

TORTILLA CHILI BAKE

This is a very filling casserole that makes a complete dinner if served with a fresh green salad. If you have any leftovers they freeze well. After the leftovers have cooled, slice them into individual servings, wrap each serving in cling wrap, and place them in a large ziplock bag. They reheat easily in the microwave. This recipe will work equally well with ground big game meat or with ground game birds.

Ingredients

1½ pounds ground game meat
1 tablespoon canola oil
1 small onion, chopped
½ green pepper, chopped
1 large can enchilada sauce
1 can black beans, drained
1 small can corn, undrained
½ can black olives, drained and slice

1 small can chopped green chilies, undrained
2 tablespoons chili powder
2 teaspoons ground cumin
1 teaspoon oregano
2 cups shredded cheese, cheddar or Mexican mix
12 6-inch corn tortillas

Preparation

PREHEAT the oven to 350 degrees.

IN A large skillet, brown the ground game meat in the canola oil over medium-high heat. Remove and set aside. Turn the heat to medium, and sauté the onion and green pepper until the onion is translucent. Return the browned meat to the skillet and add all the ingredients except the cheese and the tortillas. Stir well to combine. Bring to a boil, lower the heat and simmer the mixture for about 10 minutes.

LIGHTLY coat the bottom and sides of a 9 x 11 baking dish with oil. Place 6 of the corn tortillas on the bottom of the pan, overlapping if necessary. Spread half of the meat mixture over the tortillas and sprinkle with half of the cheese. Layer the other 6 tortillas in the same manner, and cover them with the rest of the meat mixture and then the rest of the cheese. Place in the 350-degree oven and bake for 30 minutes. Remove the dish and let cool for a few minutes.

SERVE with sides of salsa, sour cream, and chopped green onions.

Serves 8

***Wine Suggestions: Gnarly Head Zinfandel
or Nine Walks Sauvignon Blanc***

WILD GAME BURGERS

This can be made with any big game meat. We butcher our own big game and have found that our meat stays tastier if we don't grind up a whole bunch of burger and then freeze it. After cutting out our roasts, steaks, and chops, we freeze the tougher cuts and the scraps in packages of 1 to 1¼ pounds. We label these packages "Stew/Burger Meat" so that we can have the option of turning the meat into stews, burgers, or soups as the year goes by. You can have your wild game butcher do the same thing, but if you already have ground meat, you can still add the ingredients to make a very tasty burger. Just eliminate the bacon, since the butcher already added fat to your ground meat.

Ingredients

1-1¼ pound wild game meat, still partially frozen	½ teaspoon dried basil
4 strips of bacon, cut in pieces	¼ teaspoon garlic powder
½ teaspoon dried oregano	¾ teaspoon seasoned salt
¼ teaspoon dried thyme	1 egg, lightly beaten
	½ onion, cut into medium-sized pieces

Preparation

COMBINE all the spices in a small bowl and then divide in half. Using a sharp knife while meat is still partially frozen, cut it into small chunks of about ½ to ¾ of an inch. Remove any tendons or silverskin at this time. Having the meat partially frozen makes it a lot easier to cut.

PLACE one half of the meat in a food processor with a chopping blade. Add one half of the bacon pieces and one half of the spices. Repeat the process with the other half of the ingredients. Cover and pulse the mixture 10 to 12 times. Add the beaten egg and pulse 5 to 6 more times. Add the onion chunks and pulse just enough to mix the onion in. If you pulse too much, the onion will turn to liquid and your meat will become tough.

REMOVE the mixture to a plate and form 4 burger patties. Since there is so little fat in game meat, the bacon and the egg are added to help bind the mixture.

OVER high heat, grill the burgers 3 to 4 minutes per side for medium rare burgers. If adding cheese, add the slices for the last 1½ minutes.

Serves 4

*Wine Suggestions: George Duboeuf Beaujolais-Village
or Handcraft Cabernet Sauvignon*

VENISON POT PIE

You can use any big game meat in this pot pie: venison, elk, antelope, moose, caribou, etc. Just as in the sharptail pot pie, the key to a game pie is not overcooking the meat. With much less fat than domestic meats, it will turn tough if cooked too long. So, the meat is seared quickly in the pan and then added back into the mixture just before popping it into the oven. You can save washing extra pans and skillets if you have a large braising pan that can go from stovetop to oven. I find this pan indispensable in cooking dishes like this.

Ingredients

2-3 pounds venison round steak, cut into
   ½-inch cubes
2 tablespoons butter
1 tablespoon olive oil
½ cup chopped onion
2 ribs celery, chopped
3 garlic cloves, minced
1 cup mushrooms, sliced thin
2-3 cups frozen vegetables, such as a mix
   of peas and carrots, thawed
¼ cup port wine
4-5 tablespoons flour

3 cups game or beef stock
1 teaspoon tarragon
½ teaspoon thyme
¼ teaspoon allspice
1 jar pearl onions
¼ cup chopped parsley leaves
½ cup half and half cream, or heavy
   cream if preferred
1 egg white
   pastry dough for large crust, rolled out
   to fit top of pan

Preparation

PREHEAT oven to 450 degrees.

HEAT a large braising pan or range-proof casserole dish over medium-high heat and add the butter and olive oil. Quickly brown the venison pieces and remove them to a covered dish. Turn the heat down to medium and add the onion, celery, and garlic to the pan, sautéing the mixture for 3 to 4 minutes. Add the mushrooms, and sauté another 2 minutes. Add the vegetables and turn the heat down to low and add the port, stirring to scrape up any brown bits. Sprinkle the flour evenly over the mixture in the skillet. Continue slowly stirring for about 2 minutes, while the flour browns slightly.

NOW slowly add the stock, stirring constantly. The mixture will start to thicken the stock as soon as it is added to the pan. Keep stirring to avoid forming any lumps. Now add the spices, pearl onions, and parsley, stirring to combine. Simmer a few more minutes, then remove from heat and stir in the cream. Return to heat and simmer until thickened. Return the venison cubes and any accumulated juices, stirring to combine. If the sauce is too thin, sprinkle a little more flour on top and stir in, letting the mixture simmer at least another minute. If too thick, add a little more stock or wine.

REMOVE the pan from the heat, and make sure that the sides of the pan are as clean as possible, so that the area above the crust doesn't end up with burned bits.

PLACE the pastry dough gently on top of the mixture. Brush the dough generously with the egg mixture, and pierce the dough in a circle just as you would a fruit pie, so that some steam can escape.

PLACE the pan in the oven at 450 degree for 15 minutes. Turn the heat down to 325 degrees, and continue cooking for another 10 minutes, or until the crust is browned. Remove from the oven and let it cook on a rack for about 15 minutes.

Serves 8
Wine Suggestions: Massimo Malbec or Josh Cellars Cabernet Sauvignon

©Brett Smith

VENISON MEATBALLS AND SPAGHETTI SAUCE

This recipe works well with any big game ground meat. You can adjust the taste and consistency in a couple of ways. If you find that the sauce is too thick for your tastes, you can thin it by adding a little more port or red wine, or by adding a little tomato sauce. If you like a sweeter spaghetti sauce, you can add a dash of brown sugar. The wine you use will also regulate the sweetness. Use port if you like it sweeter, or use a dry red wine if you don't like it as sweet.

I always make a big batch of this recipe, because it's so easy to freeze and then defrost for a great dinner on a busy day.

For the Meatballs

3 pounds ground venison, or other
  ground game meat
3 eggs
1 tablespoon oregano
2 teaspoons basil
½ teaspoon thyme

1 teaspoon garlic powder
½ teaspoon onion powder
½ teaspoon savory
  salt to taste
2 tablespoons olive oil

For the Sauce

1 large onion, chopped
4 garlic cloves, minced
1 pound fresh mushrooms, sliced
  olive oil
½ cup port wine or dry red wine,
  depending on your taste

3 29-ounce cans tomato purée
4 12-ounce cans tomato paste
1 15-ounce can diced tomatoes
2 tablespoons oregano
2 tablespoons basil
1 bell pepper, chopped (optional)

Preparation

PLACE the ingredients from the cans of tomato purée, tomato paste, and diced tomatoes into a large stockpot. Stir to combine and set aside.

BEAT the eggs in a large bowl. Add all of the spices for the meatballs and whisk to blend. Now add the ground meat, mixing thoroughly, but gently. If you mix too long, you will toughen the ground meat. (Or, that's what my mother always said!) Using your hands is probably the best way to mix this. Salt lightly if at all. There is plenty of salt in the tomato paste and purée.

TAKE a piece of this mixture that is about half the size of an egg and roll it into a ball. Place on a platter, and continue doing this with the rest of the ground meat.

HEAT a large skillet, preferably cast iron, over medium heat. Add a little olive oil, and brown the meatballs in the skillet, turning to brown all sides. This will take some time, and must be done in batches. Don't hurry the process. If the meatballs are nice and brown on all sides, they will hold together during the cooking process. You may need to add more olive oil as you go along, since ground game meat has so little fat. When each meatball is done, use a slotted spoon and transfer it to the large stockpot with the tomato mixture. Stir the mixture gently a couple of times during this process, in order to get the meatballs mixed evenly through the tomato mixture.

AS YOU get most of the meatballs into the sauce, turn the heat under the stockpot to medium-low.

ADD a little more olive oil to the skillet and sauté the onions and pepper (if using) over medium heat until they turn translucent, adding the garlic during the last few minutes. Do not brown this mixture. When translucent, transfer to the stockpot, and stir in gently. Add the mushrooms to the skillet and sauté them for a few minutes, adding a little wine if the skillet gets too dry. Transfer to the stockpot and gently stir to combine. Put the ½ cup of wine into the skillet and stir to scrape any browned bits loose. Transfer this mixture to the pot and stir. Now add oregano and basil, again stirring gently.

BRING the stockpot to a low boil. Turn the heat down to low and gently simmer, covered, for at least 2 hours. During this time, watch the pot to be sure that the bottom is not burning. Using a long-handled spoon, stir the mixture gently. If you feel a crust forming on the bottom of your pot, remove it from the heat and gently stir with the spoon or a spatula until the crust is removed. If you catch it early, it will not be a problem. If too much has burned on the bottom, remove the burned pieces as soon as you scrape them up. Otherwise, they will turn your sauce bitter. Return the pot to the stove, but lower the heat a little, and check more frequently.

AFTER about an hour and a half, taste the mixture to see if you need any more seasoning.

Serves 10 to 12

Wine Suggestions: Castello di Monastero Chianti Superiore
or
Handcraft Petite Sirah

WILD PEPPERS

Stuffed peppers seem to be a happy memory from our childhood for most of us. We've adapted that recipe to one that features wild game and wild rice. Instead of the tomato-based sauce, we use a brown gravy sauce. To speed the process up, we use a packet of gravy mix if we don't have any leftover gravy on hand. Don't add any salt to the recipe if you use the packet. Traditionally, stuffed peppers were made with green peppers, but with the variety of red, yellow, and orange peppers in our markets today, we enjoy using the latter for this recipe. It adds a colorful touch to the plate, and the red, yellow, and orange peppers seem to be a little sweeter than the green variety.

Just a tip on wild rice: It takes some time to cook wild rice, and I hate to add the extra time to making this dish. Instead of cooking it just for this dish, I cook extra rice when I need it for a dinner. Then I freeze the extra wild rice in 1-cup amounts in ziplock bags. It seems to hold its taste well when frozen, it defrosts quickly, and then you have it on hand for recipes such as this, as well as to add to soups.

Ingredients

4 large bell peppers, tops cut off and seeds removed	½ teaspoon thyme
1 pound ground game meat	½ teaspoon rosemary, crushed
½ pound ground pork sausage	1 can beef consommé
2 tablespoon butter	1½ cups water
1 samll onions, chopped	¼ cup Marsala wine
1 large garlic clove, minced	2 teaspoons arrowroot
¼ pound mushrooms, chopped	1 package Hunter's Sauce, or other brown gravy mix
1 cup cooked wild rice	

Preparation

PREHEAT oven to 350 degrees.

BLANCH the bell peppers in boiling water for 6 minutes. Remove them with tongs, run cold water over them, and place upside down to drain.

IN A large skillet, sauté the ground game meat and pork sausage in the 1 tablespoon of the butter over medium-high heat for about 3 minutes. Add the onion, garlic, and mushrooms, stirring to combine. Sauté for another 2 to 3 minutes. Add the wild rice, rosemary, and thyme, stirring to combine. Add a little of the consommé to this mixture, and keep warm.

IN A small saucepan, combine the Marsala wine, the water, and the rest of the consommé. Sprinkle the Hunter's sauce mix over the liquids, along with the arrowroot. Whisk the mixture until it is combined, with no lumps. Bring the mixture to a boil, turn down to a simmer, and simmer according to package directions, until it thickens.

LIGHTLY oil a small shallow baking pan. Put the peppers cut side up in the pan, and fill with the meat and rice mixture. Put a small dot of butter on top of the mixture in each pepper. Spoon some of the gravy over the peppers. Bake in a 350-degree oven for about 30 minutes.

BEFORE serving, reheat the gravy left in the saucepan. Pour the gravy around the base of the peppers, and serve.

Serves 4
Wine Suggestions: Noble Vines 337 Cabernet Sauvignon or
Yellow Tail Sweet Red Roo

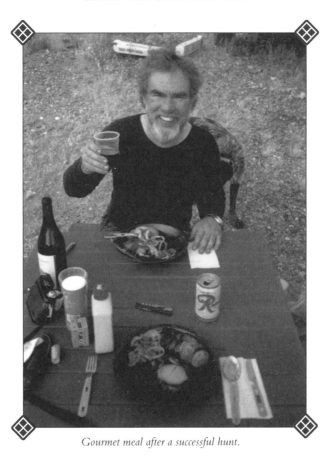

Gourmet meal after a successful hunt.

BIG GAME MEAT LOAF

This meat loaf can be made with any ground big game meat – deer, elk, antelope, even sheep. The meat loaf freezes well for a quick weeknight meal accompanied with homemade cognac mustard or a brown gravy (see section on sauces).

Ingredients

4 ounces bread, such as French, Italian, or sourdough
1 cup whole milk
olive oil
1 medium onion, finely chopped
¼ cup celery, finely chopped
¼ cup fresh mushrooms, finely chopped
¼ cup bell pepper, finely chopped
2 large garlic cloves, minced

½ cup sherry
2 eggs, beaten
1 tablespoon Worcestershire sauce
¼ cup green onions, finely chopped
½ cup Parmesan cheese, grated
1-2 teaspoons herb mix – combination of thyme, rosemary, & oregano
2 pounds ground venison
9-10 slices bacon (enough to cover top of meat loaf)

Preparation

HEAT oven to 350 degrees. Place bread slices in a pan in one layer and pour milk over them. Let them soak for 5 - 10 minutes, turning to be sure they soak evenly.

MEANWHILE, heat a small amount of oil in a large skillet and cook onion, celery, mushroom, bell pepper, and garlic over medium to medium-low heat. Stir frequently to keep from burning until soft – about 7 minutes. Stir in sherry and continue cooking until most of the liquid has evaporated. Remove from skillet and place in a large bowl to cool.

GENTLY squeeze the milk out of the bread so it is still wet, but not dripping. Chop the bread finely and add to the cooled vegetables. Add beaten eggs, Worcestershire sauce, and salt & pepper to the bowl and mix to combine. Now add green onions, cheese, and herbs and mix again. With your hands, gently mix in the ground venison just until combined.

LINE a baking pan with parchment. Put the mixture on to the parchment and shape into a rectangular loaf. Place bacon strips crosswise over top of loaf and tuck ends underneath. Place pan on center rack of oven and bake for 45 to 55 minutes, or until the internal temperature of the loaf reaches 160°. If bacon is not done, place 6 inches under broiler and broil for about 3 minutes, or until bacon has crisped. Remove from oven and let rest for 10 minutes before cutting into slices.

Serves 6 – 8
Wine Suggestions: Ramón Bilbao Edición Limited Tempranillo
or Brazin Old Vine Zinfandel

WILD TURKEY POT PIE

Ingredients

1   16-ounce bag frozen peas and carrots, thawed
1½   cups pearl onions, frozen or canned
5-6 tablespoons butter
½   red onion, chopped fine
5-6 tablespoons flour
¼   cup brandy or cream sherry
1½   cups gamebird or chicken stock, more if needed
1   cup heavy cream or half-n-half

2-3 large brown mushrooms, chopped
1   small to medium Yukon gold potato, cut in small cubes
1   tablespoon dried tarragon
1½   pounds cooked wild turkey meat, cut into bite-size pieces
1   pie pastry for top
1   egg, beaten with a tablespoon of water

Preparation

HEAT oven to 400 degrees. If using frozen pearl onions, defrost in microwave or set out at room temp to thaw. If using canned pearl onions, rinse and drain and set aside.

MELT butter in skillet over medium heat. Add onion and sauté for about 5 minutes, until soft. Sprinkle flour over top and cook, stirring constantly for another 5 minutes. You may have to turn heat down to keep flour from browning. While constantly whisking, add brandy or sherry and, as soon as this thickens, add stock and continue to stir as it thickens. Stir in cream and add mushrooms, potato, and pearl onions. Cook over medium heat for about 5 minutes, stirring regularly. If mixture gets too thick, add a little more stock. Stir in tarragon and simmer for 1 minute. Adjust seasoning with salt and pepper.

PLACE turkey meat in an oven-proof casserole and add peas and carrots. Pour the onion and potato mixture over all and stir to combine. Bring to a simmer so all ingredients are heated through. Remove from heat and place pastry round over top of mixture, sealing pastry against sides of casserole. Brush pastry with egg wash and cut 4 vents in pastry.

PLACE in oven for 35 minutes, or until crust is browned. Remove from oven and let sit 5 minutes before serving.

Serves 6 to 8, depending on side dishes

Wine Suggestions: Domino Pinot Grigio
or
Girard Sauvignon Blanc

HONKER MEAT LOAF

The richness of goose meat is a perfect substitute for beef in meat loaf. It's a great way to introduce people to wild game – using a favorite comfort food. The leftover slices freeze nicely for a quick weeknight meal, or can be used in sandwiches.

Ingredients

1½ pounds ground goose breast
½ pound ground pork
½ pound pork sausage
 olive or canola oil
1 medium onion, chopped
2 large garlic cloves, minced
4 brown mushrooms, chopped
¼ cup green onions, chopped
¾ cup bell pepper, chopped
1 small jalapeno pepper, seeded and minced
¾ cup port

4 ounces French bread, chopped into 1-inch pieces
1 cup whole milk
2 large eggs, lightly beaten
1 tablespoon capers, chopped
½ cup Parmigiano reggiano, grated
¼ cup mix of chives and parsley, chopped
¾ teaspoon smoked paprika
½ teaspoon ground allspice
10 ounces bacon

Preparation

OVER medium heat, place a small amount of oil in a skillet and sauté onion, garlic, mushrooms, green onion, and peppers for 6 to 8 minutes. Add port and lower heat to medium-low. Simmer for 5 minutes. Put mixture in a large bowl to cool.

PLACE bread in a single layer in a 9-inch square pan and pour milk over all. Let soak for 4 or 5 minutes and turn bread over. Continue soaking bread for another 3 or 4 minutes. With your hands, squeeze the bread to eliminate milk so that bread isn't soggy. Tear bread into smaller pieces and add to bowl, stirring to break bread up into tiny pieces.

ADD the rest of the ingredients, except the meats, to the bowl and gently stir to combine. With your hands, gently stir in the goose and pork until thoroughly combined.

HEAT oven to 375 degrees. Line a 9-inch by 12-inch pan with parchment. Place the mixture on the parchment and shape it into a rectangular loaf. Cut bacon strips in half and lay over the loaf, tucking ends underneath.

BAKE in oven for 50 to 60 minutes, or until the internal temperature of the loaf reaches 160°. Turn oven to broil and place pan on top rack underneath broiler. Broil for a couple of minutes to crisp the bacon.

REMOVE loaf from oven and let rest for 10 minutes before slicing. Serve with a good honey or cognac mustard.

Serves 8

Wine Suggestions: Cosentino Cigar Zin
or
Noble Vines 181 Merlot

Duke retrieving a duck.

Duck Pot Pie

Although the recipe calls for just duck breasts, you can also use the meat from the legs of ducks. This recipe also works well for dark-meat upland birds like sharptailed grouse and sage grouse. See note on alternate method of cooking the pastry topping at end of recipe. This alternate method produces a crisper topping.

Ingredients

2-3 pounds duck breasts, meat removed from bones and cut into large bite-sized pieces
2 tablespoons butter, divided
1 tablespoon olive oil
2 stalks celery, chopped
½ onion, chopped
1 carrot, chopped
3-4 mushrooms, chopped
2 cloves garlic, minced
¼ cup brandy
3-4 tablespoons flour
3 cups stock

½ cup port
1 tablespoon sweet paprika
1 tablespoon turmeric
¼ teaspoon ground ginger
¼ teaspoon ground cloves
¼ teaspoon ground allspice
½ cup half & half or heavy cream
1½ cups pearl onions
1½ cups peas
2 cups cooked wild rice
pastry dough, enough to cover the skillet or Dutch oven
egg white

Preparation

HEAT oven to 400 degrees. In a skillet or Dutch oven, melt the olive oil and 1 tablespoon of the butter over medium-high heat. Try to dry the duck chunks as much as possible before searing. The drier they are, the better. Working in batches, so you don't crowd the meat, sear the duck chunks for about 2 minutes, turning as needed to brown all sides. Remove to a dish and add the next batch. When finished, do not put meat in oven – just set aside.

LOWER heat to medium and melt remaining butter in skillet. Add celery, onion, carrot, and mushrooms and sauté until onion is translucent – about 5 to 10 minutes. Stir in garlic and sauté 1 more minute. Stir in brandy and deglaze the pan.

SPRINKLE flour evenly over mixture and stir for about 2 minutes, letting flour brown slightly. The darker the flour, the richer the taste, but do not let it burn or the taste will turn bitter. Now slowly add stock and then port, stirring constantly to keep the flour from clumping. The mixture will start to thicken.

STIR in the spices and gently simmer for a few more minutes. Remove from heat and stir in the cream. Return to heat and simmer until the desired thickness is achieved. Add pearl onions, wild rice, and peas and heat through. Now return the duck meat and all juices to the mixture and combine.

REMOVE from heat and place pastry dough over mixture. Brush the egg white on the top of the pastry with a pastry brush. Place in 400-degree oven for about 15 minutes, or until pastry has browned.

Alternate Pastry Method

WHILE the sauce is thickening, place the pastry round on a cookie sheet that has been lined with parchment. Pre-cook the pastry in the 400-degree oven for about 5 minutes. This helps the pastry to cook completely through, so the sauce doesn't make the bottom of the pastry too doughy. Then place the pre-cooked pastry top on the skillet or Dutch oven and return to oven for about 10 minutes more.

Serves 8 – 10

Wine Suggestions: Massimo Rioja
or
Windsor Sonoma Russian River Chardonnay

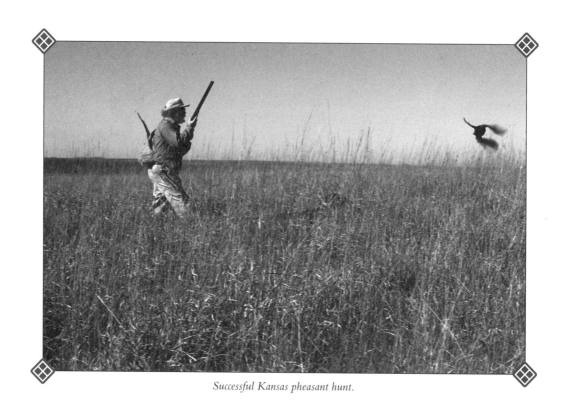

Successful Kansas pheasant hunt.

Soups & Stews

ANTELOPE CARBONADE

Of Flemish origin, a carbonade usually refers to a meat dish that is cooked in beer and onions. Beer is a nice alternative to wine in wild game recipes, especially dark beer. When choosing a dark beer for this recipe, avoid porters and stouts.

Ingredients

4 pounds antelope meat, cut in 1-inch cubes
2 tablespoons olive oil
1 large onion, chopped
2 green peppers, chopped
2 cloves garlic, minced
¼ cup brandy
4 plum tomatoes, chopped
2 bay leaves
½ teaspoon oregano
½ teaspoon allspice
1 12-ounce bottle of dark beer
1 14-ounce can beef broth
1 11-ounce can beef consommé
2 large yams, peeled and cubed
2–3 white potatoes, peeled and cubed
1 29-ounce can peach halves, drained and cut into large cubes

Preparation

BROWN the antelope cubes in the olive oil in a large stockpot over medium-high heat. Take your time, working in batches. As the meat is browned, remove it to a bowl. Turn the heat down to medium, and sauté the onions, peppers, and garlic until the onions are translucent. Pour in the brandy, and scrape the bottom of the pot to loosen any browned bits.

ADD the tomatoes, spices, beer, broth, consommé, and meat, stirring to combine. Bring the mixture to a boil, reduce the heat, cover, and simmer for 40 minutes. Add the cubed yams and potatoes, stirring to combine. Return the mixture to a boil, reduce the heat, cover, and simmer for 20 minutes. Now add the peaches, following the same process and simmer for an additional 15 minutes.

DURING these last 15 minutes, preheat the oven to 375 degrees. When the peaches have simmered for 15 minutes, put the covered stockpot into the oven for another 30 minutes.

REMOVE the stockpot from the oven and let it cool for about an hour. If you want the liquid to be thicker, spoon some of the potatoes into a blender and purée them. Add these back to the carbonade, and stir to combine.

LIKE most stews, the flavor improves as the carbonade sits. You can serve this over pasta, noodles, or my favorite – spaghetti squash tossed with a little butter, cinnamon, and allspice.

Serves 12 – 14
Wine Suggestions: Llai Llai Pinot Noir
or
Noble Vines 181 Merlot

Black Bean Soup with Venison Sausage

When we have some of our big game meat made into sausage, we like to make a big pot of this soup so that we have it in the freezer for quick lunches or light dinners. There's something special about putting up your own game soup. Now we use a freezer, but I often think of my grandparents from Minnesota who used to can all their vegetables in the late summer and early fall. It was a comforting feeling to know that you were stocked up for the long winter ahead.

This makes a very large pot of soup. If you're not feeling that ambitious, you can cut the ingredients in half and still come out right.

Ingredients

2 pounds black beans, soaked overnight in cold water
2 cans beef broth
2 cans beef consommé
2 cups red wine
5 quarts water
6-8 strips bacon, chopped
4 stalks celery, chopped
2 yellow onions, chopped
2 red onions, chopped
4 tablespoons flour

4 smoked ham hocks
½ bunch fresh parsley, chopped
4 bay leaves
1 tablespoon ground chipotle pepper,
1 teaspoon ground cumin
4 garlic cloves
4 carrots, chopped
4 small parsnips, chopped
6-8 venison sausages, halved lengthwise and sliced
Madeira wine, to finish
sour cream, to finish

Preparation

DRAIN and rinse the beans after soaking overnight. Put them in a large stockpot, cover with the beef broth, consommé, red wine, and water. Bring the mixture to a boil, reduce heat, cover, and simmer for about 1 hour.

WHEN the beans have simmered for about 40 minutes, put the bacon in a large skillet and fry until the pieces are crisp. Pour off excess fat, leaving about a tablespoon or two of bacon fat in the skillet. Add the celery and onions, sautéing them over medium heat until the onions are translucent. Remove the skillet from the heat and stir in the flour, then return to medium heat and continue cooking for about a minute, stirring constantly.

SCRAPE all the contents of the skillet into the bean mixture. Add all the rest of the ingredients, except the sausage, stirring to combine. Bring to a boil, reduce heat, cover and simmer very gently for 3 hours, adding water if the mixture gets too thick. Add the sausage during the last hour.

Black Bean Soup with Venison Sausage
CONTINUED

REMOVE the stockpot from the heat and let it cool down a little. Carefully remove the ham hocks, letting them cool enough so that you can cut out the meat. Before you add the ham back to the pot, if you want a thicker soup, you can scoop out some of the soup mixture (avoiding the sausage pieces) and purée in a blender. Now add the ham back into the stockpot and reheat.

SERVE in a soup bowl. Just before serving, swirl in a tablespoon of Madeira, and top the soup with a dollop of sour cream.

Serves 20 to 24

Wine Suggestions: Brazin Old Vine Zinfandel or Patch Block Pinot Noir

Goose and Sausage Gumbo

Making gumbo might seem to be an intimidating thing to the amateur cook. Although it takes patience, it is really no more difficult than most recipes, once you understand how a roux is made. The roux is the secret to a gumbo. It is really only a combination of some sort of fat (bacon fat, lard, shortening, olive oil, canola oil, etc.) and flour. However, the key is the patience to keep stirring and to watch as the flour browns. The darker the color of the flour, the richer the flavor of the gumbo as the nutty flavor of the wheat comes forward. But, if you let it burn, you have to throw out the entire batch and start again!

Besides the roux, the other thickening agents that are used are okra and filé gumbo. Okra is not included in this recipe, but could easily be added. If you use filé gumbo, be sure to add it at the last few minutes of cooking. If it is added in the beginning, the simmering process will break it down and make it bitter. Many Southerners simply serve the filé w gumbo at the table and let their guests use it according to their individual tastes.

You can use commercial chicken stock for this recipe, but since you will be using all the meat from a goose carcass, you might make the homemade stock the day before. Just put the goose bones and any scraps into a large pot, cover it with water, and add a couple of celery stalks, a carrot or two, and a half of a large onion. Simmer this for two or three hours, strain, and use this stock.

This recipe is also great for ducks. Just substitute 4 to 5 mallard ducks for the goose.

Ingredients

- 1 large goose, meat cut from the bones and into bite-size chunks
- 6 strips bacon, chopped
- ¾ cup fat, comprised of the bacon fat and olive or canola oil
- 1 cup flour
  olive or canola oil
- 2 cups chopped onions
- 3 stalks celery, chopped
- 3 carrots, chopped
- 2 large garlic cloves, minced

- 1 green or red bell pepper, chopped
- ¼ cup parsley leaves, chopped
- 2 quarts chicken or game bird stock
- ¼ cup port wine
- 2 bay leaves
- ¼ teaspoon thyme
- 2 teaspoons Creole Seasoning
- 1 pound Andouille sausage, chopped into small pieces
- 1 teaspoon filé gumbo

Preparation

FRY the bacon in a large stockpot until crisp. Remove with a slotted spoon and drain on a paper towel. Carefully pour the bacon fat into a glass measuring cup. Add olive or canola oil to make a total of ¾ cup of fat. Return to the stockpot and reheat the fat for about 2 minutes on medium-high heat. Start sprinkling the flour over the fat, whisking constantly until all the flour is mixed in with the fat. Continue stirring with a whisk or long-handled spoon as the flour starts to brown. This will take about 15 minutes, so be patient. You need to watch this step closely. It will start to smell as if it is burning; but unless the flour starts to show black specks don't worry. When the flour turns a rich caramel brown, you are getting close. If you're nervous about your first try at a roux, you can stop here and still have an absolutely delicious dish. If you let it brown just a little longer, it will be even better.

AS SOON as the roux reaches the deep brown color, add all the vegetables at once and stir to combine. This will stop the cooking process of the flour so that it won't burn. Now add the stock and the port, whisking to combine, and then add the seasonings, the sausage, and the fried bacon pieces. Do not add the filé gumbo at this point.

BRING the mixture back to a boil, reduce the heat, cover, and simmer for about 1 hour. Add the goose meat, cover and simmer for about 15 to 20 minutes. Remove the bay leaves and sprinkle the filé gumbo over the mixture and stir to combine. Keep warm until ready to serve.

GUMBO is traditionally served over a bowl half filled with white rice, but we often use wild rice.

Serves 10 to 12

Wine Suggestions: Ramón Bilbao Valiñas Albariño
or
Foghead Pinot Noir

ELK BLACK BEAN SOUP WITH CREOLE SEASONING

Because we butcher our own big game, we have the luxury of using the bones to add extra flavor to soups and stews. If your wild game butcher will not process the bones for you, you can use beef bones as a substitute. You can also make this soup without the bones; just increase the amount of elk meat a little. Of course, any soup is better if it is simmered with bones.

Ingredients

1 pound dry black beans
7 cups, or 4 14-ounce cans beef broth
3 pounds elk neck, joint, or shank bones, cracked
6 strips bacon, cut in small pieces
2 leeks, split in half, rinsed, and chopped
2 large onions, chopped
2 carrots, chopped
2 parsnips, chopped
2 cloves garlic, minced
½ cup parsley, chopped

1-2 tablespoons canola oil
1½ pounds elk stew meat, cut in small pieces
black pepper
4 tablespoons flour
½ cup sherry
2 ham smoked ham hocks
1 bay leaf
1 tablespoon Creole Seasoning (recipe follows)
1 can black beans, drained (optional – for thickening agent)

Preparation

THE night before, rinse the black beans and put in a large pot or Dutch oven. Pour cold water over the beans so that there is at least 2 inches of water over the top of the beans. Cover, and let soak overnight.

WHEN ready to make the soup, drain the beans and put them in a large stockpot with the beef broth and the water. Simmer, covered for 1 hour.

PREHEAT the oven to 400 degrees. Place the elk or beef bones in a shallow roasting pan and roast them in the oven until they are browned and crusty on the edges. Add a little sherry to the pan to keep the drippings from burning. When done, put the bones in the stockpot and add the sherry to the pan, scraping to loosen any browned bits.

IN A large skillet, fry the bacon pieces until crisp. Remove with a slotted spoon and dry on a paper towel. Drain off all but about 2 tablespoons of the fat. Sauté the vegetables in the fat until the onion is translucent, adding the garlic for the last minute or so. Add the vegetables to the stockpot. Put the canola oil in the skillet and brown the elk meat over medium high heat, stirring occasionally. When brown, grind some black pepper over the meat and sprinkle it with the flour. Add this to the stockpot. Pour a little sherry into the skillet and stir to loosen the browned bits, adding to the stockpot.

NOW add the smoked ham hocks, the bay leaf and the Creole seasoning to the pot and stir with a long-handled spoon to combine. Cover and bring to a boil. Reduce heat and simmer slowly for about 4 hours, checking occasionally to be sure nothing is sticking to the bottom of the pot.

REMOVE the elk bones and ham hocks from the soup, and let cool. Cut any meat from the bones and chop into small pieces. Add back to the soup. If the soup is too thin, continue simmering without covering until the liquid is reduced. If you wish to keep the volume, but want to thicken the soup, purée the can of black beans, and add this to the soup. Cover and simmer for another half hour.

SERVE in individual soup bowls with a splash of sherry and a dollop of sour cream.

Serves 10 to 12

Wine Suggestions: Gnarly Head Zinfandel or Hob Nob Pinot Noir

For Creole Seasoning

4 tablespoons ground pepper, preferably tricolor	1 tablespoon onion powder
1 tablespoon sugar	1 teaspoon ground celery seed
1 teaspoon salt	2 teaspoons oregano
1 tablespoon paprika	1 teaspoon thyme
1 tablespoon garlic powder	1 teaspoon red cayenne pepper
	½ teaspoon nutmeg

THIS makes about 1 cup of seasoning. Keep in a jar with a tight-fitting lid. It's great for seasoning steaks, as well as using in soups and stews.

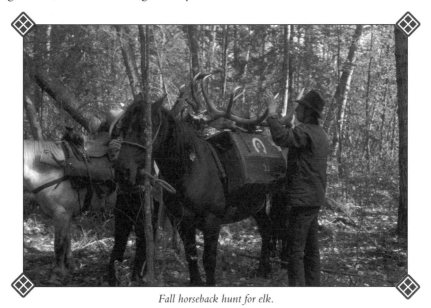

Fall horseback hunt for elk.

ELK STEW

A big, hearty game stew served over buttered noodles is the perfect touch on a cold winter night. There is something deeply fulfilling to those who hunt to know that their efforts in the field can create such a soul-satisfying dish. Stews freeze so well, that we always make a big pot just so we can have leftovers for a quick, easy dinner, especially if we have spent the day in the field. Every stew I make seems to be a little different than the one before. It all depends on what I have handy in the kitchen as far as vegetables. Don't feel you need to follow this recipe exactly. Be creative. You can always thicken the stew with a little more flour, or thin it with a little more wine, water, or broth.

Ingredients

6 strips of bacon, cut in small pieces	2 jars pearl onions, drained
3 pounds elk meat, cut in cubes	2 cans beef consommé
⅔ cup flour, seasoned with	1½ cups water
1 teaspoon onion powder	1 cup red wine
½ teaspoon garlic powder	1 cup port wine
1 tablespoon paprika	1 teaspoon tarragon
1 tablespoon seasoned salt	½ teaspoon thyme
¼ teaspoon allspice	15 mushrooms, chopped
butter or olive oil	1 large portobello mushroom, chopped
1 large onion, chopped	2 tablespoons butter
4 stalks celery, chopped	salt and pepper
4 carrots, chopped	2 tablespoons brandy
2 leeks, split in half, rinsed and sliced thin	2 tablespoons tomato paste
4 garlic cloves, minced	2 tablespoons flour

Preparation

IN A large skillet, fry the bacon pieces until crisp. Remove with a slotted spoon and drain on a paper towel. Pour off the bacon fat, reserving 2 tablespoons in the skillet. Dredge the elk cubes in the seasoned flour and, working in batches, slowly brown the cubes in the bacon fat over medium heat. Do not hurry the process. Make sure each cube has room in the skillet. When browned, transfer to a large stockpot or Dutch oven.

ADD the onion, celery, carrots, and leeks to the skillet and sauté until the onion is translucent. Add more oil or butter if necessary. Add the garlic for the last minute. Transfer to the stockpot. Add the pearl onions to the skillet and pour a little of the wine in to deglaze the pan. Add this to the stockpot. Now add the consommé, water, the 2 wines, and the herbs to the pot and stir to combine. Bring to a boil, lower the heat, and simmer the mixture, covered for about 3 hours, or until the meat is very tender. Check the pot every 20 minutes or so, to be sure that the bottom of the pot is not burning. Be sure to stir well with a long-handled spoon. If it starts to thicken on the bottom, scrape free and lower the heat a little.

ABOUT a half hour before the stew is done, sauté the mushrooms in the skillet over medium heat with the butter for about 5 minutes. Add the 2 tablespoons brandy, the tomato paste, and salt and pepper. Stir to combine. Sprinkle the flour over the mushrooms, and stir, adding a little broth or wine if the mixture gets too dry. Add this mixture to the pot for the last 20 minutes or so, stirring to mix it thoroughly throughout the stew.

WHEN the meat is tender, remove the pot from the heat, stir one more time and keep covered until ready to serve. As it sits, the flavors will continue to improve.

SERVE with buttered noodles sprinkled with parsley.

Serves 12 to 15

Wine Suggestions: Girard Artistry or Irony Chardonnay

SMOKED GOOSE AND DUCK GUMBO WITH SAUSAGE

Smoked meats add another layer of flavor in a gumbo, and smoked wild game is exceptional. For the sausage, you can use Andouille sausage, but we've also enjoyed this dish with smoked venison sausage made from our own big game harvests. Be sure to have all your vegetables cut up before you start the roux. Adding all the vegetables at one time will halt the browning of the flour so that it doesn't burn. You can use the duck and goose carcasses to make a quick stock, or you can use either chicken or beef broth, depending on your tastes.

Ingredients

8 strips bacon, chopped	1 red bell pepper, chopped
1 smoked large goose	1 green bell pepper, chopped
2 smoked mallard ducks	2 cans chopped okra
1¾ cup flour	6 cups chicken or beef broth
olive or canola oil	1 cup port wine
2 large onions, chopped	2 pounds sausage, sliced thin
5 stalks celery, chopped	¼ cup parsley leaves, finely diced
3 carrots, chopped	4 bay leaves
4 garlic cloves, minced	3 teaspoons Creole Seasoning

Preparation

REMOVE the meat from the smoked birds and chop into bite-size pieces. Set aside.

FRY the bacon in a large stockpot or Dutch oven until crisp. Turn off the heat and remove with a slotted spoon and drain on a paper towel. Carefully pour the bacon fat into a glass measuring cup. Add your choice of olive or canola oil to the cup to make a total of 1½ cups fat. Pour back into the stockpot and heat over medium-high heat for 2 minutes. Turn the heat

SMOKED GOOSE AND DUCK GUMBO WITH SAUSAGE
CONTINUED

down to medium. Whisk some of the flour into the oil and continue this until all the flour is combined with the oil. Continue stirring the mixture with the whisk or a long-handled spoon with a flat edge. Keep scraping the bottom of the pot to keep the flour from burning. It takes about 15 minutes of constant stirring to get the flour browned to the right color. You will smell the nutty flavor of the wheat coming out as it starts to brown. Do not stop stirring, or the flour will blacken and you will have to start over.

WHEN the flour is a rich deep brown, add all the fresh vegetables at once, stirring to combine. Heat for about 2 minutes, then add the okra and stir for a couple more minutes. Add the stock and wine, stirring to keep the mixture smooth. Finally, add the sausage, bacon, parsley, and seasonings. Bring the mixture back to a boil, cover, and simmer for about 1 hour. Add the smoked goose and duck pieces, cover, and simmer for another 20 minutes.

IF YOU have time, cool the gumbo overnight in the refrigerator. The next day, scrape off the fat and reheat the mixture.

WHITE rice is the traditional starch to serve with the gumbo, but wild rice is also delicious. Fill a bowl about one-third full of rice, pour the gumbo on top, and sprinkle some fresh parsley and chopped green onions on top.

Serves 18 to 20

Wine Suggestions: Massimo Rioja or The Crossings Sauvignon Blanc

Duke retrieving greater Canada goose.

Soups & Stews

224

SHARPTAIL CHILI BLANCO

This is a white chili made with white northern beans instead of the usual pinto beans. It has a totally different flavor than regular chili, and would work with any game bird, including waterfowl. Since you purée half of the beans to thicken the chili, you can add a can or two of great northern beans if you like to have more whole beans in the chili.

Ingredients

1 pound dry white northern beans
3 sharptails, meat removed and cut in small chunks
7 cups chicken broth
1 large white onion, chopped
4 cloves garlic, minced
1 tablespoon oregano
1 tablespoon ground cumin
½ teaspoon ground cloves

1 teaspoon ground coriander
1 teaspoon Creole seasoning, such as Emeril's
2 small cans chopped green chilies
1 jalapeno pepper, cored, seeded, and minced
1 tablespoon chili powder
1 can white northern beans, drained (optional)

Preparation

THE night before, rinse the beans and place in a large pot. Cover the beans with water so that the water is at least 2 inches over the beans. Cover, and let them soak overnight.

WHEN ready to start cooking, drain the beans and put them back into the pot. Add 5 cups of the chicken broth along with the onion, garlic, oregano, cumin, cloves, coriander, and Creole seasoning. Stir to combine. Bring the mixture to a boil, reduce heat, cover, and simmer for 4 hours. Stir the beans frequently, to be sure that they don't stick to the bottom of the pot.

LET the mixture cool for a little bit. Being careful with the hot mixture, purée one half of it in a blender or food processor and return it to the pot. Add the chilies, jalapeno, chili powder, and 2 cups of chicken broth. At this time, you can add the canned beans if you want more whole beans.

BRING mixture to a boil, reduce heat, and simmer for 30 minutes. Now add the sharptail, and simmer for another 20 to 30 minutes.

SERVE in bowls, with or without white or wild rice. Any of the following garnishes can be served in small bowls: chopped green onions, shredded cheese, sour cream, salsa, chopped tomatoes, and sliced black olives.

Serves 14 to 16

Wine Suggestions: Sauvion Sancerre or Irony Chardonnay

SPLIT PEA AND GAME BIRD SOUP

This recipe is a great one to use when you have leftover meat from any kind of game birds, including smoked birds. It makes a hearty hot soup for lunch, or a satisfying dinner with a green salad and dinner rolls.

Ingredients

4 slices bacon, chopped	¼ teaspoon thyme
1 tablespoon olive oil	¼ teaspoon savory
1 medium onion, chopped fine	1 tablespoon Dijon mustard
2 large carrots, chopped fine	1 tablespoon tomato paste
2 shallots, chopped fine	7 cups chicken broth
4 cloves garlic, minced	1½ cups Andouille sausage, sliced
2 stalks celery, chopped fine	1 pound split peas
¼ cup brandy	¼ cup Madeira
1 bay leaf	1½ cups cooked game bird meat, chopped
¼ teaspoon marjoram	½ cup small pasta, such as orzo

Preparation

FRY the bacon pieces in a large pot until crisp. Remove with a slotted spoon and drain on a paper towel. Drain off all the bacon fat except 1 tablespoon. Add 1 tablespoon of olive oil to the pot and sauté the vegetables and garlic until the onion is translucent. Add the brandy to deglaze the pan. Now add the herbs, Dijon mustard, tomato paste, chicken broth, sausage, and split peas, stirring to combine. Bring the mixture to a boil, reduce the heat, cover, and simmer for 45 to 50 minutes.

ADD the game bird meat, the Madeira, and the pasta, stirring to combine. Bring back to a boil, and simmer for another 15 minutes. If the soup is too thick, add a little more chicken broth or Madeira.

Serves 12 to 15

Wine Suggestions: Noble Vines 446 Chardonnay
or
Mar de Frades Albariño

VENISON BLACK BEAN SOUP

When we butcher our big game, we save all those small scraps of meat that are trimmed off the roasts and steaks. We freeze these along with the other cuts of stew meat, so that we can use them for either burger meat or stew meat. These also work great in soups, where the long cooking time breaks down the fibers and renders the meat tender.

Ingredients

1½ pounds venison stew meat, cut in very
    small pieces
3   tablespoons butter
2   cups dried black beans
8   cups cold water
3   medium to large onions, chopped
2   cloves garlic, minced
1   carrot, chopped

2   stalks celery, chopped
3   tablespoons fresh parsley, chopped
1   smoked ham hock
2   bay leaves
5   cups game stock or beef broth
    optional: sherry or Madeira
    sour cream

Preparation

RINSE the black beans and put in a large pot with the water. Bring to a rapid boil, cook 2 minutes, and turn off the heat. Cover the pot and let it stand for 1 hour. Drain and rinse the beans and set aside.

IN A stockpot, brown the venison pieces in the butter over medium-high heat in batches. Take your time to be sure each piece is browned completely. Add the onion, garlic, carrot, and celery to the pot and sauté until the onion is translucent. Stir occasionally to be sure that the garlic does not brown. This takes about 5 to 7 minutes. Add the parsley, ham hock, the bay leaves, and the black beans. Pour the stock or beef broth over all, and stir to combine and to loosen any brown bits stuck to the bottom of the pot.

BRING the mixture to a boil, reduce the heat, and simmer, covered, for at least 2 hours. Check the soup and stir it occasionally to make sure that the black beans do not stick to the bottom of the pot. After 2 hours, remove from heat and let cool slightly. Discard the bay leaves. Remove the ham hock, reserving any meat to be added back into the soup later. Being careful with the hot mixture, purée half of the soup in a blender and add back to the pot. This will thicken the soup naturally. Return any ham pieces to the soup.

AS with any soup or stew, the longer the soup sits, the more it blends and improves in flavor.

SERVE in a soup bowl, stirring in a drop of sherry or Madeira, and topping it with a dollop of sour cream.

Serves about 10
Wine Suggestions: Yellow Tail Shiraz-Grenache
or Handcraft Pinot Noir

Venison Stew with Cranberries

Fresh cranberries are available in most grocery stores from November through the height of winter, which is the best time to enjoy a hearty venison stew. You can use several different types of big game for the stew: deer, elk, or antelope. They all marry well with the ingredients. The tougher parts of your meat can be used, including the bottom round.

Ingredients

2 pounds venison stew meat or round steak, cubed
flour, seasoned with garlic powder, onion powder, salt and pepper
2 tablespoons olive oil
2 tablespoons butter
1 large onion, chopped
2 cloves garlic, minced
1½ cups beef broth or gamestock
1¼ cups tawny port

3 juniper berries, crushed
¼ teaspoon powdered ginger
½ teaspoon orange zest from fresh orange peel
2 cups fresh mushrooms, sliced
¼ cup brown sugar mixed with 2 tablespoons flour
2 tablespoons balsamic vinegar
1 12-ounce bag fresh cranberries

Preparation

HEAT Dutch oven to medium-high and add olive oil and butter. Dredge venison cubes in the seasoned flour. Working in batches so that you do not crowd them, brown the cubes in the oil and butter, removing to a plate until all are browned.

SAUTÉ the onion and garlic, adding a little port or beef broth to keep the pan bottom from burning.

ADD the rest of the port, and scrape up any crusted bits from the bottom. Return the browned venison to the pan, and add the rest of the broth, the juniper berries, ginger, and orange zest. Stir to combine and add the mushroom slices, again stirring. Cover and simmer for 1½ to 2 hours, or until tender.

ADD the brown sugar and flour mixture, the balsamic vinegar, and the cranberries, stirring to combine. Simmer another 20 minutes, until cranberries have popped open.

Serves 6 to 8

Wine Suggestions: Château de Cruziau
or
Noble Vines 446 Chardonnay

MULLIGATAWNY SOUP

There are a wide variety of mulligatawny soups made with an amazing amount of different ingredients, mostly based on Indian influences. They are usually curry-based, which is why I call this mulligatawny. If you are unfamiliar with curry, it is in itself a multi-based spice with infinite variations. It can be very hot or more on the sweet side. If you are not familiar with curry, start out with a smaller amount and add more until you are happy with the heat level.

Ingredients

- 2 pounds venison stew meat or round steak, cut in bite-size pieces
- 1 tablespoon vegetable oil
- 2 carrots, chopped
- 2 onions, chopped
- 1 turnip, chopped
- 1 bell pepper, chopped (or equivalent of various colors)
- ¼ cup brandy (optional)
- 2 tablespoons flour
- 2 tablespoons curry powder, or to taste

- 2½ quarts chicken broth, or more, based on how much final liquid you want
- 1 tablespoon tomato paste
- 4 tablespoons fresh parsley, chopped
- ½ teaspoon thyme
- 1 bay leaf
- 2 garlic cloves, minced
- 1 pound dried lentils, or half and half lentils and cooked barley
- 2 tablespoons lemon juice

Preparation

HEAT a non-stick skillet to medium-high and brown venison pieces in oil, in batches so they are not crowded. As they finish browning, place in soup pot. Add a little more oil into the skillet and add the vegetables, cooking over medium heat until onion is translucent. If using brandy, add to skillet to deglaze and continue cooking until liquid is almost evaporated. Combine the flour and curry powder and sprinkle over the vegetables, stirring to combine. Add 2 cups of the broth and continue stirring until mixture thickens. Pour all into the soup pot.

ADD to this mixture the tomato paste, parsley, thyme, bay leaf, and garlic, stirring to combine. Bring to a simmer, cover, and simmer slowly for 1½ hours. Add lentils and extra liquid if desired and simmer for 1 more hour, until lentils are tender. If using cooked barley, add just before lentils are tender, so barley can heat through.

BEFORE serving, add fresh lemon juice and simmer for 5 minutes.

Serves 10 to 12

Wine Suggestions: Ramón Bilbao Crianza
or
Loredona Riesling

BISON STEW WITH MUSHROOMS AND CRANBERRIES

Winter stews and cranberries are a great match, especially when cranberries are in abundance in the fall through the holidays. Just like blueberries, cranberries freeze very well, so I buy extra bags at holiday time and freeze them right in the bags for use all year.

Ingredients

3 pounds bison stew meat, cut in chunks
1 cup flour, seasoned with salt and freshly ground pepper
6 slices thick-cut bacon, chopped olive oil, as needed
2 large onions, rough chopped
3 large carrots, chopped
2 small parsnips, chopped
¼ cup brandy
8 brown mushrooms, sliced

1 cup beef broth or game stock
1 cup port
½ teaspoon marjoram
¼ teaspoons thyme
½ teaspoon rosemary
⅛ teaspoon nutmeg
1 2-inch cinnamon stick, broken in half
½ cup cranberry sauce
1 pound fresh or frozen cranberries

Preparation

HEAT oven to 300 degrees. In a deep skillet or Dutch oven, fry bacon until just crisp. Remove and drain. Pour off all but about 2 tablespoons of fat. Pat bison meat as dry as possible with paper towels. This helps to get a good seared crust on the meat. Place seasoned flour in a plastic bag, and working in batches, dredge meat in flour. Place in skillet and brown meat in batches, using a little olive oil if needed. Remove from skillet and set aside.

ADD a little oil and sauté onions, carrots, and parsnips until onions are just soft. Add brandy and scrape up crusted bits in pan. Cook until brandy has evaporated. Add mushroom, broth, port, seasonings, cranberry sauce, and cooked bacon, stirring to combine. Return bison and any accumulated juices to mixture and stir.

COVER with a tight-fitting lid and place in oven for 2 to 2-1/2 hours, or until meat is tender. Remove from oven and place over medium-low heat. Adjust for desired thickness by adding water or stock if too thick. If a thicker stew is desired, mix a little cornstarch or arrowroot with a little water and add to skillet, stirring to combine evenly. Add cranberries, stir, and cover. Simmer until berries start to pop – about 20 minutes.

Serves 8 to 10

Wine Suggestions: Brazin Lodi Zinfandel
or
Kunde Estate Reserve Century Vine Zinfandel

Goose Breast Stew with Beans and Kale

Too often wild goose meat is overcooked and loses its rich flavor. The secret is to cut the meat into small bite-sized pieces and add toward the end of the cooking time, leaving the meat still rare, but in a rich slow-cooked stew.

Ingredients

- 1 pound white beans, soaked overnight and drained
- 4 strips bacon, chopped fine
- 1 onion, chopped
- 1 carrot, chopped
- 2 stalks celery, chopped
- 1 small leek, white & light green part cut in half and sliced thin
- 4 garlic cloves, minced
- ¼ cup bourbon
- 4 cups beef broth
- 4 cups water
- 1 ham hock
- 2 sprigs fresh rosemary or 1 teaspoon dried
- 2 bay leaves
- 3 large Roma tomatoes, chopped
- 1 tablespoon Worcestershire sauce
- 2 pounds squash, cut in cubes
- 2 goose breast filets (1-1/2 to 2 pounds), cut into bite-sized pieces
- 2 tablespoons butter
- ½ bunch kale, washed and cut in strips

Preparation

BROWN bacon in Dutch oven or heavy soup pot until crisp. Remove and drain on paper towel. Discard all but 1 tablespoon bacon fat. Sauté onion, carrot, celery, and leek in fat for 4 - 5 minutes over medium heat, until onion is translucent. Add garlic and sauté 1 more minute. Add bourbon and continue cooking until liquid is almost evaporated. Add broth, water, beans, ham hock, spices, and tomatoes. Stir in Worcestershire sauce and bacon. Heat mixture on medium-low until it comes to a slow simmer. Cover and cook 1 hour and 15 minutes. Add squash and cook another 20 – 30 minutes, depending on the type and size of squash pieces. You don't want them to get too squishy.

WHILE squash is cooking, thoroughly pat goose pieces dry and season with salt and pepper. Melt butter in skillet over medium heat and, working in batches, sear the goose chunks for 2 - 3 minutes, stirring to cook evenly. Set aside.

REMOVE ham hock from stew and let cool. Cut meat from bone and return meat to stew. Before adding the goose to the stew, check the thickness. Add water or broth if too thick. If a thicker consistency is desired, put some of the beans, veggies, and liquid in a food processor, blend, and add back to stew. Add seared goose to mixture, along with chopped kale and cook about 5 minutes more.

Serves 6 to 8
Wine Suggestions: Sonoma Coast Vineyards Greestone Hills Pinot Noir
or
Handcraft Petite Sirah

WILD TURKEY BONE SOUP

While growing up, my mother always made turkey bone soup after the Thanksgiving and Christmas meals of roast turkey. I remember the rich and homey scent of that soup filling the house, as we waited for the soup to finish cooking. That pot stayed hot on the stove and warmed our stomachs with its rich essence for days after the holidays. This recipe is based on her original recipe, with a few additions of my own.

Ingredients

- 1 wild turkey carcass with any leftover meat attached
  leftover gravy and/or dressing (optional)
- 1 large can chicken stock (optional)
- 2 celery stalks, chopped
- 1 large onion, chopped

- 2 carrots, chopped
- 1 bay leaf
- 6 whole allspice, or 1/2 teaspoon ground allspice
  dash of nutmeg
- 1 cup brown mushrooms, chopped
- 2 cups cooked barley

Preparation

BREAK up the turkey carcass into pieces – wings, drumsticks, thighs, back, breastbone) and place in a large stockpot. Pour in some water and the chicken stock (if using). Add celery, onion, carrot, bay leaf, and allspice. Cover with water and bring to a slow simmer. Cover and simmer for 24 hours – adding more water to cover bones.

REMOVE from heat and taste. Add dash of nutmeg if desired, along with salt and pepper to taste. Let soup cool until the bones can be worked with. Discard the bay leaf. Remove bones from soup and pull any meat off and return to pot, discarding the bones.

PLACE pot over medium heat and return to a fast simmer to reduce until the desired flavor intensity is achieved – about a reduction of a quarter of the volume. Add mushrooms to soup and continue simmering until reduced another quarter. Cook barley according to directions and add to soup.

Serves 16 to 18

Wine Suggestions: Gnarly Head Chardonnay
or
The Crossings Sauvignon Blanc

Sharptail and White Bean Stew

This can be called either a stew or a soup, depending upon how thick you want it to be. If you prefer soups, just add more chicken broth. If you like a thicker stew, just mix some flour with a little chicken broth and add it to the mixture to thicken as it cooks.

Ingredients

- 2 sharptailed grouse
- 2 tablespoons peanut oil, divided
- 2 cups cooked ham, cut in ½-inch chunks
- 1 ham hock (optional)
- 1 large red onion, rough chopped
- 2 stalks celery, rough chopped
- 2 large carrots, rough chopped
- 1 medium jalapeno pepper, thinly sliced with seeds & membranes removed
- 1 green bell pepper, rough chopped
- 5 garlic cloves, minced
- ¼ cup brandy
- ½ cup very dry sherry or vermouth
- 1 15-ounce can diced tomatoes with liquid
- 4 cups chicken broth
- 5 tablespoons tomato paste
- 2 cups cooked white beans
- Madeira wine to finish

Preparation

REMOVE the sharptail meat from the bones and cut into 1/2-inch chunks. Set aside in refrigerator. Heat 1 tablespoon of the peanut oil in a soup pot over medium heat. Add ham cubes and sauté for 2 to 3 minutes. Add onion, celery, carrot, bell pepper, and jalapeno and sauté for 5 minutes, or until onion is translucent. Add garlic and cook 1 more minute. Add brandy, stirring to scrape up any browned bits, and cook until liquid is almost absorbed. Add ham hock if using. Add wine, tomatoes and liquid, and broth, stirring to combine.

BRING mixture to a low boil, lower heat, cover, and simmer slowly for 2-1/2 hours. Stir in tomato paste, stirring to combine, and cook a few more minutes as the liquid thickens. Adjust thickness of liquid to your taste by adding more broth or stirring in some flour mixed with broth. Add cooked white beans.

REMOVE sharptail from fridge and pat dry. Put remaining peanut oil in a skillet over medium-high heat and sear sharptail chunks for 1 minute per side. These need to be rare. Add to stew and heat through.

TO SERVE, ladle stew into bowls and add a dash of Madeira wine to the center of each bowl.

Serves 10

Wine Suggestions: Yellow Tail Cabernet Sauvignon-Merlot or Loredona Riesling

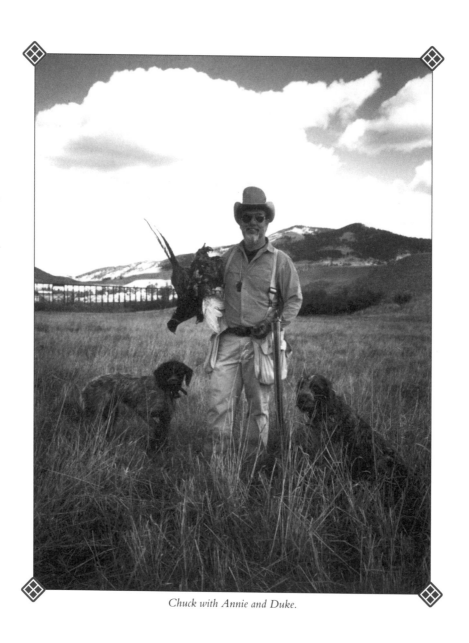

Chuck with Annie and Duke.

Sauces

Apple Delight

This apple dish works wonders with grilled game of all kinds. It is a natural with venison dishes, but goes equally well with Hungarian partridge and sharptailed grouse.

Ingredients

3 Granny Smith apples, sliced horizontally to 1½ inch thickness, core removed
3 tablespoons butter
½ cup brown sugar

3 tablespoons ginger schnappes
½ teaspoon cinnamon
¼ teaspoon nutmeg
red currant jelly for garnish

Preparation

MELT butter in large saucepan. Add the brown sugar, schnappes, cinnamon, and nutmeg. Stir to combine, and simmer for about 3 minutes. Add the fruit slices, spooning the sauce over them. Simmer for about 5 minutes until slices start to soften. Serve slices stacked with a dollop of red currant jelly in the center.

Blackberry Brandy Sauce

This sauce is a variation of the Port-Brandy Reduction that compliments grilled big game dishes. It works equally well with waterfowl and prairie grouse.

Ingredients

¾ cup cognac or brandy
½ cup tawny port
2 shallots, sliced thin
½ cup fresh or frozen blackberries

¾ cup game bird or chicken stock
3 tablespoons butter, cut in small chunks & chilled
½ cup fresh blackberries (optional)

Preparation

IN A small saucepan, combine the brandy, port, shallots, and blackberries. Simmer and reduce until the liquid is about ¼ cup. Add the stock and reduce until it thickens slightly. Strain the sauce into another small saucepan, pressing with the back of the spoon to release all the blackberry flavor. Discard the solids.

BRING the strained sauce back to a slow simmer. Slowly whisk in the butter chunks until they are combined with the sauce. If you wish, you may add ½ cup fresh blackberries at this time. Simmer gently for about 1 minute to heat through.

Serve 4

Brown Sauce

This takes a couple of hours, but it can be done at any time. The mixture can be refrigerated for several days, and it can also be frozen.

Ingredients

3½ cups beef bouillon
½ cup dry red wine
1 tablespoon tomato paste
¼ teaspoon thyme
1 bay leaf
4 tablespoons butter

½ cup finely chopped onion
1 small carrot, finely chopped
1 small stalk celery, finely chopped
¼ cup parsley leaves, finely chopped
3 tablespoons flour

Preparation

IN A medium saucepan, combine the bouillon and wine. Whisk in the tomato paste and add the thyme and bay leaf. Heat this mixture to just below a boil, and keep warm.

IN another saucepan, sauté the onion, carrot, and celery in the butter over medium-high heat until the onion is translucent. Turn the heat down to medium-low, and slowly add in the flour, blending with a whisk. Continue stirring while the flour starts to brown. When it has turned a nice rich brown, remove the pan from the heat and start adding the bouillon mixture, stirring constantly with a whisk, so that each addition does not clump the flour.

WHEN all the liquid is incorporated, cover the pan and simmer gently on very low heat for about 2 hours. If necessary, add a little more water or wine if it starts to get too thick.

Makes about 2½ cups

Blanche with Cody and Baron.

CHERRY/MARNIER SAUCE

This rich cherry sauce goes well with just about any game, especially when it has been grilled. It originally was made for waterfowl, but we have used it on grilled big game steaks, as well as roasted or grilled pheasant. Sometimes it's hard to find real dried cherries in the grocery stores, so when I do, I stock up on them since they can be stored for a long time.

Ingredients

½ cup orange juice	1½ cups game bird or chicken stock
1 cup dried Bing cherries	1 cinnamon stick, broken in half
4 tablespoons Grand Marnier, or Cherry Marnier	1 tablespoon balsamic vinegar
	1 tablespoon arrowroot
1 cup dry red wine	2-3 tablespoons butter, to taste, cut in
dash of tarragon	small chunks & chilled

Preparation

IN A medium saucepan, soak the cherries in the orange juice and 2 tablespoons of the Grand Marnier for at least 20 minutes. Add red wine, tarragon, stock, and cinnamon stick pieces. Bring to a boil and reduce by half. Turn heat down to a simmer. Remove the cinnamon sticks and add balsamic vinegar and the rest of the Grand Marnier. Simmer for 3 to 5 minutes.

PUT arrowroot into a small bowl and add some of the sauce to dissolve the arrowroot. Combine with the wine mixture to thicken. Turn down heat, and keep warm until your meat is about ready to serve.

WHEN you are just about ready to serve, increase the heat for the sauce. When it is just about at a simmer, slowly swirl in the butter in small chunks until you achieve the desired consistency. You do not have to use all the butter if you prefer a leaner sauce.

WHEN serving, drizzle a little of the sauce over the meat and serve the rest of the sauce on the side.

Serves 6

Coconut-Lime Sauce

The sweet-tart flavor of this sauce adds a new dimension to both upland birds and waterfowl. The amount of chili pepper in the recipe adds only a small amount of heat. Increase the heat to create a zestier sauce.

Ingredients

1 tablespoon finely chopped jalapeno pepper or dried Ancho chili pepper
4 garlic cloves, minced
2 tablespoons butter
¼ cup dark rum
1 cup game bird or chicken stock

½ cup coconut cream
2 tablespoons lime juice
zest of 1 lime
2 tablespoons fresh ginger, grated
1 cup of green grapes, halved

Preparation

IN A medium saucepan, sauté the peppers and garlic in the butter over medium heat for about 2 minutes. Add the rum, stock, coconut cream, lime juice, lime zest, and ginger. Stir to combine, and then bring back to a simmer. Reduce by half. Add the grapes, stir, and bring back to a simmer. Taste to adjust for sweetness. If too sweet, add a little more lime juice.

Serves 4

Ed Gerrity's Red Currant Sauce

Ed Gerrity was a friend and customer of ours for many years. He lived here in the Gallatin Valley, where he spent his spare time breeding an exceptional line of golden retrievers that were bred for hunting. Ed created this sauce for grilled waterfowl, but we found that it works just as well for grilled big game steaks. It's so handy, since it uses ingredients that are usually always on hand in the kitchen, and it takes only a few minutes to prepare.

Ingredients

4 tablespoons unsalted butter
1 10-ounce jar red currant jelly

¼ cup ketchup
¼ cup light brown sugar, packed

Preparation

OVER low heat, melt the butter in a saucepan. Stir in the jelly, ketchup, and brown sugar. Heat until the jelly melts and the mixture boils. Turn down heat and keep warm until ready to serve

CRANBERRY-ORANGE SAUCE

This sauce is perfect for Christmas dinner with a roasted wild turkey, but it works equally well with the dark meat of prairie grouse and waterfowl.

Ingredients

1	12-ounce package of fresh cranberries	¾ cup water
½	cup packed brown sugar	1 tablespoon orange peel zest
½	cup white sugar	¼ cup Grand Marnier

Preparation

IN A saucepan, combine all the ingredients except for the Grand Marnier. Bring to a boil and simmer for about 15 minutes, or until most of the cranberries have popped open. Remove from heat and stir in the Grand Marnier. Cool, and put in a serving bowl or mold in the refrigerator until chilled and ready to serve.

GINGER-RHUBARB SAUCE

We first tried this sauce on a grilled wild turkey breast. It was so delicious that we now use it on all types of upland birds and waterfowl. Since fresh rhubarb is usually plentiful in the fall, it's a great accompaniment to game dishes. If you want a little more zing, add more fresh ginger. This sauce makes a nice change from the traditional cranberry sauce.

Ingredients

2	cups rhubarb, chopped into small pieces	½ cup brown sugar
¼	cup orange juice	2 teaspoons fresh ginger, grated
		1 tablespoon rum (optional)

Preparation

IN A large saucepan, combine all of the ingredients and bring to a boil. Reduce heat to medium-low and simmer, stirring occasionally, until the rhubarb is tender. This should take about 15 to 20 minutes.

REMOVE from heat and let the mixture cool to room temperature. The sauce can be served at room temperature, or it can be chilled.

Serves 4

HUCKLEBERRY SAUCE

This is really a dessert sauce that is especially tasty if made with wild huckleberries, but can also be made with blueberries. It's great served over cheesecake, angel food cake, or ice cream. If you make the sauce a little on the tart side, it is also good served with smoked game birds.

Ingredients

2 cups huckleberries or blueberries
2 tablespoons cornstarch
⅓ cup water
⅓ cup Chambord, or blackberry brandy
½ cup packed brown sugar

2 teaspoons lemon juice
¼ teaspoon nutmeg
½ teaspoon cinnamon
3 pieces candied ginger, minced

Preparation

IN A medium saucepan, mix the cornstarch with the water. Add the rest of the ingredients except the berries. Cook on medium heat until the mixture starts to thicken. Add the berries and keep simmering until thickened, stirring frequently. Taste and adjust based on the sweetness level of the berries, adding a little more lemon juice if too sweet, or a little more brown sugar if too tart. If the berries tend to be too watery, you can add a little more cornstarch and heat to thicken.

MANGO–ORANGE MARMALADE SAUCE

Another great sauce for all grilled, smoked or roasted game birds. Substitute apricot marmalade for a slightly different taste.

Ingredients

½ cup orange marmalade
1 ripe mango, chopped with juices
½ cup game bird or chicken stock

1 tablespoon Dijon mustard
1 tablespoon soy sauce
2 tablespoons chopped chives

Preparation

COMBINE all ingredients in a small saucepan and simmer over low heat for 15 minutes. Keep warm until ready to serve.

MUSHROOM-RED PEPPER SAUCE

This is a versatile sauce that could be served on its own as an accompaniment to hearty game dishes, or it can be served over pasta. The heartiness of the sauce will vary depending on the type of mushrooms you use. We usually include at least one portobello mushroom in the mix. Shiitakes also add to the richness of the sauce. However, it can work equally well with just the ordinary fresh mushrooms in the grocery store. For the roasted red peppers, you can roast your own or use the roasted red peppers in jars. Just pat them dry before using them.

Ingredients

3 cups mushrooms, sliced
6 green onions, finely chopped with at least 2 to 3 inches of the green tops
1 garlic clove, minced
1 tablespoon butter
2 teaspoons basil
¾ teaspoon thyme

¼ teaspoon salt (do not add if using commercial stock)
¼ cup sherry
1 cup game bird or chicken stock
1 cup roasted red peppers, puréed
1 tablespoon brown sugar (optional)
2 tablespoons fresh parsley, chopped (optional)

Preparation

IN A large saucepan over medium heat, sauté the green onions and garlic in the butter for about 1 minute. Add the mushrooms and ¼ cup of the stock. Sauté until the mushrooms become limp. Add the basil, thyme, salt, sherry, and the rest of the stock. Simmer on medium-low for about 5 minutes, stirring occasionally. Add the puréed peppers and stir. Taste to adjust seasonings. If you prefer a little sweeter taste, add a little brown sugar at this time.

SIMMER for another 5 to 10 minutes, and then add the parsley, if desired.

SERVE over penne rigate or other large pasta.

Serves 4

MUSTARD DIP

This dip is delightful with any smoked game birds. It is also great with raw mushrooms as an hors d'oeuvres. It's easy to make, and will keep in the refrigerator for weeks.

Ingredients

1   8-ounce jar Dijon mustard
½   cup mayonnaise

1   tablespoon Worcestershire sauce
2   teaspoons horseradish

Preparation

BLEND together and refrigerate until ready to serve.

STRAWBERRY-SHALLOT SAUCE

We rejoice when those first fresh strawberries show up in the market in late spring. Besides reviving your morning cereal, they bring a totally new flavor to the game birds that we still have in our freezer. This sauce works wonders with pheasant, quail, chukar, and wild turkey. Of course, you can always use frozen strawberries during the winter, but just like summer vine-ripened tomatoes, the fresh spring strawberries are much more flavorful.

Ingredients

1   small shallot, chopped
1   tablespoon butter
½   cup game bird or chicken stock
6   ounces fresh strawberries, halved
2   teaspoons confectioner's sugar

2   teaspoons balsamic vinegar
½   teaspoon arrowroot
1   tablespoon Grand Marnier or
    Chambord

Preparation

IN A small saucepan over medium heat, sauté the shallot in butter until it is limp. Discard about half of the shallot pieces. In a blender, purée the strawberries and sugar. Add the purée and the stock to the saucepan, stirring to combine. Simmer until reduced by half. Turn the heat down, and add the balsamic vinegar and Grand Marnier or Chambord, stirring to combine. Taste to adjust for sweetness, adding a little sugar or balsamic vinegar to balance. Add the arrowroot and bring to a simmer until the mixture thickens slightly.

Serves 2

Plum Sauce

This rich and fruity sauce goes well with all dark meat game birds and waterfowl.

Ingredients

4 tablespoons butter
¼ cup packed brown sugar
¼ cup brandy (or to taste)

1¼ cups plum jam
     balsamic vinegar (optional)

Preparation

MELT the butter in a small saucepan. Add the sugar and 1 tablespoon of the brandy, and the plum jam, stirring to combine. Gradually add more of the brandy to your taste. As the mixture simmers slowly, the alcohol taste of the brandy will disappear.

IF YOU want a little tang to the sauce, or if you find it too sweet, add a little balsamic vinegar. Keep warm until ready to serve.

Port-Brandy Reduction

We developed this sauce for grilled buffalo steaks, but is also works well with any big game steaks. We also found it's great drizzled over fresh tuna steaks grilled rare. We like to add the green peppercorns to the sauce, as it adds another layer of flavor as well as some zing.

Ingredients

¾ cup cognac or brandy
½ cup tawny port
¾ cup game bird or chicken stock

3 tablespoons butter, cut in small chunks
     & chilled
3 teaspoons green peppercorns, drained
     (optional)

Preparation

IN A small saucepan, combine the brandy and the port. Simmer and reduce to about ¼ cup. Add the stock and reduce until it thickens slightly. Add the peppercorns, if desired. Then, slowly whisk in the butter and simmer gently for about 1 more minute.

Serves 4

PRAIRIE GROUSE SAUCE

This sauce can be used for any game birds, but we find it especially appealing when paired with the dark meat of sage grouse and sharptails.

Ingredients

½ cup game bird or chicken stock
⅓ cup orange marmalade
4 tablespoons honey
¼ cup Drambuie

3 tablespoons butter
1 tablespoon flour
raspberries (optional)

Preparation

PUT the stock, marmalade, honey, and Drambuie in a small saucepan. Heat on low until honey thins. Melt the butter in a glass container in the microwave, or in another small saucepan. Whisk the flour into the butter until it is thoroughly blended with no lumps.

SWIRL the butter/flour mixture into the sauce and blend with a whisk. Cook over medium-low heat until it thickens; about 2 to 3 minutes. Keep warm until ready to serve.

THE sauce is great just as it is, but if you have fresh raspberries available, swirl some into the sauce just before serving. Heat on low long enough to warm the raspberries but making sure they stay solid.

MUSTARD SAUCE FOR GRILLED OR ROASTED GAME

This sauce is great for big game dinners, but also works well with upland and waterfowl dishes.

Ingredients

8 tablespoons mayonnaise
3 tablespoons Dijon mustard
2 tablespoon honey mustard

½ teaspoon tarragon
2 tablespoons chopped parsley
2 teaspoons horseradish

Preparation

COMBINE all ingredients and chill for several hours to blend the flavors. Bring to room temperature just before serving. This can keep in the refrigerator for an extended time.

BOURBON-MUSHROOM GRAVY FOR ROAST VENISON

This is a versatile sauce that could be served on its own as an accompaniment to hearty game dishes, meat loaf, or it can be served over pasta. The heartiness of the sauce will vary depending on the type of mushrooms you use. We usually include at least one portobello mushroom in the mix. Shiitakes also add to the richness of the sauce. However, it can work equally well with just the ordinary fresh mushrooms in the grocery store. For the roasted red peppers, you can roast your own or use the roasted red peppers in jars. Just pat them dry before using them.

Ingredients

1   tablespoon olive oil
1   large shallot, thinly sliced
3-4 large brown mushrooms, halved and thinly sliced
¼   cup Kentucky bourbon
¼   teaspoon thyme

1   tablespoon capers, chopped
1   cup venison stock or beef broth
1-2 tablespoons butter, cut in pieces and chilled (optional)
½   cup sour cream (optional)
1-2 teaspoons cornstarch (optional)

Preparation

HEAT oil in a saucepan over medium heat. Add shallot slices, and sauté for 4 minutes, stirring occasionally. Stir in mushrooms and sauté mixture another minute. Stir in bourbon and simmer mixture slowly until liquid has almost completely evaporated. Add thyme, capers, and stock and simmer, covered, over low heat for 15 minutes.

Finish the gravy in one of the following ways:

1.   REMOVE the gravy from the heat and swirl in butter pieces a few at a time. Put back on low heat, and continue stirring until it thickens.

2.   PLACE sour cream in a small bowl and add a couple of spoonfuls of the hot liquid, stirring to combine. Add this mixture to the gravy, stir, and heat through before serving.

3.   IN A small bowl, combine cornstarch with a little water until there are no lumps. Stir into gravy and continue cooking until gravy thickens.

Serves 6

COGNAC MUSTARD

This recipe is one I found in the March, 2011 edition of *Sunset Magazine*. We use this with a lot of wild game – sometimes as is, and sometimes softened with a little sour cream.

6 tablespoones yellow mustard seeds	⅔ cup white wine vinegar
2 tablespoons brown mustard seeds	¼ cup brown sugar
⅓ cup water	1 teaspoon salt
3 tablespoons cognac	

PLACE the mustard seeds, water, cognac, and vinegar in a bowl and stir to combine, completely submerging seeds. Cover and let sit at room temperature for 2 to 3 days

PLACE mixture in a blender with the sugar and salt and whirl until thickened.

Makes about 2 cups

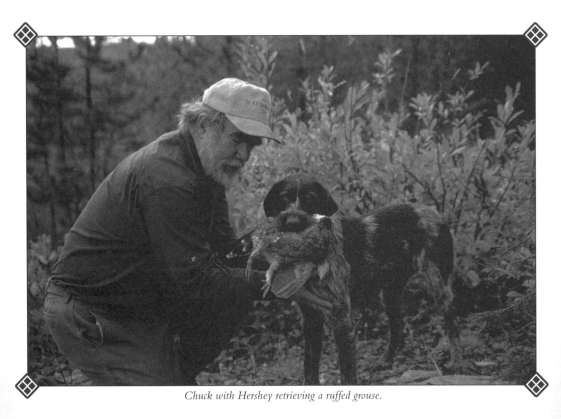

Chuck with Hershey retrieving a ruffed grouse.

SHIITAKE AND JUNIPER BERRY SAUCE

This sauce goes well with grilled big game meats.

Ingredients

2 tablespoons peanut oil
2 cloves garlic, minced
2 teaspoons fresh ginger, minced
2 shallots, sliced thin
2 cups shiitake mushrooms, stems removed and sliced thin
1 tablespoon soy sauce
2 tablespoons lemon juice

2 tablespoons brown sugar
1 teaspoon juniper berries, crushed
1½ cups game stock or beef broth
1 ounce gin
1 ounce scotch
1 tablespoon arrowroot mixed with ¼ cup water

Preparation

HEAT a small skillet over medium-high heat. Add the peanut oil and sauté the shallots, garlic, and ginger for about 1 minute. Add the mushrooms and sauté, stirring constantly, for about 2 more minutes. Reduce the heat and add the rest of the ingredients except the arrowroot mixture. Simmer for about 5 minutes. Add the arrowroot to the sauce, and simmer for a couple of minutes to thicken.

RASPBERRY GAME SAUCE

This sauce is especially delicious with grilled game birds.

Ingredients

1 cup raspberries, fresh or frozen
1 cup game bird or chicken stock
1 small cinnamon stick
1 tablespoon raspberry vinegar

2 tablespoons balsamic vinegar
brown sugar or raspberry jam to taste
4 tablespoons butter, cut in small chunks & chilled

Preparation

IN A small saucepan, combine the raspberries, stock and the cinnamon stick. Bring to a simmer and reduce the mixture by half, smashing the raspberries to release their flavor. Strain the sauce, mashing the raspberries with the back of a spoon. Return to pan and bring to a simmer. Add the vinegars and stir. Cook 2 minutes more on low. Taste the mixture and add either a little brown sugar or a little raspberry jam if it is too tart. Now slowly swirl in the butter chunks until the mixture thickens slightly and has a silky appearance.

Stocks and Marinades

GAME BIRD STOCK

If you really want your game dishes to stand out, making your own stock is the best way to achieve this. I know it's so much easier to just open a can of prepared chicken broth or beef broth, but the fantastic flavor of homemade stock made with all those wild game bird carcasses will make you a believer once you make a batch. You will also have stock that is not as salty as most commercial stock. Spend a weekend making a big stockpot full, and you can then freeze the stock in ice cube trays. As each tray freezes (it takes a little longer than water), you can pop the cubes out and store them in quart ziplock bags in your freezer. Now you don't even have to bother with opening a can! Each cube is about an ounce of stock, so it's easy to count out approximately 8 cubes for a cup of stock. Put them in a glass measuring container and microwave for a minute and you've got your stock.

Most professional chefs keep a stockpot simmering on their range, and they just keep replacing the bones and ingredients. This isn't practical for home use. Instead I save up carcasses and make one very large stockpot at a time. Every time we have a roast game bird, I collect the bones and freeze them in a ziplock bag. When using a recipe that just calls for duck or pheasant breasts, we will defrost the birds just enough to fillet out the breast and keep the rest of the bird frozen for the stockpot. Of course, the carcass of a wild turkey will fill one stockpot and makes absolutely wonderful stock. If we have a lot of ducks, I will try to make a separate stock with the duck carcasses, but I have also mixed upland game birds with waterfowl carcasses. Just because the stock is made with game birds doesn't mean that it can only be used in bird recipes. The stock is so rich that it can easily stand up to most big game meats.

You will notice in the ingredients listed below that dried mushroom stems are listed. Mushrooms go so well with wild game recipes that I found I had a lot of stems that were being thrown away. Some of the best are shiitake stems. I keep a small brown paper bag in my spice cupboard. When I am preparing a dish with mushrooms, I save the stems and put them in the paper bag. They dry out in the bag and can be kept indefinitely.

So, try making this stock. I think you will be amazed at the difference it makes in your cooking, and you will also have the satisfaction of making your stock from scratch and utilizing the entire game bird.

Ingredients

game bird carcasses (backs, wings, legs, etc.) enough to fill a large stockpot
4 stalks celery, cut in half
2 large onions, unpeeled, cut in half with 1 whole clove stuck in each half
4 carrots, quartered
10–12 black peppercorns

½ bunch of parsley, including stems
2 bay leaves
4–6 sprigs of fresh thyme
1–2 cups dried mushroom stems (see above)
1 bottle of white wine
2 cups sherry
water to cover

Preparation

IF THE game bird carcasses have not been previously roasted or cooked, put them in a roasting pan and roast in a 350-degree oven until they are brown. If they stick to the pan, add a small amount of water, loosen the bones, and then combine the water and brown bits to add to the stock pot.

loosen the bones, and thencombine the water and brown bits to add to the stock pot.

PUT the roasted carcasses in a large stockpot. Add all the ingredients and fill with water to cover. I sometimes add a small can or two of Swanson's low-salt chicken broth to boost the flavor even more. Bring the mixture to a boil, lower the temperature to a simmer and cover. Let this simmer gently on the stove for 10 to 12 hours, stirring once in a while with a long spoon. You can either do this in the evening and let it simmer overnight, or you can turn it off in the evening, store it covered in your refrigerator overnight, and reheat and continue cooking the next morning. Start counting your cooking time when the mixture is back to a boil.

WHEN the stock has simmered for 10 to 12 hours total, remove from heat and let the mixture cool down enough to handle. Put a large strainer over a second stockpot. With tongs, remove most of the large bones and place in strainer, letting any of the stock drip through. Discard the bones. Continue removing the contents of the stockpot with either tongs or a large spoon, putting them in the strainer. Use the back of the large spoon to flatten the vegetables in the strainer, so that their flavor is imparted to the stock. Doing this will make the finished stock cloudy instead of completely clear, but I like the extra flavor that is imparted with this method. Discard the solid remains before you put the next batch in the strainer. As you work through the large bones and vegetables, you can then start pouring the mixture into the strainer.

ONCE you have emptied the first stockpot, place the strained liquid in the second stockpot back on the stove and bring to a low boil. Simmer uncovered to reduce the liquid and concentrate the flavor. When the flavor reaches the strength that you want, add salt to taste, if needed. You will probably reduce the liquid by close to half of the original volume.

REMOVE the stock from the heat and cool it enough so that you can put it in your refrigerator to cool completely. When cooled, it will form a thin layer of fat on top that can be skimmed off and discarded. Now you can take your time and fill ice cube trays with the stock and freeze them. When they are frozen solid, remove from the freezer. Put some warm water in your sink. Immerse just the bottom of the tray into the warm water and count to 10. Remove and turn the tray upside down over a large bowl or plate, twisting the tray to pop out the cubes. Immediately put them in a ziplock bag and place them in the freezer.

EACH cube is approximately an ounce of stock. When you are ready to use it in a recipe, just count out the number of cubes you need. Place in a glass measuring cup and microwave on high for about 1 minute. When the cubes melt, you will be able to tell if you need another cube or two to make the amount of stock that you need. Now you can relax and enjoy the appreciative comments from your guests and family when you use the stock in your wild game recipes.

GAME STOCK

As with the game bird stock on the preceding page, there is nothing better than having your own stock to use in your wild game recipes. It far surpasses any commercial stock or broth you can buy, and doesn't have as much salt in it.

If you are lucky enough to have a wild game processor who will custom butcher your big game, you might be able to talk him or her into saving some bones for your soups and stock. If so, ask the butcher to save the leg joints, and split them open to expose the marrow. The rib bones can also be saved. We have always used the neck bones that often have delicious meat attached to them. Freeze these bones until you are ready to make your stock. You can also save any bones from chops and steaks you have cooked. If you are short a few bones, ask your grocery butcher if he has any veal shanks. Even though most grocery butchers are now only working with pre-cut slabs of meat, they can often special order some veal bones for you. These add a great flavor to the stock.

Ingredients

	big game bones, with joints cracked (elk, deer, antelope, etc.) enough to fill a large stockpot	10-12	black peppercorns
		½	bunch of parsley, including stems
		3	bay leaves
4	stalks celery, cut in half	4-6	sprigs of fresh thyme
2	leeks, cut in half lengthwise, and rinsed out	1-2	cups dried mushroom stems (see above)
2	large onions, unpeeled, cut in half with 1 whole clove stuck in each half	1	bottle of red wine
		2	cups tawny port
4	carrots, quartered		water to cover

Preparation

IF THE bones have not been previously roasted or cooked, put them in a roasting pan and roast in a 350-degree oven until they are brown. If they stick to the pan, add a small amount of water to loosen the bones. Then stir the water to loosen the brown bits. Add both bones and liquid to the stockpot.

PUT the roasted bones in a large stockpot. Add all the ingredients and fill with water to cover. I sometimes add a small can or two of Swanson's beef broth to boost the flavor. Bring the mixture to a boil, lower the temperature to a simmer and cover. Let this simmer gently on the stove for 10 to 12 hours, stirring once in a while with a long spoon. You can either do this in the evening and let it simmer overnight, or you can turn it off in the evening, store it covered in your refrigerator overnight, and reheat and continue cooking the next morning. Start counting your cooking time when the mixture is back to a boil.

WHEN the stock has simmered for 10 to 12 hours total, remove from heat and let the mixture cool down enough to handle. Put a large strainer over a second stockpot. With tongs, remove most of the large bones and place in strainer, letting any of the stock drip through. Discard the bones. Continue removing the contents of the stockpot with either tongs or a large spoon, putting them in the strainer. Use the back of the large spoon to flatten the vegetables in the strainer, so that their flavor is imparted to the stock. Doing this will make the finished stock cloudy instead of completely clear, but I like the extra flavor that is imparted with this method. Discard the solid remains before you put the next batch in the strainer. As you work through the large bones and vegetables, you can then start pouring the mixture into the strainer.

ONCE you have emptied the first stockpot, place the strained liquid in the second stockpot back on the stove and bring to a low boil. Simmer uncovered to reduce the liquid and concentrate the flavor. When the flavor reaches the strength that you want, add salt to taste, if needed. You will probably reduce the liquid by close to half of the original volume.

REMOVE the stock from the heat and cool it enough so that you can put it in your refrigerator to cool completely. When cooled, it will form a thin layer of fat that you can skim off and discard.Now you can take your time and fill ice cube trays with the stock and freeze them. When they are frozen solid, remove from the freezer. Put some warm water in your sink. Immerse just the bottom of the tray into the warm water and count to 10. Remove and turn the tray upside down over a large bowl or plate, twisting the tray to pop out the cubes. Immediately put them in a ziplock bag and place them in the freezer.

EACH cube is approximately an ounce of stock. When you are ready to use it in a recipe, just count out the number of cubes you need. Place in a glass measuring cup and microwave on high for about 1 minute. When the cubes melt, you will be able to tell if you need another cube or two to make the amount of stock that you need.

Blanche and Duke.

Basic Waterfowl Marinade

Ducks and geese benefit greatly from being marinated for several hours or overnight. It's fun to vary the ingredients in a marinade to produce subtle differences in the finished dish. The basis of a good marinade is a combination of some type of oil with an addition of a little acid from citrus or wine. The oil helps to keep lean game meat from drying out, and the citrus or wine will help tenderize the meat. There is no preparation to most of these marinades, because you simply combine the ingredients, pour them over the meat, and keep in the refrigerator until about an hour before cooking. The suggested additions can be added as desired.

Basic Ingredients

1 cup olive oil, peanut oil, or canola oil	2 tablespoons soy sauce
2 tablespoons lemon or lime juice	salt and pepper

Suggested Additions

2 tablespoons sherry	2-3 garlic cloves, minced
dash of Tabasco sauce	1 teaspoon powdered ginger, or
dash of thyme	1 inch piece of fresh ginger, grated
4-5 green onions, chopped	

Game Roast Marinade

This marinade works well for any big game roast. The ingredients are for roasts up to about 5 pounds. As with most roasts, it is best to marinate them overnight if you can. To help the marinade permeate the roast, I will often use a fork and a spoon after I have poured the marinade over the roast. I spoon the marinade over the top of the roast, and at the same time, I pierce the roast with a fork. I continue doing this on all sides. This especially helps if you cannot let the roast marinate overnight.

Ingredients

½ cup olive oil	1 shallot, chopped
2 tablespoons soy sauce	1 garlic clove, minced
1 tablespoon Worcestershire sauce	½ teaspoon tarragon
1½ tablespoons Hoisin sauce	½ teaspoon thyme
⅔ cup red wine	½ teaspoon rosemary, crushed
1 tablespoon balsamic vinegar	cracked black pepper

GAME STEAK MARINADE I

This is another marinade that works well for all cuts of big game, from steaks to roasts. If doing steaks, marinate for at least 1 hour up to overnight. If doing a roast, it is best to marinate overnight.

Ingredients

⅓ cup olive oil
2 tablespoons soy sauce
4 cloves garlic, minced
1 teaspoon lemon juice
½ cup brandy

¼ cup Madeira
12 juniper berries, crushed
6-8 fresh sage leaves, chopped and crushed
1 teaspoon cracked black pepper

Preparation

COMBINE all ingredients except the juniper berries, sage leaves, and pepper in a bowl. Separately combine the crushed juniper berries and crushed sage leaves, along with the cracked pepper. Rub this mixture over the steaks or roast. Add the remaining mixture to the marinade.

PUT the steaks or roast in a bowl and pour the marinade over.

GAME STEAK MARINADE II

This marinade can work equally well for steaks and roasts. Just marinate a roast for a longer period, preferably overnight.

Ingredients

⅓ cup olive oil
⅓ cup tawny port
4 cloves garlic, minced
2 tablespoons soy sauce
1 tablespoon lemon juice
1 tablespoon Tabasco sauce

2 teaspoons chipotle pepper or red cayenne
1 teaspoon sage
1 teaspoon curry, such as Rogan Josh
1 teaspoon coriander

GAME BIRD MARINADE I

Use this marinade for a minimum of half an hour, or up to 4 hours, depending on the type of bird: white meat less and red meat more.

Ingredients

¼ cup olive oil
2 tablespoons lemon juice
2 tablespoons soy sauce
1 tablespoon Dijon mustard

1 tablespoon red currant jelly
2 tablespoons port
½ teaspoon tarragon
½ teaspoon thyme

GAME BIRD MARINADE II

This marinade works especially well for pheasants, but can be used for just about any game bird. The amount in this marinade is enough to marinate 2 pheasants, 4 chukars, or 8 quail. Marinate the birds for 1 to 3 hours. You can vary the Tabasco and pepper based on your own personal heat level.

Ingredients

⅓ cup olive oil
⅓ cup tawny port
4 cloves garlic, minced
1 tablespoon lemon juice

1 tablespoon Tabasco sauce
1 teaspoon sage
1 teaspoon chipotle pepper or red cayenne

Salty Pete on retrieve in Idaho.

Stocks and Marinades

Jack Daniels Game Marinade for Waterfowl

This marinade will cover up to 4 duck breasts or 1 goose breast, split. It is preferred that the game is marinated overnight, but you can marinate for as little as 2 hours if pressed for time.

Ingredients

⅓ cup olive oil
⅓ cup Jack Daniels
2 tablespoons soy sauce
1 tablespoon horseradish
2 tablespoons Worcestershire sauce

2 tablespoons lemon juice
2 tablespoons orange juice
3 cloves garlic, minced
1 teaspoon rosemary
1 teaspoon thyme

Lemon Marinade for Pheasant

This marinade works equally well for chukar and quail. Its flavors don't overpower the delicate flavors of these birds. Marinate the birds for a minimum of half an hour up to 2 hours, turning occasionally. You can also vary this marinade by substituting pineapple juice for the lemon juice.

Ingredients

¼ cup olive oil
⅓ cup lemon juice
¼ cup white Worcestershire sauce
1 tablespoon dry vermouth or dry white
   wine

1 tablespoon sugar
1 teaspoon lemon zest
1 tablespoon fresh rosemary, or 1
   teaspoon dried
salt and cracked pepper

Marinade for Goose Breast

This marinade can work for duck breasts as well as geese. Just be sure if you are marinating a goose breast to be grilled, that you split the breast in half. If you are doing ducks, you only need to marinate 2 to 4 hours. If you are marinating a much larger goose breast, it is best to marinate overnight, or at least 4 hours.

Ingredients

½ cup peanut oil
1 inch piece of fresh ginger, minced
1 lemon, sliced
2 tablespoons brandy or cognac

2 tablespoons soy sauce
2 shallots, sliced thin
4-5 sprigs of thyme, or 1 teaspoon dried

Marinade for Upland Birds

This marinade is great for pheasant, chukar, and quail. While we usually marinate big game meats and waterfowl overnight, if possible, we marinate the lighter meats of pheasant, chukar, and quail for 1 to 3 hours at the most. If left in a marinade too long, the marinade overpowers the delicate flavor of these birds. The amounts below will easily marinate up to 2 whole pheasants, 4 chukars, or 8 quail.

Ingredients

½ cup olive oil
½ cup orange juice
2 tablespoons soy sauce
2 tablespoons sherry (optional)

1 garlic clove, minced
½ inch fresh ginger root, minced
1 tablespoon Dijon mustard
1 teaspoon brown sugar

MUSTARD GLAZE FOR GAME MEAT

This glaze is great for all game meat, big and small, as well as duck and goose breasts that you are going to grill. We have used it for years, and never grow tired of it.

As with other marinades, just combine the ingredients and marinate the meat at least 2 hours or as long as overnight for larger pieces. Remove from refrigerator at least one hour before cooking. If grilling, just put the marinade-covered meat right on the grill without wiping the marinade off.

Ingredients

⅓ cup olive oil
¼ cup dry red wine
2 tablespoons lemon juice
3 tablespoons Dijon mustard
2 tablespoons soy sauce

¼ teaspoon salt
　cracked black pepper
2 cloves garlic, minced
1 teaspoon thyme
1 teaspoon rosemary

MUSTARD MARINADE FOR SMALL GAME

This marinade will work for 1 large rabbit or 2 large squirrels. Marinate for 2 to 6 hours before cooking.

Ingredients

4 tablespoons canola oil
4 tablespoons Dijon mustard
1 teaspoon sage
1 teaspoon chipotle pepper or red
　cayenne

1 teaspoon Tabasco sauce
3 cloves garlic, minced
4 tablespoons brandy

PEACH MARINADE

This sweet and tangy marinade is perfect for game birds of all kinds. Marinate white-meat birds for 1 to 3 hours at most. For darker meat birds, you can keep them in the marinade for anywhere from 2 hours to overnight. Remove from the refrigerator at least 1 hour before cooking. You can also use the marinade as a basting sauce by simmering it in a saucepan for about 15 minutes. You can increase the heat level of this marinade/basting sauce by increasing the chipotle pepper. When peaches are in season, you can substitute two fresh peaches for the canned variety.

Ingredients

1	8½-ounce can peaches	2	tablespoons light molasses
2	green onions, chopped	¼	teaspoon salt
¼	cup canola oil	½	teaspoon ground chipotle or cayenne pepper
¼	cup cider vinegar		
¼	cup bourbon	2	tablespoons chopped parsley

Preparation

COMBINE the peaches, green onions, canola oil, cider vinegar, and bourbon in blender. Blend on high for 45 seconds. Add the molasses, salt, and chipotle pepper and blend for about 15 seconds. Add the parsley and blend for about 10 seconds.

PRAIRIE GROUSE MARINADE

This marinade works especially well for sharptails and sage grouse, but could also work for waterfowl. The ingredients will marinate 2 sharptails.

Ingredients

½	cup olive oil	4	cloves garlic, minced
½	cup port	1	tablespoon sage
2	tablespoons Dijon mustard	1	tablespoon tarragon
2	tablespoons soy sauce	1	tablespoon ground pepper
2	teaspoons lemon juice	1	teaspoon salt
2	teaspoons Tabasco sauce		

Preparation

COMBINE all ingredients well. Pour over birds. Marinate 6 hours to overnight, turning birds every 2 hours.

RASPBERRY MARINADE

This marinade is great for all game birds, but especially for grilled or roasted forest grouse, such as ruffed or blue. As with other marinades, the dark-meat birds can be marinated overnight. If you are using for light-meat birds, marinate for 1 to 4 hours. You can also use the marinade for a basting sauce. Just simmer in a saucepan for about 15 minutes after removing the birds.

Ingredients

3 cups fresh or frozen raspberries
1 cup raspberry vinegar
1 cinnamon stick, broken in half

½ cup olive oil
1 bay leaf
1 teaspoon thyme

Preparation

IN A medium saucepan, combine the raspberries, vinegar and cinnamon stick. Bring to a boil, reduce heat and simmer for 2 minutes. Stir in the rest of the ingredients. Cool to room temperature before pouring over birds.

WATERFOWL MARINADE WITH ORIENTAL FLAVOR

The meat of ducks and geese blends well with oriental flavors. The list of ingredients in this marinade may seem long, but most are usually on hand in the kitchen. Since the marinade is simply a combination of these ingredients, there is very little work, but the different ingredients will add a subtle flavor to grilled birds. They also work well in preparing the meat for use in any Asian-type recipe. Ducks and geese are best if marinated at least 4 hours or overnight in the refrigerator. Remove from the refrigerator at least 1 hour before cooking.

Ingredients

½ cup peanut oil
½ cup olive oil
1 heaping tablespoon fresh ginger, minced
3 green onions, chopped with the green tops
2 tablespoons lemon juice

3 tablespoons soy sauce
1 tablespoon Hoisin sauce
2 tablespoons honey
¼ cup red wine
1 tablespoon Worcestershire sauce
dash of Tabasco sauce

Bourbon-Chipotle Marinade

This can be used for any kind of big game steaks or chops, and also works with birds with dark meat, such as ducks, geese, and sharptailed grouse. You can increase or decrease the amount of chipotle pepper depending on your own heat scale tolerance.

Ingredients

¼ cup olive oil	4 fresh sage leaves, chopped
½ cup Kentucky bourbon	1 teaspoon lemon juice
⅓ cup brown sugar	1 tablespoon Worcestershire sauce
1 teaspoon ground chipotle pepper	3 garlic cloves, minced

Preparation

COMBINE all ingredients in a bowl or plastic bag. Season the steaks or birds with salt and pepper and place in the marinade for 4 hours to overnight.

Marinade for Big Game Roast

Ingredients

2-4 pound big game roast, such as a sirloin tip	¼ cup olive oil
salt and freshly ground pepper	3 ounces Kentucky bourbon
pinch of nutmeg	½ teaspoon dried thyme
	2 garlic cloves, minced

Preparation

PAT roast dry and season with salt and pepper. Lightly sprinkle nutmeg over all sides. Mix rest of the ingredients and pour into a self-sealing bag. Place bag in a bowl, and add the roast to the bag. Seal the bag, squeezing out as much air as possible and letting the marinade surround all sides of the meat. Place in refrigerator to marinate overnight, turning occasionally. Remove from refrigerator at least 1 hour, so that the roast can come to room temperature. Remove from marinade and grill or roast in the oven according to your favorite recipe.

BRANDY MARINADE FOR VENISON CHOPS AND STEAKS

This marinade works for all types of venison – elk, deer, antelope, etc. Then the chops or steaks can be grilled, broiled, or pan fried.

Ingredients

4 garlic cloves, minced	2 tablespoons sea salt
8 juniper berries	2 tablespoons cracked peppercorns
1 teaspoon dried thyme	½ cup olive oil
1 teaspoon ground cinnamon	2 cups red wine
1 teaspoon ground chipotle pepper	2 tablespoons brandy

Preparation

WITH a mortar and pestle, grind the garlic, spices, salt and pepper into a paste. In a bowl or marinating container, whisk together the olive oil, wine, and brandy.

PAT the chops or steaks dry and cover them with the garlic paste. Place them in the wine-brandy mixture, cover, and refrigerate. The meat can marinate anywhere from a couple of hours to overnight, turning them at least twice.

Camas on point.

©Brett Smith

Stocks and Marinades

263

SMOKED GAME BIRD MARINADE

This works well for all dark-meat birds, from ducks through sharptail grouse. Smoked birds can be enjoyed warm, right out of the smoker. They are especially good with a side dish of cooked apples. When we smoke birds for a dinner, we usually add extra birds for use later. Smoked birds will keep in the refrigerator much longer than regularly cooked meats. They are great for snacks and hors d'oeuvres, especially with a mustard dip.

Ingredients

⅓ cup olive oil
2 tablespoons soy sauce
1 teaspoon lemon juice
4 cloves garlic, minced
1 teaspoon ground sage

2 teaspoons ground chipotle pepper or red cayenne
½ cup Calvados or apple brandy
dash of Tabasco sauce
salt and pepper

Preparation

COMBINE ingredients and marinate birds at least 6 hours or preferably overnight. This makes enough marinade for 2 sharptail or 1 goose breast.

Chuck preparing field lunch.

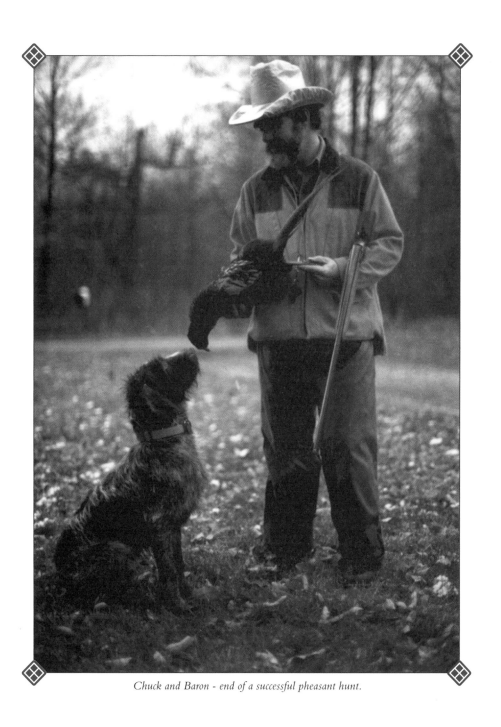

Chuck and Baron - end of a successful pheasant hunt.

DEUTSCH FAMILY WINE & SPIRITS

Here at Deutsch Family Wine & Spirits, our family company represents the many families who grow, produce, and make the products we sell. Our portfolio currently numbers 33 different brands from eight different countries around the world, plus the United States.

Our wines are grown in France, Italy, Spain, Portugal, Chile, Argentina, Australia, New Zealand, and of course, California. We have all manner of delicious wines to choose from – red, white, still, sparkling, sweet, and dry priced for every budget.

Our spirits are produced in France, Italy, Spain, Poland, Mexico, and the United States and are the harbingers of quality, diversity, and value.

Whether you're looking for a wine or a spirit to complement a recipe, a meal, or an entire menu, look no further! Our range of products offers you the perfect selection opportunity, for all wild food, whether finned, feathered, or furred.

Like hunting and fishing, the process of choosing wines and spirits is an intensely personal experience, as is the consumption of all of these products. Both involve the appreciation of nature's work, the environment, and often, the camaraderie of good friends and family. It is this spirit of sharing the many pleasurable aspects of food, wine, and spirits, together or separately, that unites us all. With this in mind, we can look forward to the enjoyment of good times and the creation of many happy memories!

Cheers!

Jorge Hernandez
National Director of Wine & Spirits Education
Deutsch Family Wine & Spirits

DEUTSCH FAMILY
WINE & SPIRITS

deutschfamily.com

Please Drink Responsibly. ©2012 Deutsch Family Wine & Spirits, White Plains, NY 10604

DFV WINES

FAMILY FARMED SINCE 1924

D FV Wines is a family-owned winery committed to its 80-plus year California winemaking and winegrowing heritage. Three generations of the Indelicato family have overseen vineyard operations and winemaking at their California properties. The winery harvests grapes from Napa, Lodi, Monterey, and Sonoma to craft wines that express the diversity of these appellations.

The Indelicato family has always understood that wine quality starts in the vineyard, and a vineyard is first and foremost a living thing. The DFV Wines' Family Farmed philosophy reflects its unwavering dedication to environmentally sensitive and economically sustainable business practices.

In 1924, Gasparé Indelicato emigrated from the small village of Campobello in Italy and, in the tradition of his father and grandfather, planted the first grapes of the Delicato Family Vineyards. Within a few years, winemakers across the country knew of the quality of Gasparé's California grapes. Through the decades, the family continued the winemaking tradition with Gasparé's three sons – Frank, Vincent, and Anthony. Today, Anthony's sons – Chris and Jay Indelicato – are leading the business into the future.

The Indelicato family is devoted to its California winemaking heritage of family farming, environmentally sensitive winegrowing practices, and economically sustainable principles. It is with an eye for the continued success of the family winery, and the success of their business partners, that they have developed a strategic direction that protects and enhances the things they hold most dear – family, farming, and quality wine for consumers.

DFV Wines Facts:
Website: www.dfvwines.com
Address: 12001 South Highway 99, Manteca, CA 95336
Telephone: 888-599-4637 or 209-824-3500
Email: info@dfvwines.com
Tasting Room Hours: 9:00am to 5:30pm daily
Tastings: No charge
If you can't visit us personally, contact us at info@dfvwines.com to find out about our exciting new Vino della Famiglia Wine Club.

Indelicato Family Casual Dinner.

Hondo pointing a covey of sharptails.

CULINARY SOURCES

This list is only provided for your convenience. While many of the suggested suppliers have been recommended, not all suppliers have been individually checked out. We do not endorse any particular vendor or supplier.

WILD GAME
Broken Arrow Ranch
Antelope, venison, and wild boar.
P.O. Box 530
Ingram, TX 78025
www.brokenarrowranch.com
800-962-4263

Exotic Meats USA
Alligator, antelope, buffalo, caribou, cobra, duck, elk, frog, goose, kangaroo, lamb, ostrich, pheasant, quail, rabbit, rattlesnake, snapping turtle, squab, New Zealand venison, wild boar, and wild turkey.
1330 Capital Blvd.
Reno, NV 89502
www.exoticmeatsandmore.com
800-444-5687 – ask for Russ McCurdy

Nicky Game USA
223 SE 3rd Ave.
Portland, OR 97214
www.nickyusa.com
503-234-4263
800-469-4162

Oakwood Game Farms
Fresh and smoked pheasants, chukar partridge, quail, and duck.
P.O. Box 274
Princeton, MN 55371
www.oakwoodgamefarm.com
800-328-6647

Prairie Harvest Specialty Foods
Buffalo, elk, venison, wild boar, rabbit, pheasant, quail, duck, and goose.
350 Hillsview Drive
Spearfish, SD 57783
www.prairieharvest.com
800-350-7166

SPICES and SAUCES
Bronco Bob's
Chipotle-fruit sauces and marinades
www.lwcbrandsinc.com
800-552-8006
214-630-9101
email: orders@ladywaltons.com

Grandma Hoot Products
Chipotle-fruit sauces and marinades, plus pickles, jellies, and relishes
P. O. Box 684
Florence, Montana 59833
www.grandmahootproducts.com
email: hopeproducts@yahoo.com
406 544-1425 or 406 544-264

Hicountry.com
Hi-Country Snack Foods, Inc.
Jerky and sausage seasonings, brine mixes, and sausage casings
P.O. Box 159
Lincoln, MT 59639
www.hicountry.com
800-433-3916 or 406-362-4203

Penzey's Spices
Online spice store with retail stores throughout the country.
1200 W. Capitol Drive
Wauwatosa, WI 53222
www.penzeys.com
800-741-7787

Saltworks
America's Sea Salt Company
Source for smoked salt
16240 Wood-Red Rd NE
Woodinville, WA 98072
www.saltworks.com
800-353-7258

GLOSSARY

blanch	To plunge food (usually vegetables and fruits) into boiling water briefly, then into cold water to stop the cooking process.
bouquet garni	A bunch of herbs, usually including parsley, thyme, and bay leaf, in a cheesecloth bag for flavoring soups, stews and broths.
braise	Browning food (usually meat or vegetables) first in fat, then cooking in a small amount of liquid, covered, at low heat for a long time.
brown	To cook quickly over high heat, causing the food's surface to turn brown while the interior stays moist.
Calvados	A dry apple brandy from Calvados, the Normandy region of northern France, often used in dishes with chicken, pork, and veal.
chipotle	A dried, smoked, jalapeno with a sweet, almost chocolaty flavor.
clarified	The process of clearing a cloudy substance, such as in stocks or wines, or melting butter until the foam rises and is skimmed off.
curry powder	Popular in Indian cooking, curry powder is a mixture of as many as 20 spices, herbs, and seeds. It comes in two basic styles — standard, and the hotter of the two, "Madras."
deglaze	Adding wine or water to the skillet to loosen browned bits on the bottom to make a sauce.
dredge	To lightly coat food with flour, cornmeal, or bread crumbs, usually prior to frying.
epazote	A strongly flavored wild herb with a unique taste, available from Latin markets. It is used in Mexican and Caribbean cooking, especially when cooking black beans.
filé powder	A seasoning made from the ground, dried leaves of the sassafras tree, used in Creole cooking.
fillet	To remove the bones from a piece of meat or fish, thereby creating a boneless meat or fish fillet.
french, to	To trim fat or bone from a cut of meat.
hoisin	A sauce of soybeans, garlic, chili peppers, and various spices used in Chinese cooking.
infuse	To introduce, steep, or soak one ingredient with another.
kosher salt	An additive-free coarse-grained salt.
macerate	To soften by soaking in liquid.
parboil	To partially cook ingredients prior to adding them to other ingredients in order to have them complete cooking simultaneously.
purée	To grind or mash food until it's completely smooth, using a food processor, a blender, or by forcing the food through a sieve.
reduce, reduction	To boil a liquid rapidly, reducing it until its thickened and flavorful.

roux	A mixture of equal parts flour and butter used to thicken sauces. Cooking different lengths of time results in different flavors and colors.
sauté	To quickly cook food over direct heat in a small amount of hot oil.
sec	This French word means "dry".
shallot	Member of the onion family.
simmer	To cook food at a low temperature with gentle surface bubbling.
sweat	To cook vegetables slowly in a tightly covered pan so that they literally stew in their own juices.
Tabasco pepper; Tabasco Sauce	A small, hot, red pepper originally from the Mexican state of Tabasco. The word, meaning "damp earth," is trademarked by the McIlhenny family.

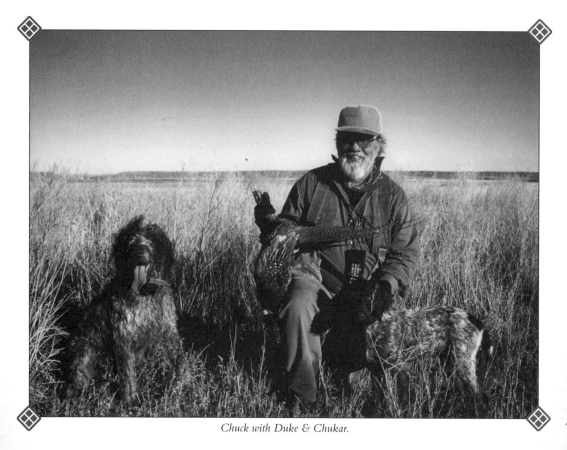

Chuck with Duke & Chukar.

INDEX

W

Five-month-old Hondo's first duck retrieve.

About the Publishers and Authors

Chuck and Blanche Johnson started Wilderness Adventures Press, Inc. in 1993, publishing outdoor and sporting books. Along with hunting and fishing, they love fine dining, good wines, and traveling. They have always been able to "sniff out" the most outstanding and interesting restaurants in any city they visit.

Chuck and Blanche have been hunting wild game for close to 50 years. They travel the country hunting in a number of states each year. On weekends, they experiment in the kitchen, cooking a variety of fish and meats, as well as preparing the harvest from their time in the field.

Chuck is also the Versatile Gun Dog columnist for *Pointing Dog Journal*. Blanche is an outdoor photographer whose work has appeared in various hunting magazines.

Chuck and Blanche make their home in Gallatin Gateway, Montana, along with their German wirehaired pointers.

About Fred McCaleb

During the mid-1900s Fred McCaleb was considered by some as a consummate sporting artist. When he wasn't at his easel, his bachelorhood allowed him to fish the bayous and rivers of his home state, Louisiana, shooting ducks in its marshes, or hunting game birds in its flatlands. He translated these life-long experiences into numerous paintings, drawings, and etchings – many of which appeared in the pages of *Field & Stream*, *Outdoor Life*, and *Sports Afield* magazines. And whereas his art reflected a variety of themes, it was his ability to portray the hunting dog as an almost regal subject that has won this artist his unique place in the world of sporting art fifty years after his death.

About Brett Smith

Brett James Smith is considered among today's best sporting artists for his ability to capture today's sporting experience with yesterday's sense of adventure. Sportsmen nationwide collect his work for its visual excitement and authenticity. His work has appeared in Wilderness Adventures Press' reprints of William Faulkner's classic *Big Woods*, Nash Buckingham's *De Shootinest Gent' man*, and the Archibald Rutledge collection *Bird Dog Days, Wingshooting Ways*. His work also regularly appears in publications such as *Gray's Sporting Journal*, *Ducks Unlimited* magazine, *Sporting Classics*, and *Shooting Sportsman*. Smith currently resides with his wife and two children in Covington, Louisiana.

More examples of his fine artwork can be seen at www.brettsmith.com